Serving Up Excellence

Creating Meaningful Dining Experiences through the Power of Connection

Joshua Farrell

Serving Up Excellence: Creating Memorable Dining Experiences through the Power of Connection

Copyright © 2026 by Joshua Farrell

All rights reserved. No part of this book may be used, reproduced or transmitted in any manner or form whatsoever, electronic or mechanical, including photocopying, recording, or any future means of reproducing text, without written permission from the publisher. The publisher does not have any control over and does not assume any responsibility for author or third-party websites, applications, or their content.

Published in the United States by Schellville.

Contact Email: info@schellvillepublishing.com

ISBN: 978-0-9899345-8-9

Edited by Dean Kuipers

Cover Design: Christo Downs

The business of business is relationships; the business of life is human connection.

-Robin Sharma

Contents

INTRODUCTION		XI
PART 1: CASUAL RESTAURANTS		1
1.	THE RUNDOWN Casual Restaurants	3
2.	VALUE Price, Expectation, and the Guest Experience	31
3.	LEWIS ROSSMAN COO/Partner, Shenkman Hospitality	33
4.	HALF A BUCK Providing an Engaging Work Experience	35
5.	WE Keeping Teams Unified and Connected	37
6.	THE FINGERPRINT Attention to the Smallest Details	40
7.	PAIGE REILLY Owner, Upside Pub	43
8.	PLAN B Adjusting to the Back-Up Plan	45
9.	COMMON CONVERSATIONS All Day, Every Day	48

10. THE SCOOP — 51
Knowing the Neighborhood

PART 2: UPSCALE RESTAURANTS — 55

11. THE RUNDOWN — 57
Upscale Restaurants

12. THE GREETING — 96
The Strength of the Host

13. DOUG WASHINGTON — 100
Principle/Creative Director at Doug Washington Design

14. DESCRIBING FOOD — 103
Bringing the Menu Off the Page

15. ADAM COLE — 105
Chef, Consultant

16. CREATING TIME — 107
Efficiency, Time Blocks and Linking Tasks

17. MARVIN WELLS — 110
Director of Hospitality, FAO Hospitality

18. MANAGING AND MONEY — 112
Navigating the Areas of Costs

19. CAROLINE STYNE — 115
President and Wine Director- The Lucques Group

20. THE GREAT DELEGATOR — 118
Prioritizing and Communicating with Teams

21. JOSH GOLDMAN — 120
Hospitality & Beverage Consultant

22. ATMOSPHERE — 122
Maintaining Great Service in Lively Rooms

23.	ROBIN KIRBY	124
	Operations leadership team- Kokkari and Evvia.	
24.	SHARED PLATES	126
	The Challenges of Upscale Family Style	
25.	GARRETT HARKER	129
	Restaurateur- Eastern Standard, Standard Italian, Equal Measure	
26.	TURN AND BURN	133
	The Real Estate of a Dining Room	
27.	JACKSON CANNON	136
	Beverage Director- Eastern Standard, Standard Italian, Equal Measure	
28.	EVOLVING TECHNOLOGY	138
	Embracing Innovations	
29.	MICHAEL VOLTAGGIO	143
	Chef, Author, and Restaurateur	
30.	WHAC-A-MOLE	145
	Smarter, Not Faster	
31.	DAVIS CAMPBELL	147
	Founder- Wines Together	
32.	THE CHALLENGING FOLKS	150
	Professionalism and the Search for Similarities	
33.	RECOVERY SITUATIONS	153
	Winning the Guest Back	
34.	GARY OBLIGACION	157
	Former Director of Operations- The Alinea Group	
35.	LEARNING TOGETHER	159
	Creating a Culture of Becoming Better	

36. HERE TO SERVE ME — 162
   Ego, Status, and the Words We Choose

37. PASCALINE LEPELTIER — 166
   Master Sommelier

38. EFFORTLESSNESS — 168
   Practice, Repetition, and Confidence

39. ALICE WATERS — 171
   Chef, Author, Restaurateur- Chez Panisse

PART 3: ELEVATED RESTAURANTS — 175

40. THE RUNDOWN — 177
   Elevated Restaurants

41. VISION — 219
   The 8 Rings

42. JOANN CLEVENGER — 223
   Restaurateur- Upperline

43. CAPO — 226
   Learning a Fast Room and Selling an Experience

44. STEVE SCOTT SPRINGER — 230
   Former General Manager- Spago

45. SHORT MEMORY — 232
   The Benefits of Forgetting

46. JOSIAH CITRIN — 235
   Chef/Owner- two-starred Michelin restaurant Melisse

47. LARRY NADEAU — 237
   Dining Room manager- Two-starred Michelin restaurant, Enclos. Former Maitre'd- The French Laundry.

48. WHY SO SERIOUS? — 240
   The Importance of Keeping a Playful Attitude

| 49. | DAWN AGNEW | 242 |

Former Maitre d'- One-starred Michelin restaurant, Gary Danko

| 50. | REFRESHING ENTHUSIASM | 244 |

Inspiring Employees Back to Standards

| 51. | SARAH CLARKE | 247 |

Wine Director, Republique

| 52. | DIRECTOR OF SERVICE | 249 |

Coaching, Auditing, Leading

| 53. | DONATO POTO | 251 |

Co-owner/GM- Three-starred Michelin restaurant, Providence

| 54. | GREAT WHEN I NEED TO BE | 253 |

The Consistency of Performance and Behavior

| 55. | DOMINIQUE CRENN | 255 |

Chef and co-owner- Three-starred Michelin restaurant, Atelier Crenn

| 56. | STAYING AHEAD | 257 |

Creating a Culture of Innovation

INTO ACTION: PROMPTS   259
Building Engagement, Connection, and Culture

RECOMMENDED RESOURCES   267
Books and Podcasts

INDEX   271

ACKNOWLEDGEMENTS   281

ABOUT THE CONTRIBUTERS   283

ABOUT THE AUTHOR   289

INTRODUCTION

ALL ABOUT A STORY

All we are doing is creating a series of little stories. I have my story, you have your story and if our paths cross, we have our story. I've always pictured my interactions with guests as this story we are creating. A story our team is going to build with our guests so the guest can share it with their friends and families. The story can range from simple, to more detailed, to complex. As we know from life, our stories can change in an instant, and what was simple now becomes complex or the other way around. All we do is tell stories —to ourselves, to our friends, parents, co-workers, anyone who will listen. For example:

- I went to the store and picked up some bread.

- I went to the store and picked up some bread and noticed that all the bread is on sale this week.

- I went to the store and picked up some bread and while I was in the isle I met a woman who was also shopping for bread. We talked. I'm in love.

See how fast that happened?

The narrative – the way we present the story – can change quickly too. We can see how a story is going and participate in changing it, so it moves in a different direction. We do it for ourselves all day long. Out of protection, fear, love, desire—you name it. We avoid someone, we pick up the phone, we dare to stand up for a cause. All these little decisions happen a bazillion times a day.

Focusing on Others

What I like about hospitality is it gives me a break from my own narrative and allows me to participate in someone else's. Sure, my story is still going; that's life. But my focus, when I'm in service of others, working with a team, is on someone else's story. This pursuit puts me in the present moment; it's similar to when I used to play sports or perform in front of large audiences. There is a rush because I'm outside of myself a bit, I'm less selfish, I'm in a place of trying to connect with someone, to be of service.

In hospitality, we are simply looking to positively affect a story. We are either building a positive story from scratch, enhancing a story that already exists, taking a bad story and making it better, or taking a good story and making it great. And that story usually has to do with someone else. You can never completely take yourself out of it, but the story is theirs, they are the lead, and you are a key player.

That story, whatever it is, might be played over and over in that person's mind, be shared with co-workers, friends, and family, or it may just be a brief, pleasant blip in a person's day. In hospitality, we always hope that the story is positive, creates a great memory, and is shared with others. The flip side is the story you don't want — the bad experience that you couldn't turn around or the fact that that person will never walk in your business again and will tell others an awful story.

This is the world we live in. These are the stories that are told when someone leaves our restaurants, hotels, and places of business. These are the stories of guests and employees. These stories, good and bad, go on to be told on social media: Instagram, Facebook, TikTok, Yelp, etc., the list goes on. And they stay there. Our goal is that the positive stories we help create, will bring more people to have a great experience with us. That's it. It's that simple. The more positive experiences a guest has in a restaurant, the more likely they are to return again, spend money, and share that great experience with others who will visit the restaurant. It's the same for the employees: the more positive experiences an employee has in a restaurant, the more likely they are to keep coming back with a great attitude, effect the team with that upbeat energy, create return customers, and grow their career with the restaurant or company.

A Moment to Connect

Here's the thing: over 30 years of experience in the hospitality industry have taught me that, if you care, you can positively affect a guest experience and their story every day. It doesn't have to be a massive celebratory flash mob in the restaurant or a Tiki drink on fire. It can be a tiny moment. Just a warm hello with a nice smile or a handwritten note with a simple recommendation for other things to do in the neighborhood. Our job isn't to simply place a plate of food in front of someone and walk away. That's not hospitality. We are here to change a story. To positively affect our guests and to move the needle. It's as simple as making sure our guests leave feeling a little better than when they walked in our door.

I want you to care. I want you to know that you have the power to affect someone's story, and to connect to them — remembering their favorite dish, introducing them to a new flavor or beverage. And the cool thing is that when you do affect the guest's story in a positive way, your story changes too. When you make people feel good, you feel good. That's a win-win.

I wrote this book to inspire you to care more about the service you give to people and to coach teams to do it: helping them reignite their passion for service, improve communication with each other, and find joy in those brief interactions with guests. This book is about their story, mine, and yours, so let's get into it.

A JOB

In my first hospitality book, *Counter Culture: An Essential Guide to Service*, I explored working in fast food, coffee shops, and fast casual establishments. Having worked in those myself, my next natural step, as it is with most restaurant folks, was to move into waiting/serving tables. For the purpose of this book, I will use the phrases "serving" and "server" instead of "waiting," "waiters," or "waitresses." It took me a while to be a server at a restaurant. I started at 15 as a dishwasher in a pizzeria. I then went from working at Sizzler, to working for multiple catering companies, to landing a great job as a bartender. I worked at a few more restaurants and finally landed at one of the most sought-after server jobs in Los Angeles. It was a long journey to a Michelin-starred restaurant with a small team that were nominated James Beard semifinalists for the "Outstanding Service" in the United States.

Moving Forward

Let's be clear about the motivations: I like details, being of service, connecting with people...and yes...making money. I don't want to oversell you on my good nature; while it does tie into everything I do and integrity is very important to me, I got into restaurants because I wanted to make money and I like restaurant and bar people, so it seemed like a good fit.

Since I wanted to continue to make MORE money, I had to adapt, learn more complex styles of service, improve my education, and move my way up through different types of restaurants that had higher prices. The higher the check average per guest, the more money I was going to make. That led me to the world of upscale and elevated dining.

Connecting

My last job in restaurants was serving very wealthy, super-famous people for many years in a Santa Monica restaurant with over 2,500 wines on a Wine Spectator Grand Award list. And as much as I thoroughly enjoyed my time working there and in some of the best restaurants in Los Angeles, I have to say that my favorite experiences were working in more casual places.

That's where I learned the secret to hospitality: how to connect with people. Casual restaurants and bars draw people from all walks of life, with varying viewpoints. I learned most of my life skills and people skills in those places. As I moved through more complex restaurants, I added many tasks to my position, more steps of service, more knowledge about food and beverage, all the things you need to be successful and make more money. But without learning the skills to connect with people, co-workers, and guests, I don't think I would have gone all that far. I certainly wouldn't have had as much fun.

People and relationships are what it's all about. That's what make stories interesting. It's rarely the place; it's always the people. One of my favorite restaurants is Black Bear Diner. Super casual, and I love it! I like to find that perfect butter-to-syrup ratio on the waffles, let it soak in a bit, but not too soggy, and then go to town on a stack. The last time I was there, in my hometown a couple of months ago, it was super busy. It always is. But the servers always have a nice comment for the table. The connection, while sometimes very brief, feels genuine. I've had a few different servers that are unique, maybe even a little quirky, but I'm down with the quirkiness. It's the connection that I most respond to and a server being present with us, even if it's quick, in the middle of a busy breakfast, is great service. And that moment, that connection that I enjoy when I dine out, is exactly the same moment managers should be encouraging their employees to achieve with guests, regardless of whether they're serving a $4 breakfast sandwich or a $75 Copper River salmon. Make a connection. Make a person smile. Improve their story.

DISCOVERING STYLES

In college I worked at Sizzler, one of the original restaurants to use a fast-casual concept. Guests would order at the counter, sit down with a number, and we would bring the food to them when it was ready. We, the servers, would get their drinks for them and check on them periodically throughout the meal: refilling drinks, clearing dishes, bringing their entrées to the table. The process involved just a few streamlined steps of service and the costs to dine were very reasonable.

Casual

In my early twenties we used to hang out late nights in Hollywood at places like Swingers, Canter's or the local Denny's or Mel's Drive-In Hollywood. These places were packed as people were exiting shows, clubs, and bars. Here you could sit down at the table, order your food from the server, the items were usually served in less than 15 minutes, and you could be out the door in 40 minutes to an hour. These were casual, full-service, sit-down style restaurants.

In my mid-twenties, when I had a little more money and I was looking for a different atmosphere, I started going on dates at restaurants. The great thing about Los Angeles is there is food from all over the world, at every price point imaginable. So, I explored more casual restaurants but with a little more atmosphere and interesting foods than a diner, but still within my budget. Thai, Mexican, Peruvian, Argentinian, Greek, Filipino, Italian, Korean, the list goes on. L.A. is a great food city!

Upscale

Eventually I ramped it up a bit and started looking for romantic restaurants for dates and finding the right atmosphere, low lights, good music, great vibe, with a little more upscale food. This is where my life really shifted, and I started to feel a sense of enthusiasm about finding a great place. I was introduced to wine and started to enjoy it with dinner. I wanted to have a different type of experience. I had to pay more, but I was okay with it. That's part of the deal.

And this is around the time I started to understand the difference between types of restaurants and what I was paying for. I had been to plenty of casual places, was just starting to explore nicer upscale restaurants, and hadn't really been to a fine-dining restaurant.

Elevated

I grew up in Sonoma, California, thirty minutes away from the French Laundry. I had some friends that worked there and knew I would probably never be able to afford to eat there. That place was what I'd call elevated. To be honest, I worked in elevated/fine dining restaurants well before I could even afford to have that type of experience.

These were the types of places I discovered: Casual, Upscale, Elevated. For the purposes of this book, I will use the term "elevated" dining instead of "fine dining." I use this because now there are so many types of restaurant offerings that fall into this category, and I think "fine dining" has become a bit of an antiquated and limited term that doesn't quite encapsulate all the types of experiences you can have at the high end of the restaurant spectrum.

Casual, Upscale, and Elevated are the areas I'll explore in the book and use as a rough guide to service and how it is refined and grows more complex with each step up in style. The cuisine and food costs will also be different, of course, involving varying quality of ingredients, cooked using different techniques, plated in specific styles, served in different atmospheres. But this book is going to focus primarily on the service standards and ways we make memorable, connecting experiences at any level of dining.

In my book, *Counter Culture: An Essential Guide for Service*, I go into detail about fast food, fast casual, and coffee shop concepts. If someone wants to experience a restaurant atmosphere where they can sit down and then order from a server, as opposed to doing it at the counter, they would be in what is referred to as a "full-service" restaurant. Guests expect a distinct set of service standards when they sit down in a restaurant: the steps of service shift to a bigger focus on table service and how the server, team, and kitchen can meet those expectations.

NAVIGATING THIS BOOK

You can read this book front to back, or you can simply look for a very specific subject from the Contents section in the front or the Index section in the back. If you've had some experience in restaurants and are trying to brush up on some skills, jump around and find a topic that motivates you or makes you nervous. Other amazing people offer plenty of wisdom, thoughts, and advice in interviews throughout. This may be a book you are using because you want to move up to a different level of restaurant. You may be a new supervisor or manager navigating the ideas and practices of communication and other important topics. You could be an owner or seasoned manager looking to use this book as a guide or tool with a new supervisor or manager. You may simply keep it in the office to pick a topic or idea to use at line-up, as you inspire your team to connect with each other and guests. I hope you can continue use this book as a reference as you grow in your roles and throughout your career in hospitality.

Many restaurants blend styles of service from each of the sit-down categories I present in the book. The vision of the owner, chef, or franchise will determine this choice. There is always a vibe or style they are presenting to guests, and a targeted price point they will fall into...so I tried as best I could to keep the categories separate, staying aware restaurant owners will mix and match according to their own style.

Style and Price

It's hard to talk about service without talking about style and price. When you look at some of the popular websites for dining and travel, such as Trip Advisor, OpenTable, Resy, SevenRooms or Yelp, you find they break down restaurants into price ranges and various categories. However, those lines have completely melded into each other in the last decade of dining. I like that. So many amazing chefs and restaurateurs have been pushing the limits to provide different experiences at different price points. What is considered fine dining in Minneapolis may be different in Seattle. A casual restaurant in Nashville may be different than a casual restaurant in San Francisco. For the sake of this book, I continue to use these categories so the reader can have some sort of framework to find what they're looking for.

In my first hospitality book, *Counter Culture*, I loved it when fine dining chefs took elements they had in their elevated restaurants and peppered the fast-casual dining experience with those. That's the beauty of crossing between categories. You don't have to just be in one. The elements are interchangeable depending on your budget, service ability, and business model.

Last year I was in Atlanta and had some amazing BBQ at a sit-down restaurant. Our server had on flip-flops, shorts, tank top, sleeved tats, and looked a little unkempt. As soon as our server opened their mouth to explain the menu, I knew we were in great hands. The server guided us skillfully through the menu with great knowledge of ingredients and descriptions of the dishes, portion sizes, and flavors. It wasn't an inexpensive restaurant, and based on the service provided, it seemed to be an upscale experience.

TO BE OF SERVICE

My friend Fredo Vita, the first Concierge I ever worked with, was the first person I watched sign on a signature line, "Yours in Service." Initially, I thought it was kind of hokey. Since he had worked at some very high-profile luxury hotels, was a member of the renowned Les Clefs d'Or, and had served as the president of the Los Angeles Concierge Association, I figured maybe this is just a thing they say in fancy places.

What it meant was "I will always put you first and I will always find a way to be of service to you." And after working with Fredo for a year, I got to see exactly what it meant in action. This was how he approached hospitality. He lived it. He taught me how important each detail is and that the name of the game is repeat guests. "How are you going to make sure they come back? How are you going to anticipate their needs and make this a memorable moment for them." He taught me how to hunt for opportunity, to be a hospitality detective, to find connection points with guests and personalize my service to their unique needs.

Nick Peyton, the well-known restaurateur from Cyrus in Healdsburg told me, "For the service industry, you are a people pleaser. You actually want that to the very edge of dysfunction. That is going to drive your intuition and anticipation because you want that. We work for that little thrill—that we enlivened somebodys' life. You know when you hit it. Oh my god, those people went out of here floating on a cloud—and part of that was because of how I orchestrated that meal. How I made that happen for them."

In a service economy that seeks to please customers and guests though service, I see a lot of opportunity missed. If we aren't connecting with guests, why would they come back? How are we creating return guests and sustaining revenue streams? We don't want to fall into the trap of thinking another customer will just walk through the door. The National Restaurant Association estimates a 20% success rate for all restaurants, and 80% fail within five years of opening. (Wells, Andrea. Squeezed from All Sides: Restaurants, Pressured by Labor, Food, Insurance Costs. Insurancejournal.com. 18/3/2024.

https://www.insurancejournal.come/magazines/mag-features/2024/03/18/764913.htm.)

With those kinds of failure rates, we can't take our guests for granted or make assumptions. In order to be part of the successful 20%, we need to personalize our interactions, anticipate our guests' needs, and ensure they return.

On the Lookout

Being proactive and looking for "little red flags" will help us see possible issues before our guests do. Pay attention. This is the service part. I think it's dangerous to create a false narrative, telling ourselves: "They didn't say they hated it, so they must have loved it." Or "They didn't mind, or they would have definitely said something." Or my least favorite saying of all time; "It was good enough."

Most people are not big fans of confrontation. They aren't going to tell you to your face that their steak was overcooked, or that they are annoyed they had to wait 30 minutes for their entrées or 17 minutes for a cocktail. When a server or manager comes to the table and asks a generalized question like, "How is everything?" or "Sorry about the wait, but it's a great steak isn't it?" they will just receive a generalized response: a nod, a grunt, or possibly, "It's fine, thanks." Most of the time people are going to avoid being direct. They won't tell you, "You really dropped the ball" or "You should have someone paying closer attention to ticket times and ensure the server writes the order down correctly." They are simply not going to return. And they may decide to post their negative experience on social media.

We should be searching for feedback. All of us: servers, runners, supervisors, managers, chefs, owners. The phrase "no feedback is great feedback" may sink you. That's the equivalent of a company canceling their reporting and feedback channels so no one can see the numbers or measure experiences. I don't know of any customer-driven business where that model leads to success. You should be looking for real-time information - any information that can help the restaurant and team do better.

Being of service means we are on the lookout to make the guest experience great. Trying to read a table, read a room, read a person and fix a situation before it becomes one. Owners and managers should be coaching teams to pay attention to guests, details, and the systems in place to create a nice dining experience.

This doesn't mean your team has to hover and over-service every table, but they do need to have their radar on. It's essential to ask the right questions. Is your service effective? Are your food and service consistently up to standard? Are you paying attention to the verbal and nonverbal cues of each guest? If you can beat the guest to the issue, while focusing on making small connections, your service will bring people back. Coaching and training on these types of questions is essential.

That training and coaching requires an investment, and the guest will know the difference. I asked restaurateur Thom Crosby, known for his company's diligent training practices, "What if you put all this effort into training your employees and they leave?" He responded with seven words. "What if I don't, and they stay?" Mic drop.

Consistent and Accountable

While we are going to delve into a lot of aspects of service, it's very important to come back to three simple things.

- Do your employees know the steps of service and standards you want them to execute?

- Do they know the details of the menu items and drinks you serve?

- Are you consistently coaching on service and holding them accountable when they don't know these details of the role?

I think this book provides some very useful information. But if this book is to be used in the best way, then it should be coached consistently. Over time, I guarantee you will see amazing results in both your own growth as a leader and your teams' overall performance.

1 to 10

One of my first jobs in an upscale restaurant was in a place called Blue Velvet in downtown Los Angeles. It was a cool, hip restaurant. I got put on lunches to start because that's what happens when you're the new guy. During my third lunch shift, the chef, Kris Morningstar, came out and pointed to a couple waiting at the host stand and said, "What number would you assign to those people based on how you think they are feeling?"

I was confused: "What? What do you mean?"

He responded a little more abruptly, "That couple, there, waiting to be sat, on a scale of 1 to 10, how would you say they are feeling?"

I looked at them and responded, "I don't know, maybe a 7."

He replied, "Great. Your job is to make sure that number is an 8, 9, or 10 by the time they leave. Understand?"

"Yes, Chef."

And he walked back into the kitchen.

I think that might be the simplest and most spot-on lesson in service I'd ever had.

It was time to move into action. Change a story. Be of service.

PART 1: CASUAL RESTAURANTS

1

THE RUNDOWN

Casual Restaurants

Casual restaurants are some of my favorite places to eat. It's difficult to precisely define a full-service sit-down casual restaurant because there can be so many different types: diners, family-oriented, brewery restaurants, themed restaurants, 10 tables, 50 tables. Typically these are at a lower price point, but that's not a given. It's a wide range. Some are simple and streamlined, others with big teams adept at handling large volumes of guests.

Team: The restaurant team may consist of the following:

- Host: Greets guests and seats the room

- Busser: Clears tables, resets tables, and refills drinks

- Runner: Takes plates from the kitchen to the tables

- Expeditor: Manages the kitchen pass where plates land before being taken out to the dining area. This role is more common in high-volume casual restaurants. Usually, this position is fulfilled by the chef, sous-chef, or lead runner.

- Server: Explains menu items, takes orders, takes food to tables

- Bar Preppers/ Batchers: These positions will prep ingredients and/or create batches of popular cocktails to use during service. Depending on the complexity and volume of the restaurant bar, managers of these positions may also be needed.

- Bartender/Beertender: Makes drinks for the entire restaurant and serves guests who may be eating at the bar

- Dishwasher: Washes dishes and assists with cleaning the restaurant

- Prep Cook: Cook who comes in early and focuses on prepping items for that other cooks will use during service

- Line Cook: A cook that is assigned a certain station on "the line" tasked with preparing and cooking food for service

- Chef: May design menu items and/or oversee the cooks on the line

- Owner: May be a full owner, franchise owner, partner, or investor

Since casual restaurants vary in size, you may have employees taking on multiple roles. In a smaller restaurant, a server may be asked to execute most roles: greeting, bussing, and running. If you are a supervisor or manager, you should know how to perform the roles in the Front of House (FOH) operations. Understanding these details will allow you to navigate and guarantee the guest has a great experience. You will be able to give direction to your employees, side coach when necessary, and in the event that someone calls out sick or the restaurant is busy, this skill will only enhance your ability to assist the team.

Training

Once you are hired as a new employee you should receive a description of all the menu items: food and drinks you are expected to know. New managers will also usually train this way, to understand the processes of the restaurant. It's important to start studying as soon as possible. Some quick ways to start memorizing and retaining this information are:

- Flashcards: Write everything down and continue to test yourself

- Phone voice recorders: Record menu item descriptions and play them back

- Pictures: If the chef allows, pictures are a great way to memorize if you are a visual learner

- Discuss: It's never too early to start getting your mouth around the words; role-play with someone at home and start describing dishes

Training will depend on the restaurant and the management. In most restaurants, employees will learn the food and beverage, shadow someone in the kitchen or at the window where food is picked up, shadow a server on the floor, discuss special cocktails and wine offerings, as well as learn the computer system. Most training occurs during service with staff but may be done via computer tutorials as well.

Point of Sale system

Most items in a restaurant are entered/ordered into a computer system call a POS—a Point of Sale system. Some large systems include Micros, Aloha, and Squirl. A POS system can also operate through a tablet, phone, or other mobile device, such as Square, Clover, Lightspeed, TouchBistro, and Toast. Employees will either be using pad and pen to take the order tableside and then type that information into the POS system at a station somewhere in the restaurant, or they may be using the POS mobile devices tableside.

Modifications

Practice and repetition are the quickest way to get a handle on the Point-of-Sale system. Understanding the framework and how items are listed is important, with modifiers being equally important. Modifiers are clarifications, additions or subtractions from a given dish. If a steak is ordered, a modification screen may appear asking for temperature, sides, or substitutions. Some modifiers may exist for common allergies including "Gluten Free," "Nut Allergy," "No Dairy," "No Shellfish" and "No Sesame."

- If a new hire is on the clock and has time before service starts or while waiting for the last table to leave, these are ideal times to improve on computer skills. The faster an employee is on a computer, the quicker they can navigate the operation system, and the easier time they will have adjusting to service and speed. Remember DO NOT hit "Send" or "Submit" during these practice sessions. Here are a couple other quick tips:

- Make space to practice when there are no guests in the restaurant. Practice putting in orders just as you would during service. Get used to the modification buttons and take your time. Repetition will naturally make you quicker.

- Once you feel comfortable with the layout of the restaurant, do speed rounds. Practice putting in orders just as you would in the heat of service. Time yourself. At one restaurant where I worked, a manager made it a game and each server had the same list of menu items and modifications, with seat numbers, and we had to put in the order as fast as possible without making mistakes. The competition was fun.

Some restaurants and restaurant groups use well-designed computer programs to help train their staff. These trainings may be completed on the computer at work, or employees may be able to do it from their home computer or mobile device. Some programs and companies allow employees to clock in on a device and learn the lessons needed to fulfill the training, track the time it takes, and the progress of the training.

Back Up Plan

Technology is changing rapidly and it helps us provide service in a quicker, more efficient manner, but always have a Plan B! At some point, a POS system will conk out at 8:30 p.m. on a Saturday night. It happens. It's happened at every place I've worked. Managers and servers should have a plan in place and be able to go "old school" if the computers go down. It's important for servers to know the plan prior to the issue arising, because they will most likely be the ones to implement the plan while the manager is communicating with frustrated guests. Servers should be able to answer these questions:

- How are we going to take the orders from guests and communicate that to the kitchen?

- How are we going to get payment information from the guests and keep it secure?

- How are we going to process the payment once the computers come back on?

Management Duties

Restaurant management duties may include any of the following:

- Promote and lead restaurant organization and cleanliness

- Participate in the hiring of potential employees

- Train staff in restaurant policies and service standards

- Learn restaurant's computer system, reservation system, and other programs

- Oversee restaurant liquor and food inventories

- Oversee compliance with policies, practices, and procedures

- Control costs within designated departments

- Effectively schedule employees to meet the demands of the restaurant

Beer, Wine, Cocktails

Casual restaurants will vary on how many beverage offerings they have for guests. Managers and servers should be familiar with the types and styles of beverages served. Is the beer a lager or an IPA? Is the wine white or red, light bodied or heavier? If cocktails are available, are they sweet, sour, bitter, spicy, salty? Knowing the basics of flavor profile and style allows the employee to be specific about what the restaurant has to offer.

Being able to offer beers according to style is a great detail. *"For lighter beers we offer two lagers, Coors and Corona. If you'd like a medium-bodied beer, we have a Sierra Nevada Pale Ale. Medium to heavy we have two IPA's – a Codebreaker West Coast style and Highland Park Competition, American style. For something heavier, we offer a Pizza Port Imperial Stout."*

When offering wine in a casual restaurant, knowing the body style of the wine can guide the guest. "If you'd like lighter whites, we have a dry riesling or citrus-forward pinot grigio, a medium-bodied, high-acid, crisp sauvignon blanc from New Zealand, or a full-bodied, oaky California chardonnay."

When a guest asks for a recommendation for a cocktail, I like to ask a clarification question. What do you tend to like? Something light or heavy? Sweet, sour, or bitter? Fruity, boozy, refreshing? This personalizes the interaction and gives the server or bartender a direction for guiding the guest. It's easy for us to recommend what *we* like, but clarifying with the guest about what *they* like may help filter the options down, discovering together what the guest is more likely to enjoy on your menu.

It's ideal for a restaurant to have an engaging beer, wine, and cocktail program because it improves the guest experience, while easily improving the check average. It's essential for servers to know what they sell so they can describe it well to customers. Servers should have a couple of favorites and also be able to shift recommendations, helping the bartender out when it's very busy; if the restaurant is slammed, don't recommend six of the most time-consuming and difficult drinks for the bartenders to make.

Knowing prep times for drinks, as everyone should for food items, will only help your team as you collectively curate the guest's experience. Managers and servers who can use their skills of suggestion will be able to alleviate guests waiting, expedite the drink process for your bartenders, and turn tables quicker.

Depending on the restaurant and management, employees can get as detailed as they like about the beverages offered. Who produces the wine? What brewery makes the beer? How many elements of the cocktail should someone mention when dropping it off to the table? Some casual restaurants will prefer quick and simple, while others may like employees to delve a little deeper into how they describe what they serve. I've been in restaurants where the beertenders can go full beer nerd and tell you where the hops are from, how they are grown, the pH balance of the soil, what the brewing process is like for a specific beer, and the whole history of a brewery. Just ensure this is what the guest wants. The experience offered to a guest should always entail your team reading the guest and pivoting off their cues.

When I spoke with Greg Koch, co-founder of Stone Brewing, about his approach in his tasting rooms and restaurants, he said, "The expectation is that our servers and bartenders are consultants. They can consult with a varying level of knowledge basis that our guests will have, so they can guide them. Sometimes you can suss out in the conversation that the guest knows quite a bit but are asking about beers they may not be intimate with. So, I can use some sophisticated language that they will fully understand. Or, I can tell that this person is little bit newer in the curve, and therefore I've got to modify my delivery so that I won't leave them behind or talk over them. They [bartenders] need to be able to suss out that difference."

Managers should make beverages a consistent conversation at line-ups. Ask what beverages employees are excited about or what they would pair with menu items. Can those employees that interact with guests describe the beverages really well? Can they meet the guest where they are? Quizzing should be a part of the culture. It shouldn't elicit an eyeroll and a sarcastic, "Great, Josh is going to quiz us again." Make it fun and engaging. This is how you build confidence in the team. How you build a service culture. In any restaurant, guests love an experience where they trust the server to guide them confidently to the right beverage for them.

The Floor

Ideally, a new hire, server, manager, or any front of the house employee should be prepared to memorize the layout of the restaurant as soon as possible. A floor map is usually provided. Sections, table numbers, and even seat numbers are usually included. I've always tried to get this out of the way as soon as possible, as being able to communicate about the location and seat number of a guest is going to be key in any conversation.

Be Prepared

With the many things that people do in their lives, it's important to have a conversation with employees about making a distinct shift from their personal mindset into their work mindset. It's not a big ask, but the staff are expected to be mentally prepared to support the needs of the restaurant and guests. I've always enjoyed working in hospitality because I get to put a break on what is happening in my personal life and shift my focus to working with a team and serving guests. This type of private conversation may be appropriate and needed if an employee is doing any of the following:

- Showing up to work late on a regular basis.

- Showing up to work in the nick of time, clocking in, and disappearing into the bathroom to get ready and but not being fully present with the team at the appropriate time.

- An employee that is still finishing their own tasks of the day, not relevant to the restaurant: on their phone, texting, emailing while on the clock at work. The idea isn't that the first 30 minutes of the shift is warm-up. The expectation is at the start of the shift, an employee is ready and focused to help the team.

Grooming Standards

Employees should always have a clean uniform. Grooming standards are always reviewed during onboarding of an employee, and they have to be consistently observed by managers. As a guest, when I see a server with a stain on a shirt, messy apron, or dirty shoes, my take is that no one has checked this employee before the shift. The team should look ready.

A general rule for grooming standards may be:

- Uniform cleaned and pressed, no stains

- Shoes look clean and well kept, polished if applicable

- Hair pulled back (if long)

- Facial hair groomed, so it doesn't look too unkempt
- Fingernails trimmed and clean
- No excessive perfumes or colognes
- Nametag on, if applicable

Essential Items

Along with grooming and ensuring employees look ready to work, they should have the necessary tools on them to do their job. For a manager and server, it will be common to have the following in a casual restaurant:

- 2 pens
- 1 bottle opener/wine key
- 1 Point of Sale key card
- 1 lighter (for candles, although many are battery operated)
- 1 pad of paper

Setting the Room

It's always important to have the dining room set up for lunch or dinner service. There will usually be a standard as to how everything should look. A general rule of thumb is you want it to look clean and aligned, ready to receive your guests. As with grooming, a supervisor or manager should quickly walk the room before line-up to ensure the room is ready and up to the standard of the restaurant. Some standards may be:

- Align the tables.
- Ensure the tables are balanced and the chairs are sturdy.
- Clean the chairs so they are free of dust, crumbs.
- Make sure the floor is clean and free of debris.

- Check that artwork is straight and free of dust and debris.

- Check that all lamps and lights have working lightbulbs.

- Light all candles (before service starts).

- If using battery-operated candles, ensure you have backups in case they go out during service.

- Fill water pitchers and set for service.

- If utilizing music, ensure the correct music and volume level is set.

Setting the Table

In my book, *Counter Culture*, I point out that most of us are already attentive to details and matching; we just need to apply this to restaurant tasks. That attention to detail is there in the server or busser who has an amazing fade; clean, unblemished tennis shoes; or an immaculate car. The runner or bartender that has their special shirt or blouse they only wear on a date, or the details they pay attention to when grandma is coming over to visit. All of these moments are in-focus because they mean something to those individuals outside of work. The same detailed focus needs to simply shift to the restaurant. Details matter. This is a very coachable skillset for managers. Here are a few general notes surrounding a properly set table.

- Tabletop is clean and free of debris.

- Any plates pre-set at the table should be clean and free of stains and chips/cracks.

- Utensils and glasses should be handled toward the bottom. This keeps employee's hands away from areas that may come in touch with a guest's mouth.

- All glassware should be checked to be free of stains or water spots.

- Vase, candle holder, or any other table accessory is clean and free of debris.

- Utensils should be aligned. One inch from the edge of the table is a good standard.

- Utensils, glassware, and plateware are set to match each of the other tables in the dining room.

- If paper napkins are pre-placed, ensure they are placed at identical positions around the table. If utensils are placed on top of the napkin, they should be placed evenly and identical to other settings at the table.

Line-Up

This is a pre-shift meeting, lasting anywhere from three to ten minutes and ideally involving the whole team or as many as possible. I've seen this happen mostly after the room is set and just before the doors open for service. In the event that the restaurant is already open, a private space can be utilized for this meeting to happen out of the view of restaurant guests.

Information discussed may include:

- Position assignments for the shift, how many sections the floor is broken into and who is in what section

- Any specials that are on the menu and how to describe them

- Introducing new food or drink items and their descriptions

- Menu items not available that shift, requiring a verbal warning to the guests *before* they look at the menu

- Any items that have a low count (meaning only a few more exist and will most likely run out during the shift)

- Specific points of service to focus on during the shift

- Announcing sales goals for the shift and sharing selling tactics

- Sharing positive notes, quotes, or feedback with the team

- Notification of any equipment that is out of service and will affect the team and guests

This is an ideal moment for supervisors, managers, and chefs to connect with their teams, bringing them together and focusing them for service. Consistency and repetition are key. Consistency means that it happens every day at the same time. Through repetition, discussing elements of service and using skills exercises and menu quizzes, we hone those skillsets. My friend, Tim McCracken, likes to say, "We celebrate redundancy. We hear it again and again and again and we do it again and again. Celebrate the redundancy."

Line-Up (Shift) Board

For restaurants that stay open throughout the day or have staggered in-times, a line-up or shift board is a great option to have for those employees that are unable to attend line-up. Menu changes, new specials, and any other pertinent information for the shift should be posted here.

Steps of Service

This can also be referred to as Sequence of Service. I loved the steps of service at my first server job. They were a straightforward guide, and if you followed the steps, you were usually guaranteed to provide at least B-level service as long as you brought a good attitude. In hospitality you can't just go through a checklist with an unenthusiastic attitude. This job is not to simply write down an order, put a plate of food in front of someone, and expect to have your customers come back. We have to do that with warmth and generosity. Consistently. This job asks you to bring some feeling to it.

The steps of service are a guide, a framework to follow, while you fill in that framework by engaging with the guest and ensuring they are enjoying their experience in the restaurant. For a casual restaurant, the steps of service don't differ much from any other style of restaurant. **In upscale and elevated restaurants, you are just adding more steps to the process to ensure a heightened dining experience.**

Here is an example of Steps of Service for a casual restaurant:

- Host, manager, or server greet the guests as they come in the door.

- Host, manager, or server check guests into the reservation system, if applicable.

- Host, manager, or server seats the guests and gives them their menus.

- Server greets the table, tells them of any special additions to the menu, recent promotions, and takes a beverage order.

- Server or busser brings the drinks to the table.

- Server asks the guests if they have any questions about the menu and takes the order, asking about allergies in the process.

- Server puts the order in the computer.

- Server checks back with the table to refill beverages.

- Server serves the food to the table and ensures they have any condiments or additions before walking away from the table.

- Server checks back with the table a *couple of minutes* later (people always miss this one!) to see if anyone needs anything.

- Server or busser checks back again and refills drinks throughout the meal.

- Server or busser clears the dishes promptly when the table is finished dining.

- Server offers dessert and/or coffee.

- Server or runner brings dessert and/or coffee.

- Server brings a check to the table.

- Server collects payment, processes it, and give it back to the table. (This could all be done at the table if the restaurant is using a handheld point of sale system.)

- Server thanks the guest for dining and tells them to have a good day, afternoon, or night.

- Host and/or manager thanks the guest on their way out the door

Remember, these will shift and change depending on the style of the restaurant and the complexity of service and food provided. A more relaxed place may not have a host. Guests may seat themselves when they walk in, pick their utensils out of a container on the table, and use a QR code to read a menu on their own phone. Never forget that while this may be considered okay in a casual setting, your restaurant is asking the guest to do the tasks that another competing restaurant may be fulfilling. It is vital to ramp up the service and personal engagement when you are eliminating services that other restaurants provide within the same price point.

Greeting and Seating

A reoccurring theme in my interviews is that one of the most underestimated roles is that of host/hostess. In a smaller casual restaurant, it's still important to understand that even without the position of a host/hostess, the server or manager should be able to execute this role. It's a difficult position that a lot of people think is simple. The host/hostess needs to possess many skills other than a friendly attitude and upbeat enthusiasm. It's hard to sit 80 tables a night. It's really hard to sit 200 in a large casual restaurant. This position needs to bring that friendly and engaged attitude, consistently, to each person that walks through the door while handling other tasks. A few things essential to the position are:

- Organization: knowing the guests (regulars and/or guests with reservations) that are coming in and communicating details such as guest preferences, special occasions and allergies to the server and team

- Keeping an authentic, upbeat attitude throughout the shift, without making it seem mechanical, forceful, or robotic

- Communicating in a friendly way to guests as to why their table may not be ready and/or how long they can expect to wait

- Managing the text or pager alert system for waiting guests
- Answering the telephone using friendly phone manners and energy
- Answering any questions from the guests about the menu
- Ensuring menus are clean and in great condition
- Seating guests and communicating with them any information needed before their server approaches the table
- Saying goodbye to guests and thanking them for dining

Table Presence

Table presence refers to how a server and any other position talks to the table. Some aspects of good table presence may include:

- Positive attitude
- Appropriate language
- Good posture
- Ability to engage with customers
- Skill to read the guests at the table
- Can take care of the guests in their section
- Ability to describe a dish

All managers and owners are looking for someone with good, consistent table presence. If you have awesome table presence when you have four tables, it can't all go away when you have eight tables. The goal is to get your table presence consistent no matter how busy your section is. This is a huge challenge in restaurants that do a lot of covers. "Covers" refer to the number of people who dine during a specific shift.

Professional servers are great at consistency. But it takes practice. A great manager will gradually build a new server's section as that server is learning the ropes, adding a table per night or nights and slowly getting the server up to the speed and table count they are expected to handle. This ramp-up gradually builds a server's confidence and in turn, table presence. If a restaurant doesn't have the time for this, role-playing before service is a great opportunity; working on speed, order taking, and inputting orders in pre-shift exercises should help prepare a server to ramp up more quickly. Be creative. How you practice is how you play.

Power of Suggestion

- Guests are always looking for tips on what to eat or drink. Oftentimes, when the restaurant is running low on an item, or they have multiple items that come from one part of the kitchen (the cook on pastas is very backed up on tickets) a manager and server's knowledge of similar items on the menu will come in handy. You're expected to know your menu and ingredients well, so you can offer smart options to the guest at a moment's notice. Here are some ideas when it comes to recommending alterative items on the menu:

- Find a similar alternative on the menu to suggest to them

- If it's a salad, recommend another different cold item that they may enjoy

- If it's salmon, offer another type of white fish or mild flavored fish (cod, halibut)

- If it's a steak, you could recommend another cut or another protein (pork chop)

Taking the order

I've heard a manager exclaim, "How difficult can it be to take an order at the table? It's not rocket science." Agreed. It's not rocket science - but it can be difficult. The process of taking an order can set a server up for success or break them. Here are some good rules that will never change, no matter the style of restaurant.

- If the server is using a pad of paper, pre-fill or chart the pad, so it's easy to fill in information for each order at the table. (Early in my career, I would always run out of room and start scribbling in the margins when guests changed their mind mid-order. And then, when I got to the computer to enter it, I'd get confused — sometimes by my own hurried handwriting. I'm definitely not a rocket scientist. Preparation will save a server when they are slammed or are thrown a curveball.)

- Taking orders with handheld devices may benefit service by getting the order into the kitchen quicker. Some devices offer built-in upsell prompts to assist servers. "Do you want fries with that?" "Would you like the 24-oz. option for $2 more?" If servers are reading from this device to the guest, they should remember to look up intermittently and make eye contact with guests, making the upsell more personal.

- Always inquire about allergies.

- Repeat orders back to the guest, clarifying as it's written down or being typed into the handheld device.

- Get orders in quickly to control the pace of the table and shorten the table turn times.

- Servers and bartenders should know the menu items, adjustments to the menu, and prep times for popular dishes. Prep times for dishes will vary depending on how busy the restaurant is. A pasta ordered at 5:00 p.m. when the restaurant just opened, as opposed to 8:30 p.m. when the restaurant is slammed, could vary by upwards of 10 minutes. Anyone taking orders should have a general sense of the time it takes so customers aren't waiting too long.

- DOUBLE-CHECK the order before pushing send/enter. This ensures less mistakes.

- Everyone should be conscious of their fellow team members and prepare accordingly. On a busy night, a server who isn't prepared, trying to figure out what they wrote on their pad of paper and holding up the line at the POS system, is only going to get grief from managers and other servers waiting to get their orders in.

Allergies

More ingredients mean more things people can be allergic to. Or more things people may dislike. Servers and managers need to pay close attention. It needs to be written down and relayed to the chef. People's lives depend on it. If a guest has an allergy, I take the time to put it in for each dish a guest is ordering. Is it time consuming when a server is slammed on a busy night? Yes, but it's our commitment to the guest and it's what keeps them coming back...and alive.

Delivering Food to the Table

In a busy restaurant, you want to ensure that servers and runners are delivering the food to the correct table and, ideally, to the correct seat. Most POS systems have a seat number option so the runner or server know which seat the plate is going to. When picking up the food in the pass, any employee assisting wants to ensure they know a few things.

- Does the plate have the correct food on it?

- What table is the food going to?

- What seat at the table is that plate going to?

- Are all the food items for that table ready? If you don't do this, you run the risk of taking half the order out while the rest of the table has to wait extra time for their plates to arrive. This isn't an ideal situation when a family came to the restaurant to "eat together" and they receive their food 10 minutes apart.

When an employee drops off the dish, they want to place it in front of the correct guest and announce it. A few tips I find useful:

- Say the name of the dish and one or two main items in it, e.g., "Here is your eggs Benedict with rosemary potatoes," or "Grilled

Western burger with cheddar cheese and curly fries." You want to do this for three reasons: It's a great way to present the restaurant's food by defining the dishes that are being put down; you want to ensure that each person is getting the dish they ordered; and it gives an opportunity to the runner or server to ask if they may bring anything else to the guest.

- It's always a nicer experience for the guest to receive the food they ordered as opposed to listening to someone call out dish names like they are giving away free items at the local county fair. "Who has the Santa Fe chicken?" "This chicken Caesar looks tasty, who's having it?" "I got three orders of wings. Please raise your hand."

- The caveat here is the style of the restaurant may be casual enough that this auction-style delivery is intentional. There is a place where that works and it's appropriate to the atmosphere the owners are trying to have. It should be intentional though.

Backhanding

This term is used often when referring to the act of placing something in front of a guest using the inside arm. For example: if you are standing to the left of a sitting guest and you used your right arm to place an item in front of them, they would see the "back of your hand." If you used your left (outer) arm to place the item in front of the guest, they would see the inside of your left arm, and the palm-side of your hand. The server or runner also automatically creates space when they use the arm farthest from the guest. This can be applicable when placing drinks, pouring wine or water, and placing or removing food.

Bobby Stuckey, founder of Frasca Hospitality Group in Boulder, had this to say about backhanding, "Take a casual hip spot, but since it's casual they may not think it's important to understand how to put a plate down. But if you are eating there and there are a lot of plates coming out, and every time the server backhands you with the plate and your head goes back a little bit, without even knowing it, the guest is less comfortable, because their personal space has been affected. If you have somebody who grew up in fine dining… they present a plate properly, with that skill set where you are not backhanding a guest, you have actually just moved your hand eight inches away from a guest's face. And that can be done in ANY style restaurant! Think about the guest experience. It doesn't have to be just fine dining."

Table Maintenance

Table maintenance is anything that has to do with keeping the table clean and orderly: refilling water and beverages; clearing any empty glasses, used paper napkins, dirty utensils, or dishware. Repeatedly reminding servers and bussers to maintain tables drives managers and owners a little batty. I've seen this happen at every style of restaurant, everywhere! It's essential that servers, bussers, and runners maintain the tables.

Water service

A part of table maintenance is water service. If the restaurant's standard is that you have a self-serve water station and it's clear that guests are to serve themselves, I get it. But if water is being brought to the table, the team is responsible for the refills. A precedent has been set. I know it can be busy and crazy, but to have tables with empty water glasses that customers would like filled is unacceptable. It looks forgetful and lazy. Everyone should be on the lookout: bussers, runners, servers, managers. A restaurant is based on food AND beverage. Complimentary doesn't mean the team doesn't have to stay attentive to the task. Not everyone wants water and not everyone wants a refill, but it is the restaurant team's job to find out that information and ensure the guests who do want water don't have empty glasses in front of them. Be proactive and keep people hydrated.

Managing the Pace of the Table

Timing is essential in any restaurant. Staying in communication with the team about where a table is in the process of their meal is vital to ensuring they receive their courses in a timely manner. Often in casual restaurants an order will be "order fire," which means as soon as the order is sent through the Point-of-Sale device, the kitchen will start cooking it. This alleviates a lot of issues that can arise in multi-course restaurants. That said, paying attention to ticket times (the difference between the time the order was put in and the time it arrives at the table) is important.

Anticipation of Needs

The more focused the staff is on the non-verbal communication from guests and the anticipation of what those guest's needs may be, the quicker the pace of the table. Ideally, the team should be looking for and picking up guest cues.

My former colleague, Akili Steward, a server, sommelier, and GM, told me, "The better a server is at *figuring out* what their guest needs without them asking, the better a server they will be. This applies to entertaining guests, offering side items, making them feel special, and then disappearing when not needed. My personal goal while serving is to never be asked for anything."

Utensils

Ideally, utensils should already be set at the table when the guest is seated. But when a guest has ordered soup or steak, for instance, a specialty utensil, soup spoon or steak knife should be placed down. This should happen *before* that soup or steak arrives at the table. It does not make guests happy to watch their soup or steak get cold while flagging down a server for the correct utensil.

Use a Tray

Depending on the style of a casual restaurant, trays may be used. I think it makes it easier to take items such as drinks or specific condiments to a table using a tray. This cuts down on beverages dripping and looks nicer. Different-sized trays are a nice option depending on the number of items being taken to the table. This also allows for items to be picked up from tables using a tray.

I've been in packed casual restaurants and bars where it is not ideal to use a tray. Navigating through a crowd can be impossible with a tray and it may be easier to quickly carry two drinks to a table without it. If this is the intended service style of the restaurant than by all means, deliver items without a tray.

Do a Lap

It's imperative in successful restaurants that, if time allows, a server should be checking in on other servers' sections or assist in other areas of the restaurant: clearing a dirty dish, refilling beverages, taking an order, etc. This may only be for a minute at a time, but that minute can really make a difference for a manager, co-worker, or guest. If the runners and bussers can do the same with clearing and refills, the restaurant's going to win, and the guests will win too. Guaranteed.

Great managers are able to train staff to see the room in this way. Increase the vision of the servers and get them out of their section when they have a moment. See the whole room. If a server can learn to be efficient with their service and section, they can then find time to be do a lap and assist the team.

Clearing a table

There are a couple of schools of thought: only clear the table when everyone is finished; or remove each plate as it is finished. It's up to the restaurant to have a policy on when an employee should clear the table. The point is: dirty dishes and glassware, not including water glasses, need to be cleared. It should never wait until the after the guest has paid and left the table. Leave that look for the local Moose lodge party.

Employees can choose those moments and quickly remove any empty glasses or plates as the meal is winding down. Here are a few tips:

- Ask the guest if you may take their dish away *before* you start to take it away.

- Be careful placing your hands or arms too close to guests' faces.

- Minimize the clinking of utensils as you place them on plates you are clearing from the table. This can create a lot of unnecessary noise in the room.

- Do not scrape food from one plate to another in front of guests.

- Try to not stack plates, although in high-volume restaurants this may be unavoidable.

- If you are stacking plates, don't stack too high. And be conscious of utensils sliding off the plate onto the floor or hitting guests.

- If two guests are quite close to each other or conversing, a good rule is to not put your arm in between them. Clear on either side.

- Your clearing tray should look orderly when you are walking back past tables headed to the kitchen.

- While items on a table may be difficult to reach, avoid asking guests to hand items to you.

Dessert

Dessert is a great way to extend the guest experience and finish the meal off with something sweet. In casual restaurants, there may be desserts made to order, those that are pre-made, and those that require the server to finish the dessert with an extra item e.g. whipped cream, a scoop of ice cream, or a special garnish. If desserts are on the menu, they should always be offered to guests. I've seen servers offer desserts to-go to a table that is in a hurry. A few more thoughts on dessert:

- I was recently at a restaurant and the server asked our table if we were in the mood for dessert while two of us were still eating our entrees. I was confused, to say the least. It's not the first time. Dessert should be offered *after* the entire table is finished with their entrees.

- While desserts may come out very quickly, it's important that *before* they arrive to the table, new utensils are placed in front of each person that will be enjoying dessert.

- Dessert is special and certainly when it's a special occasion. Having some candles handy for a birthday or topper picks with sayings such as, "Happy Birthday" or "Happy Anniversary" are nice touches of hospitality.

The Dishwashing station

The dishwashing station should look organized, and that relies on everyone.

- Employees should not leave a bunch of food on the plates when they place them in the station.

- Put the correct glassware in the correct glass container at the dishwashing station.

- Be careful to not accidently toss utensils into the food waste bin. (Happens a lot!)

- If placing a very hot plate in the dishwashing station, notify the dishwasher so they are aware and don't burn themselves.

- Be conscious of the system that the dishwasher has set up and be helpful to that person and their role. They are focused on getting all those items cleaned and back to the team as quickly as possible.

Hardworking dishwashers will greatly appreciate this kind of help from the team.

Dropping the check

In high-volume restaurants, I've seen many servers drop the check before the guests are even finished eating. "Here is your check, whenever you need it. No rush." *If there is no rush, and time allows, employees should hold off on dropping the check until the guest is finished eating.* Also, an employee should ask something to the effect of, "Is there anything else I may bring you?" *before* bringing a check to the table. The point of this is to make sure the guests are satisfied with the meal they just ate and ensure they have everything they want. If the guest has no additional requests, that is the green light to place the check on the table.

To be fair, at a restaurant where a guests may get up and go to the front to pay their bill or sign their bill to a room, the server may want to make sure they are not keeping the guest waiting. Breakfast and lunch are times when a guest may be in a hurry to leave. In these instances, the restaurant policy may allow for an employee to drop the check before the guest is done eating. A couple of quick points about dropping the check.

- Avoid simply sliding the check on the table as you are strolling by.

- Say thank you and make eye contact when you place the check on the table.

- Be quick. If the guest puts a card down and is ready to leave, process it as soon as possible. Making people wait for any amount of time after you place the check down is bad news.

- Don't just disappear after the bill has been processed. I get that you may be waiting to take your break, but if that's the case, make sure someone will look after your tables.

I find it odd when I pay the bill and no servers or staff acknowledges me anymore. It gives the vibe, "I've got your money, now scram!" If a guest is still under your roof, then they are still a guest. If you had a friend over to your house to watch a ballgame and the game was over and you offered them a final beverage or something to nibble on and they said no, would you just walk to the bedroom, close your door, and go to sleep? No, that would be weird. You'd wait until they actually walk out the door of your house.

Even if the bill is finished and the table is clear of all items, employees should keep an eye out. A server should be in the vicinity so they can say goodbye when the guests start to get up from the table. A guest should never leave a table without some member of the team saying goodbye and thanking them. This is how we keep people coming back and how we show appreciation that they chose to come into our restaurant.

Cleanliness and Reset

Dirty tables should be cleaned quickly, efficiently and reset completely. Here are a few tips:

- Employees should make the least amount of noise possible. A tray should be used, but a bus tub may be used to clear a table that had a large party. Clear the table and stack the tray or bus tub with the dishwashing station in mind. By that I mean, employees should think about how they are going to offload into the dishwashing station, so it is efficient for the dishwasher to do their job.

- Be aware that guests can see everything and everyone in the dining room. Cleanliness is important, so if an employee is using an old dirty towel to wipe down a table, it's not going to inspire a lot of confidence in anyone who can see that happen. Wiping crumbs off the table onto the carpet or floor looks awful too, even if it's "just a few" and even when it seems no one will see it. Everyone on the floor should assume all guests are watching.

- Almost every place I've worked, I've seen supervisors and managers get annoyed that the team would leave a table dirty for longer than a few minutes after guests leave. The most common excuse is, "It's not my job." I've even seen a server not clean their dirty tables in a timely fashion so the host couldn't sit a later table in their section. The server had a party to go to later that evening. All right, I confess...it was me! I know these tricks; I've used them myself. It's not cool.

- The point of having a table reset quickly is the team should always want the restaurant to look as good at 9:00 p.m. as it did at 5:00 p.m. Not only does ownership want to be able to sit the table again, if needed, as soon as possible, but a reset table brings the room back to looking presentable and ready. There is nothing worse than being one of the last tables in a restaurant and all the tables are completely bare. This sends a message to the guests still dining: "We want you to leave!" You might as well turn the lights up, start putting chairs on the tables and break out the vacuum. Kidding. But I've seen it done and those guests will likely never return to your restaurant.

Note: Don't put a guest in the position of having to agree to an employee's probing question: "You don't mind, do you? We are just doing our side work; we can stop if you'd like us to." Of course, most people will say they don't mind, but you are putting them in an odd position. Yes, they mind, they are trying to enjoy the end of their meal. They don't need to hear the music turned off, plates banging like crazy in the kitchen, and chairs being stacked as they are taking the last bites of their chocolate drizzled cheesecake. My bet is the restaurant will lose that return customer.

Side Work

Look, I'm a realist. Side work has to be done, and there is no way you can wait for all the guests to leave to do everything. But employees need to stay aware: side work should be done while not affecting the experience of the guest. If a server decides to disappear for ten minutes to do side work in the back, they should first ensure someone is looking after their tables. If employees can do side work in increments as the evening is winding down, without guests seeing, that is ideal. Be discreet. Employee should not assume a guest would understand, "Hey, this is a restaurant, this is just what we do at this time of night. The clock is ticking; I got a party to bounce to." They would like to finish their meal in the same restaurant atmosphere they walked into.

I mention this other issue I have about side work in *Counter Culture* because it happens everywhere: employees shouldn't leave their own, designated side work for someone else to complete! There is always someone who just does the bare minimum. It creates a lot of resentment in co-workers. If employees think co-workers don't notice that they are skimping on their side work, they are wrong. You can always tell yourself, "The condiments seem full enough. There is enough soap in the dispenser, enough rolled silver, enough folded napkins, the bar bottle rack is clean enough." "Is it enough?" is not the question. The question is: is it full and ready for a guest? Is it completely clean, not just clean enough? Employees shouldn't cut corners and leave more work for the next person. If each person completes their side work fully and quickly, the team will appreciate them.

Checklists are an ideal way to ensure tasks are completed. This may be a digital checklist on a shared device or a traditional paper checklist.

Side work, pre-shift or post-shift, in a casual restaurant may include:

- Restock supplies that may include napkins, straws, utensils, glassware, ketchup, mustard, mayonnaise, salt, pepper, teas, coffee, creamer, non-dairy creamers, sugars, sweeteners, artificial sweeteners.

- Wipe down utensils/ flatware/ silverware (these words are interchangeable)

- Roll utensils, fold paper napkins if necessary.

- Restock items in the bathroom: dish soap, hand towels, bath tissue, liner for wastebasket. Wipe down mirror.

- Clean and restock the server station including items listed above and clean menus, clean cups and glassware, clean plates, shared utensils, liners for wastebasket.

- Set and fill water pitchers.

- Wipe down tables, chairs, booths, menu QR codes, windows.

- Clean windows, mirrors, or any glass tables before service begins

- Restock any items needed at the pass: wet towel for wiping, share utensils, printer tape.

- Restock any boxes or bags for to-go items.

- Bar areas may need restocking with beverages, syrups, CO tanks, beers, wines, liquors, ice, printer tape, napkins.

- Bar area may need cut fruit (lemons, limes, peels), and restocked olives, onions, specialty items, and items used in drinks: straws, picks, decorative items.

- Restrooms are checked right before opening to ensure they are clean and restocked prior to opening the doors. If employees use the guest restroom prior to the restaurant opening, the restroom should be checked and reset after the last employee has used it, but before the first guests walk in the restaurant.)

Ideally, restrooms should be checked throughout the shift to ensure they are clean and stocked for guests.

2

VALUE

Price, Expectation, and the Guest Experience

I think of value as the place where price and expectation meet. I like to talk about money. I didn't for a long time, and I think it's because it scared me. I felt intimidated by it. When it came to saving, I never had enough. When it came to spending, I was getting by. But even when I didn't have money, I could still understand value. Was I getting what I was paying for?

Ripped off

I feel like I have a good sense of knowing if I'm being ripped off. Like when I go to the airport and a small bag of chips is $8 dollars, or a bottle of water is $7.50. My wife and I love baseball, but I can't help feeling a little taken advantage of when I see $10 hotdogs, $21 beers, and $9 lemonades.

But we know we are being taken advantage of in these places. We have to pay the high prices because, frankly, there are no other options. So then we ask the question, "Is it worth it?" At the airport, I've yet to find a way to justify the costs. But at a baseball game or a concert, I'm o.k. with the cost because I find value in it. I still feel a little annoyed, but I'm paying for an experience: the huge baseball lights, the roaring crowd, and $8 bags of peanuts being thrown over your head by a vendor into the hands of an excited neighboring sports fan. Or another awesome vendor guy meandering through Scottsdale stadium yelling about his grandma's lemonade. I'm willing to pay for the overpriced lemonade because I'm *at the game*. This experience feels better than buying a can of Minute Maid at the gas station for a fraction of the cost and drinking it in my car on the way to work. In restaurants we need to understand value and our participation in creating a dining experience surrounding the product, food, and drink.

The Whole Show

There is a reason that someone is coming to your restaurant to spend three, four, or five times the amount they would need to buy the ingredients and make it at home. They see value in buying a $14 turkey sandwich at the restaurant rather than making it in their kitchen and eating it on their couch. Yes, they are paying for the food, but there is a whole other thing they are paying for: the experience. First, someone is cooking or assembling the tasty meal. Preparing it in a way the guest can't. And then someone is serving them; asking them what they would like to eat, describing the dishes for them, making recommendations, bringing drinks, refilling the drinks, serving their food on time, hot if desired, and ensuring that it tastes good. Caring about them. Being of service. It's here, in this moment, where the value will be assessed.

But there is more. When I go out, I want to not only have the food or drinks prepared by someone who really knows how to cook, but I want a cool place to hang out. I like an ambience and vibe while I eat it. I'm also paying for the design, lighting, music, art, the feel of the space. And I want people! Connection!

It's all of these things added together. The food, service, people, and experience may change depending on the cost of the products, the services, or style of the restaurant. As a diner, I can find value from casual to elevated: I find value at Chipotle, Waffle House, Denny's, Morton's, or Alinea. The price, style, and service vary at all of these different restaurants. What's important is that the employees, managers, and owners are able to step back and ask themselves: is this experience of a specific value and is that value up to the expectation of our paying guests?

3

LEWIS ROSSMAN

COO/Partner, Shenkman Hospitality

Hosts

An initial greeting can make or break it: eye contact, the first interaction with the guests, and showing confidence that you know what you are doing and can handle the situation. People sit in traffic for a long time, drive one and a half hours, only to get here and be told there is an hour wait for their party of six. The hosts have to deal with a lot of tension and try to handle it well, with confidence. You need someone who can react well.

Reading the Guest

Our intention is not to "turn and burn" but work at the pace of the customer. So, it's important for the server to read that table really well. Pick up some cues from the guest to determine what kind of experience they want. Do they want to be in and out? Do they want to have a longer meal? If they order right off the bat, without looking at the menu, and don't want to hear about specials, they want to eat and get on with their lives. Others—they are making a day of it.

Some people want to be left alone. They know what they want to eat. [They] appreciate a server who gives them seamless service, is on top of the table, but also gives them the privacy to enjoy their moment.

Others have more needs, want to know a description for every item, and need a lot of attention. You have to read and assess each table.

Multi-tasking

Service by definition implies a level of multi-tasking. Greeting the table within two minutes. Making sure everything is set, everything is clean. The volume is so intense, and the multi-tasking is endless, everything is order-fire (*this means as soon as an order is put in, the cooks will start cooking the first course*), so it is absolutely essential for our servers to multi-task, know the fire times, and how long something takes to cook, depending on the time of day and how many guests are in the whole place. If we are at half-capacity, your food is going to come out quicker than if we are at full capacity when the kitchen has a ton of tickets on the line. The server needs to adjust accordingly. Considering the volume that we do—it's about our communication.

Teamwork

We are a team. If you have a table that is not in your section and they have not been greeted, and they are straining their neck looking around—that is your opportunity to greet them. Check in with them and then communicate to their server or a manager. It's a team. A server that is successful will work WITH the busboy. Understand they can cover more ground working hand-in-hand together. I can pour water, I can get bread, I can get beverages. It helps at our style of restaurant.

4

HALF A BUCK

PROVIDING AN ENGAGING WORK EXPERIENCE

"People are crossing the street for 50 cents an hour, Josh. It's crazy." A good friend of mine expressed this to me a couple of years ago as we were talking about our hospitality industry. He had lost a couple of employees who went to work a similar job at another place in his neighborhood for only 50 cents an hour more. This led to a bigger conversation about the economy and a smaller, more intense conversation about the work experience he was offering his employees. How were they being treated? It was a counter-style restaurant, and while it can seem like a streamlined job and not too complicated, he was losing people for reasons other than the 50 cents. We often think it's just the money, but there are almost always other reasons why employees leave. What's the job's real value, beyond the wages? So, we talked about it, looked at his program and added a few things that balanced out how to engage his employees in their work-life. Some questions we addressed were:

- Be interested. Are you asking employees about their interests outside of work?

- Are you engaging with employees that seem bored or feel they don't add value to the team?

- Are you holding engaging shift line-ups to inspire the team?

- Are you checking in with people about their goals in the restaurant, as well as overarching goals?

At the end of the day, the remaining employees were more engaged, found more value in their job, and were more apt to stay.

In fact, a great overall work environment is important to both the employees and guests dining in our restaurants. What is the value of the experience? Step back and try to see that through their eyes. Half a buck more per hour or half a buck less per entrée? Both need to be consistently gauged and scrutinized to ensure we keep our employees and guests connected to their experiences.

5

WE

Keeping Teams Unified and Connected

We should always be looking to help and support each other during service. If we are connected as team members, we can put ourselves, collectively, in a place to solve guests' issues and elevate their experience. A server can smooth things for the kitchen because they see the importance in that. And vice versa. We need each other. This viewpoint and having leaders that can build bridges where division exists will create a much stronger team. Classic restaurant battles are Front of House vs. Back of House or the bartenders vs. the servers or even servers vs. bussers and runners. This is an area of great opportunity for leaders: successful managers and seasoned employees can do a lot to mitigate these divisions, keep the team unified and goal oriented.

We are human; there will still be moments of contention, blame, and differences, but in the best places I've worked, the teams were able to quickly resolve issues or be guided by management to stay in a place of respect and gratitude for each other. It can be difficult when an employee holds onto a narrative that supports division. It can be comforting to cling to a critical viewpoint, to push this story of "if they would only do X, everything would all be fine."

I've worked with servers who were constantly playing the "complain and blame" game: "The bussers should do more. The bartenders make too much money. The kitchen is so slow." Or cooks who've said, "The servers are lazy. The manager is inept at navigating the books and managing the floor. Nobody is working as hard as we are." These frustrations can even be true and valid, but if they are not dealt with immediately, in a constructive and positive way, they have the power to divide the whole team. The longer employees stay in a place of conflict and division rather than finding connections and solutions, the longer this battle thrives, and the longer it effects performance and the guest experience.

If you are a manager, part of your job is to bridge the gap; be on the lookout for issues and find a way to move your employees and teams, constructively, into a place of solution. Find ways to remake connections and rebuild relationships. My old boss at The Dining Room, Robert Hartstein, excelled at bridging gaps in the team. Maybe because he had come up in hospitality as a chef and then moved to front of house, he had experience with many different types of teams and excelled at mending those divisions. He was a fantastic communicator and aimed to resolve an issue *as soon as* it came up. He didn't wait. Didn't let an issue fester.

He knew that we all needed each other and was able to facilitate that well. He took on the responsibility of finding ways for us to connect and rewrite the narrative. As a front-of-house team, we started to learn about each station in the kitchen; we knew every cook's name; they knew ours. We learned what dish each cook was preparing. We spent time with them on the line. When chef Michael Voltaggio joined us, we learned about Molecular Gastronomy and all that came with it: the unfamiliar ingredients, techniques, and equipment used to cook in that style. (A Robot Coupe can spin at 10,000 RPM—pretty cool!) I used to love leading FOH field trips to the kitchen!

We built new connections. We respected the amount of hustle and details the cooks were putting into each dish because we saw it with our own eyes. We understood we needed each other on a deeper level. The kitchen could see our desire to learn, sell, and share with the guests. This mindset created one of the best team experiences I've been a part of. We were led to realize we were stronger together in our ultimate goal to serve the guest.

I feel it's always important to remind the team to stay away from the blame game in front of guests. In the front of house, we want to be careful to avoid saying things like:

- "I'm so sorry your pasta is taking a while. The kitchen is a little slow tonight."

- "I'm sorry you have been waiting so long for your table, there were some issues getting going tonight."

- "Well, the hostess didn't communicate that allergy to me, I'm so sorry."

- "It's a new drink, so the bartender seems to be trying to figure it out. Sorry for the wait."

- "We were told there were 6 of you dining with us, not 8. They daytime team didn't update your reservation."

We rise together; we fall together. If a team is working well together, our fellow employee's mistake is ours. Sure, it needs to be addressed with the individual, and that can be handled privately, without the guest's involvement. Ultimately, we are all responsible for the guest's experience. Here are some ways you could rephrase the above comments to better reflect a connected team.

- "I'm so sorry your pasta is taking a while. Let me check on the progress and see when it may be ready."

- "I'm sorry you have been waiting so long for your table, we have a few guests still enjoying their meals, but your table should be ready soon."

- "My apologies, I did not see the allergy notation. I can assure you; I will be very focused and ensure your dishes do not have any of those ingredients."

- "My apologies, my understanding was there were 6 of you dining with us, not 8. Let me see how we can accommodate all of you.

These are good skills exercises to have the team do at line-up. Work on shifting from a defensive standpoint to a proactive one. Only use a "we" viewpoint. This is the type of support a manager can offer the team, keeping them unified and focused on the guest experience.

6

THE FINGERPRINT

Attention to the Smallest Details

All it takes is a smudge, the tiniest of overlooked errors, and the door is open. As soon as that "mistakes have been made" door is open, in come service detectives...guests looking for what may go wrong, can go wrong, and isn't up to par. We're not talking about inspectors; this happens with ordinary guests. You may have that one who notices the little stain on the menu, and then they start to look around for other things that are dirty or out of place. They might not have done this if they didn't see that stain on the menu. Servers and managers should see these issues long before a guest does. This is why an opening checklist or a final sweep of the dining room before the doors open is so important. Here are some common issues that will flip that switch, turning your guest into a detective:

- Dirty menu

- Stained tablecloth or napkin

- Smudge on silverware

- Fingerprints on the glassware

- Wobbly table

- Crooked artwork on the wall

- Light bulbs out in the restaurant

Or during service:

- Not having the reservation info correct

- Missed allergy

- Dishes placed in front of the wrong people

- Making a guest wait too long for drinks or food

You might be thinking, "Josh, this isn't that big of a deal. It's not fine dining. Or elevated dining, as you are calling it." Sure, but don't underestimate your guests' expectations. Somewhere in their consciousness it will leave an impression. And the fact that they couldn't have ketchup with their fries, or a server gave them a dirty menu, will factor into their decision to walk—into your competition's restaurant next time they are deciding where to eat. The details matter.

Here are three ways to make sure guests don't see errors and start looking around to find other problems:

- Create and use checklists

- Consistently communicate with the team about issues that continue to arise:
  - Dirty condiment holders
  - Empty condiment jars or holders
  - Stained napkins in rolls
  - Unpolished glasses that have water spots
  - Leaky soap dispensers in the bathroom
  - Soiled tablecloths
  - Damaged and unbalanced chairs
  - Items guests may use that need to be restocked

If a restaurant includes this type of checklist into their side work process AND keeps people accountable for using the checklist, fewer guests will have reason to look for something to be unhappy with. These are small items, but important.

Consistency is vital with the lists. If a manager isn't checking that list on a regular basis, gaps grow in the process, and the list becomes an afterthought and all of the sudden it's squeezed into the back of a drawer somewhere. Two months later another discussion ensues, "You know, we should get back to that list thing." Make and keep the routine. Keep the routine! It supports a culture of detail, and the team is going to be in a much better space to create a consistent, good, dining experience for guests.

7

PAIGE REILLY

Owner, Upside Pub

New Employees

When a regular walks in, it's not just about that person getting their drink; it's about the entire ceremony of making that person feel special and introduced properly to that new team member. With a story behind it. Equally important is that the new team member sees that this is how we treat people. This is what we do for the people that keep coming back, our regulars. This is how we get people to keep coming back. It's not just about the drink.

Observe, Observe

We want our team members to genuinely feel involved with all of our customers, regulars and non-regulars—but as involved as they get with that one guest, they have to constantly, every 30 seconds, gut-check themselves. *How is my observation going? Am I observing the bar? Am I observing the room?* And it's a hard balance. It's a learned skill of being able to stay engaged with the person in front of you, but always be observing, observing, observing. We would do exercises at [Tony's Darts Away]. One of us would stand at the corner of someone's eye, while they were talking to a guest and wait for them to recognize us and if they didn't, we would coach them. The key - and it's not a quick fix - is to constantly train yourself to observe your surroundings, not just what's in front of you.

Cleanliness

Cleanliness is so important. The beer that you are about to pour into this glass and give to someone is a piece of art. An artist made this. And they made it EXACTLY the way they want their client and the people drinking it, looking at it, feeling it, experiencing it, to have it. And so, anything that we do to adjust that experience is doing a disservice to the artist that we bought this product from and made a contract with.

And so, when we don't clean our glassware properly or when we don't put proper head on the beer, [don't] store things correctly, or don't clean the taps—or anything else that goes along with the cleanliness of beer—we are breaking a contract with these artists that have put so much effort into this beer. And I always get laughed at and I always get eyerolls, but this keeps our glassware really clean. No one forgets about it, and no one doesn't think about it every single time they pull a piece of glassware out.

8

PLAN B

Adjusting to the Back-Up Plan

My wife Kirsten and I got married in San Luis Obispo. It was a fun wedding. We are both fans of fairs and carnivals…she's from Minnesota, which has one of the country's great fairs. (I know: the Texans and Ohioans are rolling their eyes.) We like the people-watching, the food, and definitely the games and general merriment that come with visiting a big fair. We decided to have a fair-themed wedding, and since we both are pretty crafty—and not bad at construction—we decided to make our own midway games for our wedding. So, over a six-month period, we built our own Skee-Ball machine, High Striker-style hammer slam, water-gun-into-the-clown-mouth game, dime-toss game, balloon dartboard and a few more—all used for the after-wedding cocktail reception.

For $100 total in Los Angeles, we rented a popcorn machine, a cotton candy machine, and a snow cone machine. Aside from the fun flavors for the snow cones, I made alcoholic liquors so those people who drank could squirt a margarita, a cosmopolitan, or an old fashioned or Manhattan onto their crushed ice. And we had a keg of Miller High Life…the champagne of beers. We know how to party. We did all of this because it was fun, but also because we wanted to get married on the cheap and use our money to travel instead.

We had a food truck serve dinner and we had a pie-baking contest for desserts. Over 20 entries! We also decided to hire our own servers….one of whom didn't show up. No notice. On our wedding day. How dare they!!! I was a little annoyed, but here's the thing: both of us, having worked in restaurants, didn't really get fazed. We are built for this. You have to adjust on the fly. You have to have a Plan B. I've experienced being understaffed in every service job I've had - catering gig, restaurant work, bartending, etc. We stayed calm, re-adjusted assignments, consolidated a couple of stations. We improvised and we survived. This is one of the many great life skills you learn and hone while working in restaurants. Did someone forget to bring out the late-night corndogs and mustard? Yes, but hey, people were busy having a blast on the dance floor, so no one even noticed.

Are You Prepared?

When I worked at The Langham Huntington hotel, the hiring process took a long time and, subsequently, we were often understaffed. This is not a reflection on the hotel; it simply took a long time to find high-quality candidates. We created a sheet, a playbook really, that simply stated how we were going to run with different sized teams. We essentially had a different offense for whatever the makeup of the staff was. Most restaurants already have a base for this. It's a layout of all the tables in the restaurant and how those are divided between servers or teams. Essentially, if there are five servers, there is one breakdown; if four, there is another. These layouts are usually stuffed in a drawer near a POS system with olive-oil stains on them.

You need to have a Plan B; it's the first step in not second-guessing yourself or freaking out the team when you have to pivot in an unpredictable situation. Having no plan means you get stressed, crabby, and short with each other, and then it all goes south. Having a Plan B keeps you confident and moving forward. So here's a few tips:

- Be cool. Don't freak out. Take a breath. It is what it is.

- Keep your spirits up. The team needs encouragement.

- Move into action—you can dissect the past later.

- Enjoy improvising, lean into it. Savor the challenge.

- If you have a Plan B, which you should, execute it.

- A guest does not need to know the restaurant is a server, busser, or cook down. No one on the team should feel the need to blame slow service on Johnny, who is under the weather or running late.

- It's o.k. to tell a guest, "We are quite busy, items are taking a little longer," and state the adjusted time. Communication is important but think about how to frame it.

A manager or server should be very clear with the team that there is a change of plans and present it calmly. Clear communication. If the entire team can support the plan and start adjusting quickly, they won't have time to dwell on the fact that Johnny called out again. A meltdown or blame game isn't going to help the situation in the moment. A manager can figure out what went wrong later and address that with the necessary individuals. The focus should be on rallying the team and providing positive direction as Plan B is executed.

9

COMMON CONVERSATIONS

All Day, Every Day

There are a few topics I find myself always talking about in restaurants: time, anticipation, professionalism and feedback. They are common themes and are peppered through everything we do as employees and leaders, and I wanted to share a few thoughts on them.

Time

In hospitality, we are always referencing time. Did you clock in on time? Clock out on time? How long have they been waiting? How long until the order is up? How long until the table turns? When did you fire the table? Are their drinks almost ready? Did they pay their check yet? How long have they been on hold? Did you email them back yet? How long has the review been online? Time. Time. Time. Talk about it. Everybody on the team needs to be paying attention to it, but it starts with the leader. As a leader, make time a priority: "I will be dressed and ready at the correct time. We have line-up every day at the same time. I will post the schedule at the correct time. I will meet my wine reps at our set time." When you demonstrate your commitment to time, it says a lot about your character and the respect you have for others. This priority will then permeate the culture of the restaurant. It will affect the employees and the guests. But it starts with the leaders.

Anticipation

A phrase I've heard my entire career in restaurants is, "Anticipate the guests' needs." It's one of the most common phrases in hospitality. Anticipation is about paying attention. It requires team members to actively look for non-verbal indicators or clues within a conversation with a guest and then do something for that guest before the guest has to ask for it. Doug Washington uses the word, "hunting." We are hunting for clues, hunting for anything that can tell us how we can be of service to that guest. This is active. It's not a passive action. Spend time with your teams, train them to pay close attention to the details of each guest. Practice looking for non-verbal cues. Find opportunities and act on them quickly.

Professionalism and Fairness

As a new manager coming into an established restaurant, you may find yourself leaning toward a group of employees that appear more friendly than the others. This is going to happen, it's natural, but it's very important to maintain neutrality and professionalism. You can do this with warmth; don't get me wrong here. What I mean is that fairness has to be maintained when you are in a management position. I've never been a fan of managers who play favorites or gossip with employees about other staff. This creates division. We aren't in that game. We are in the game of connecting with people and facilitating connections. Managers should always maintain a balanced, professional relationship with everyone on the staff.

Feedback

How do we stay open to hearing feedback without getting defensive, and how can we find ways to have the feedback we give be impactful and retained? Most of the time, both require setting up a safe environment for feedback and ensuring the timing is right. Putting forethought into the timing and place can make people less defensive and create a space that inspires collaborative dialogue. Hint: "Sit down I'm going to tell you what you did wrong" usually doesn't do the job.

When you give feedback, remain empathetic, avoid blame, and focus on the behavior of the person rather than the person's personality. The conversation will more than likely stay balanced. Sharing the note as an observation (i.e. "I observed this, what do you think about it?") may create dialogue and promote finding a solution together. Practice this. Feedback is a learned skill. Find another manager or friend, role play, and practice giving feedback. Seek out the advice of managers that are good at constructive feedback. Most are willing to share their experience and skills.

10

THE SCOOP

Knowing the Neighborhood

My parents used to go to this restaurant/bar in San Francisco called Perry's. It is an old institution on Union Street in Pacific Heights, near the Presidio, the first neighborhood over the bridge. Anytime we were all in the city, we would go for lunch or dinner, and I will always remember the staff (and the breadsticks—they had great breadsticks!).

I remember the staff because they always remembered us. It was one of my parents' favorite spots in the city. Everyone would come over to the table and say hi — managers, bartenders, servers, even Perry himself. They would talk with my mom and dad about this and that going on in the city—Giants, Niners, concerts, plays, new restaurants, recent Herb Cain articles, you name it. Seemed like the staff knew about everything. The staff was talking with guests at every table.

I thought of the staff at Perry's years later when I started bartending in Los Angeles. When you are behind the bar, you are not just a bartender; you are someone who supposed to know what the heck is going on in town. The best bartenders have a secret to share. The scoop. If someone asks, you've got a story to tell, some advice for a dinner spot, a band that's playing, an after-dinner cocktail spot, a new brunch hangout, a late-night club. Yes, we know you can make a drink, what else do you have to offer? What do you have in your back pocket? What do you know that they haven't heard about?

Know the Neighborhood

I felt the same way about serving tables. When a guest asks, "What else is there to do in this neighborhood?" it's discouraging to hear, "I don't know, I don't live around here." That's never going to cut it. It's our business to know. You work around here—figure it out, take a walk before or after work, but have something in your back pocket to offer the guest.

We are guides. Just like the concierge at a hotel that can give a quick tip, make a reservation, call a car, or find that late-night flower shop, we are in charge of the guests' experience from the time they walk in to the time they walk out, and that includes answering questions, creating a little connection. This simple interaction may turn into a memorable experience for them. Great managers and servers excel at many versions of this, all while creating return guests.

We all have lots of phone apps and search engines to give us access to more information than ever. That isn't a reason to not have a few things to actually connect and talk with guests about—it's all the more reason. It's always better to provide some detailed information than telling someone to simply Google a name or place. While the guest may look it up later, employees don't want to a miss an opportunity to be of service and make an impactful moment for them. The answers should be quick but include a few details. People should get in the habit of quickly hitting a couple of descriptors in explaining things. Here are ideas to keep in mind:

- What is the type of food or drink?
- What is the ambience like? (music, lighting, décor)
- What is the style of the place? (chill, busy, casual, upscale, elevated)
- Is it kid friendly or for adults?
- Is it indoor or outdoor? And if outdoor, will the weather be an issue?

One way to ensure your team is prepared to make recommendations to guests is to do a skills exercise before service and simply ask questions of individuals in the group. For instance:

- Can you recommend a good place to have a drink after we leave here?

- Is there anything interesting to do in the neighborhood? Can you recommend a great place to grab breakfast or lunch tomorrow?

- Is there something fun we can do with our kids around here?

Asking a clarification question will narrow the options. The same as we would when asking about a type of wine, drink, or entrée. Asking about preferences allows us to filter out an answer. For instance:

- Are you looking for a quiet bar or something a little livelier?

- Do you think you want to do something indoor or outdoor?

- Do you want a breakfast place where you can sit-down and take your time, or a more quick, fast-casual place?

- Do want a relaxing walk or something a little more challenging?

Management should create their own questions that are appropriate to the neighborhood and surrounding area. Play with it, engage the team at line-up. Again, it shouldn't feel like a speech. A few points in the sentence should do it. For instance:

- "I love the Jade bar; it's quiet, romantic, has amazing craft cocktails, and usually a mellow DJ."

- "For outdoor activities, Lake Nero has great fishing and boat rentals and is about 20 minutes away. There is also a bike rental place next door. They have regular or the pedal assist, which can be fun."

- "Dom's is great for breakfast. It's a fun, busy room, no reservations, usually a line, but worth the wait. The Domlette is my favorite: bacon, cheddar, chive, and the special sauce."

- "If you are looking for a morning walk, there is a nice hiking trail in Allistar Park, mostly flat, that takes about 40 minutes, and the trailhead is only 10 minutes from here."

Find Joy in Sharing a Good Idea

I like to know what's happening in the neighborhood and in town. It's always created a great avenue to engage with guests. I've had so many customers come back over the years and thank me for recommendations. When I was working at Capo, a small Italian restaurant one block from the beach in Santa Monica that wine lovers flocked to, I had recommendations for other restaurants with great wine options. Even a few wineries they may enjoy, just an hour and a half north in Santa Barbara. I had various lists on my notes app on my phone. On occasion, I would email these ideas to guests. If they were driving all the way up the coast to Sonoma and Napa, I had my favorites list for those areas too. Why not? We were a well-known restaurant with one of the top wine lists in the world. It was a question people often asked, and I was prepared for it. I had it in my back pocket.

I was in San Francisco recently, and I stopped in at Perry's to have a bite to eat and catch the rest of a ballgame. I ate at the bar and chatted with the bartender. As I was heading out the door, he called out, "Next time you are in town, check out the Brazen Head Pub—they have a great French Onion soup. And they serve late!" Some things never change.

PART 2: UPSCALE RESTAURANTS

11

THE RUNDOWN

Upscale Restaurants

This section builds on information in the Casual section, so you might want to read that before proceeding. It's good stuff and it's the kind of stuff all of us need to review. I don't want you to feel like you missed anything. This chapter, Upscale Restaurants, addresses the same topics, but at the next level. They build on each other.

Upscale restaurants raise the game and the service standards quite a bit. This category has the widest range of price points, service, and experiences, as many different owners try varying models to cater to specific guests. The food styles and cuisines have an enormous variety. Since upscale menus are much more complex than casual offerings, the employee's knowledge of ingredients and product will be much larger. You have chefs and cooks making incredible food, offered in many different environments. This restaurant style is generally more expensive than casual places, but the prices range widely. Obviously that number can drastically change if the table is ordering multiple craft cocktails or going big on wine.

The dial needs to be turned up on service in these types of restaurants. The steep increase in check averages will lead to a similarly steep climb in expectations for management, servers, and staff. But it will also positively affect how much money people are going to be able to make.

To be an effective supervisor, manager, and server in a fast-paced, high-caliber, upscale restaurant, you need to be a great director, coach, communicator, and an excellent food and wine guide. Product knowledge is huge here. The team should always be improving, so they can give the guests the experience they want and introduce them to new dishes, special wines, and excellent craft cocktails. Great supervisors and managers should be facilitating this product knowledge, engaging with employees, and ensuring standards are consistently met. Everything will be larger: check averages, stress, and paychecks.

Team

The positions in this style of restaurant looks similar to casual restaurants, but there may be additional staff and certainly additional tasks for each position. The tasks increase as the expectations of the guests increase. An increase in prices usually leads guests to believe that they are in for a more detailed experience than at a casual restaurant. So, let's break it down.

FOH: Front of House

- Hosts: you may notice the addition of one or more hosts. Depending on the team, you may have two people: one to walk guests to their tables and another to stay at the stand. You should always have someone at the stand when a guest arrives. As pointed out at the beginning of the book, this is where the ball is dropped the most.

- Bussers: while clearing tables, providing water service, cleaning tables, and resetting tables are still paramount, a busser may also be asked to assist in running food or drinks to tables. If this is required, the busser will have more interaction with guests and will need to know the food and drink items being brought to the table.

- Runners: runners start to become a very important position in upscale restaurants. I'll go into more detail about the runner position in a moment.

- Back servers: the addition of back servers will most likely be reserved for the very high end of upscale restaurants. If a restaurant is particularly large and focused on the details of service, they may decide to include back servers as a position. Back servers will usually split tasks with the front server or captain.

- Front server/server: wine and food knowledge is the biggest change and challenge in this type of restaurant. Servers will be depending more on other employees who are assisting in their section. This means it's essential they have great skills in prioritizing, good communication and working with a team.

- Bar Preppers/ Batchers: these positions will prep ingredients and/or create batches of popular cocktails to use during service. Depending on the complexity and volume of the restaurant bar, managers of these positions may also be needed.

- Bartenders: the bar will most likely have a bar program in addition to beer and wine offerings. Often the bar seats may be reserved for full dinner service provided by the bartender on top of their duties making drinks for the whole restaurant.

- Barista: depending on the volume of the restaurant, this may be a designated position, or it will be fulfilled by one of the other roles — busser, runner, or servers may be asked to make coffee drinks.

- Floor supervisors and/or managers: assist the general manager with all FOH operations, overseeing the team and execution of service.

BOH: Back of House

- Cooks: in the back of the house, you may see the addition of multiple cooks, split into various stations. One may focus on salads and cold appetizers, one on hot apps, another on mains. This really depends on the complexity of the menu and standards of the chef.

- Expeditor: the duties of an expeditor usually fall to the sous-chef or a seasoned runner.

- Sous-Chef: you may have a sous-chef introduced to the BOH at this point. The sous-chef is always second in charge to the chef de cuisine and oversees the line cooks.

- Chef de Cuisine: you may also work with a chef de cuisine (CDC) who oversees the kitchen and can create dishes and changes to that menu. The chef de cuisine will answer to the executive chef.

- Executive Chef: can be the chef de cuisine as well. Creates menu concept and dishes and oversees the business decisions of the kitchen and staff.

Upper Management/Owners

- General Manager: in charge of daily operations and coordinates front and back of house operations. They are usually very involved with the FOH staff, service, and guests.

- Owner: person or group that owns the restaurant.

- Investor: person or persons who have invested capital in the restaurant and receive "shares" in return.

The Value of Great Runners

Runners are a position that can be really undervalued in restaurants. If you view runners as someone who simply brings a plate to a table, you are underutilizing and underestimating the power of the role. Often servers will act as their own runners, and they should be able to fulfill the details of the position in smaller restaurants. But in bigger and more complex restaurants, the runner becomes a vital position. So, let's break it down.

- Sometimes, depending on the size of the restaurant and the chef's preference, the runner may also be the expeditor.

- They ensure food gets from the kitchen (pass) to the table in a timely manner.

- They are the last look, ensuring the dish looks perfect before it leaves the pass.

- They ensure shared utensils are with shared dishes.

- They, hopefully with the help of the servers, make space at the table *before* bringing shared dishes.

- They can relay, if needed, seat numbers to other runners and servers assisting with running the corresponding plates to that table.

- They can announce the food as it's placed on the table.

- They can describe the dishes if a guest asks for more details about a dish.

- They can verbalize to servers, back-servers, or bussers anything that needs attending to on the table.

- If time permits, they can spot and pick up any used items that can be cleared from the table.

- Some high-volume or minimally staffed restaurants insist that every position participates in running food, provided they pass a strict test of knowing the ingredients on each dish and how to properly describe that dish at the table.

See what I mean when I say it's not just a role where they put a plate on a table and walk away? When you have a good runner or runners on your team, they free up the servers and bussers to use that extra time for table maintenance, service, and guest engagement. When a runner is added to the team, you have the benefit of:

- Delivering the food faster and hotter, not having it wait in the pass.

- Having tighter firing times for courses, leading to quicker table turns.

- Working more efficiently, giving time for other team members to attend to clearing courses, marking the table, wine service, and connecting with guests.

Training

My hope is that every restaurant has some great menu descriptions so all new hires can start memorizing the detailed information about each dish. It's not always the case. The first book I ever bought for a restaurant job was called *The Food Lover's Companion*. There was an appetizer on a menu that I thought was a dessert, and after I confided in a server, he let me know that sweetbreads were not, in fact, a dessert but a meat delicacy. He recommended the book, and it changed my whole view of food overnight. The descriptions of items were amazing. I was new to upscale restaurants and embarrassed to ask questions, so I just wrote down everything anyone said that I didn't know and looked it up when I got home. Meyer lemon: *Who the heck is Meyer?* Espelette: *What?* Sea Bream: *Huh?* Sorrel: *Shrug*. It was a clinic, and it's how I fell in love with food, chefs, and the dining experience. But hey, we have the Internet now and all this information is at our fingertips. I still reference *The Food Lover's Companion,* though…best descriptions ever! (Great to use when you are refining how you or your team describes dishes.)

Point of Sale

I go into great detail about Point-of-Sales systems in Part 1: Casual, on page 5. Please reference this section if you need guidance in this area.

Management Duties

Restaurant management duties in Upscale restaurants may include any of the following:

- Train and mentor employees
- Participate in the hiring of potential employees
- Coach employees to maintain top service standards
- Oversee restaurant liquor, wine, and food inventories
- Learn restaurant's computer system, reservation system, and

applicable programs

- Oversee compliance with policies, practices, and procedures

- Control costs within designated departments

- Effectively schedule employees to meet the demands of the restaurant

- Ensure working areas have a high level of cleanliness and follow health code requirements

- Ensure food safety and/or alcohol certifications for employees are current and up to date

- Maintain healthy restaurant relationship with outside vendors: e.g. valet company, wine and liquor reps, food purveyors, outsourced delivery drivers, cleaning companies, maintenance crews

Retention

I don't know about you, but I was not gifted with a brain that remembers everything after I've heard it or repeated it a couple of times. One of the first great chefs I worked with changed the menu daily, if not mid-shift. Kris Morningstar could not stop tinkering; it was amazing. I'd never seen anything like it. But it made me realize I had to figure out a way to retain the information. I had to memorize but also find a way I could continually study it. If items were being added and changed, this was going to be an ongoing process. And that's what it was for the rest of my time in upscale and elevated restaurants. I wanted to absorb and be able to share this information with co-workers and guests.

It's important to set your teams and new hires up for success. Talk to them about how they learn best. One way doesn't always fit everyone. People learn in different ways: auditory, visual, reading/writing, and kinesthetic. I like to make my materials reusable. Some methods I use:

- Record the menu. I quickly started reading the menu items to myself on a recorder with the ingredients as chef had explained it, not just what was listed on the menu for guests. I'd *listen* to these in the car, on the metro, on the treadmill at the gym. I would have to change this recording weekly, but I wanted to stay up to date on what was what.

- Even now, I use digital flashcards on my phone. I created them using Canva, but there are several programs available. I *write* the descriptions into the program myself, as I feel that method locks the information in my memory. I've added pictures to flashcards too, because seeing the items increases my retention.

- For me, remembering food is a combination of description, menu, and pictures. Since I was always taught by doing a few shifts on the pass before I could even set foot in the dining room, I learned by *seeing* the dishes. I had a few cool chefs who allowed me to snap pictures if I wasn't in the way, and that helped me learn quicker. Now, some places give you a picture with the menu descriptions to make it easier to learn.

- With wine, I did a lot of *audio* recordings. But honestly, discussing it with co-workers and sommeliers, and *hearing* it from other wine folks really locked tasting notes and stories into my memory.

- If digital learning isn't possible, simple index cards do wonders. On paper. Writing menu descriptions and definitions will increase retention.

As I mentioned before, training will really depend on the service culture of the restaurant. New managers and servers should be open and ready to take in a lot of information quickly. What I enjoy most about working with inventive and inspired chefs is I'm never bored. Sure, I may have to spend more time memorizing different seasonal and weekly dishes, but I will always take that over a stagnant, uninspired menu. It keeps employees connected with the special experience being offered to guests and provided by their co-workers.

Cocktails

Cocktails in restaurants keep getting better and better. As they do, bartenders are not the only staffers who need to know what the main ingredients are. Every role in the front of house has a chance to engage guests about the cocktail program and it's a great way to connect with those guests. Managers, hosts, servers, and runners should know every ingredient in each of the main signature drinks. Restaurants that have a popular cocktail program and want their employees to sell and talk to guests about those drinks usually have a great detailed description on the menu.

Bartenders and mixologists put a lot of effort into designing and executing these craft cocktails. It's important that the team presenting them to the table know the flavor profile of the drink and know how to express that to a guest. The beverage team might design cocktails from scratch or put a new spin on a classic with their own witty names like "The Burning Tree Tiger." Nobody, I repeat, nobody knows what the heck that is. Make sure the team learns the ingredients, because you can be assured people will ask. As a guest, how many times have you ordered a drink and by the time it was brought to the table, you forgot what was in it? Makes sense that you would ask the manager, host, server or runner, "Hey, what's in the 'Alabama Jackalope,' again?" Only to have them look at you sheepishly, stare at the drink, and say, "Well...an orange liquor with...let me check with the bartender." Know your drinks—it's part of the experience you are providing to your guests.

When it comes to classic or commonly requested cocktails, designated employees *must* know the ingredients. Details matter when it comes to selling. Servers, managers, and hosts also need to know this information so they can upsell! If someone orders a cosmopolitan, knowing that vodka is the base allows a server to ask, "What kind of vodka would you like?"

Many places will have a cocktail menu designed around a theme. This could be based on many things: the theme of the restaurant, the use of the building before it was converted into a restaurant, a particular time in history of the neighborhood. For instance, years ago, I was in a place called Duello, and the well-known bar director, Iain Mcpherson, had created the cocktail list based on the downtown arts district neighborhood transitioning from vineyards and citrus groves into an industrial hub in the late 1800's, and then into the Arts District. The cocktails were created around this history. Story rules! Having an anecdote of why this cocktail was created and sharing it with a guest is a great way for all employees to add depth to the cocktail experience and sell at the same time.

Wine

Wine offerings ramp up quite a bit in upscale restaurants. Again, it will depend on the beverage program. I think knowing the basic varietals of the wines by the glass when walking in the door for an interview at an upscale restaurant puts any interviewee in a stronger position. I've glanced at these lists and done minimal research so I could have a talking point if it came up in an interview. It's always come in handy. Once I was hired, I could delve deeper and get to know more, such as what wine region it's from and the name of the producer/maker.

If a guest asks, "Who is the producer of your chardonnay by the glass?" A server should be able to reply, "It's a Patz and Hall chardonnay from the Napa Valley." The expectation at this level should be to know four elements about the wines by the glass: region, price, producer, tasting notes. If you are in a restaurant that doesn't offer tasting notes, do the research yourself and pass it along. Use online wine stores or search engines for descriptions. Some stellar boutique wine stores offer great descriptions. It's easy and free. Any manager or server is responsible for this wine knowledge, and your guests expect you to know the basic information of any beverages being served. To keep it more interactive at work, explore these ways to engage employees about wine on your list:

- Can you tell me about your favorite white and red wine by the glass? (Answer should include producer, wine region, varietal, some tasting notes, and a short anecdote.)

- Pick an entrée on the menu and ask the team to tell you what wine by the glass or bottle will pair best with it and why.

- If you find an employee who is very interested in wine have them do a short briefing on a region featured on your list, a local region, or one of the producers on your list.

Beer

I address offering beer in Part 1: Casual on page 7. I've seen plenty of upscale restaurants with amazing beer lists. Again, everyone should be on point with knowing the styles of beer offered in their restaurant and it's always nice to know enough so you can play the game, "If you like this, you may like this." If the restaurant is the type of place that has unique and bespoke craft beers that guests may not know about, it might be good to create a list for servers, so they can reference a popular style or brand the guest may be familiar with and then draw the comparison. This can at least pique the interest of a guest who may be willing to try something new.

I learned the most about beer by doing the mini tastings at craft beer bars and asking questions. It was a great way to taste many styles, in small 2 oz pours, without breaking the bank. For any employee that is looking to learn more about beers, this is an ideal route and there is almost always a beertender who will tell you a lot about styles and methods of beer. For the super interested, the Cicerone certification offers four levels of certification from the basic fundamentals progressing to the very complex and demanding.

Non-Alcoholic Options

A few years ago, I walked into a non-alcoholic bottle shop called Soft Spirits. This place was amazing. They had more premium non-alcoholic spirits, beer, and wine than I'd ever seen in one place. Their zero-proof products were sourced from around the world, and I asked the owner, "Is there that many non-drinkers coming in here?" And she said, "Actually, our biggest customer is people that drink but are picking up something else that has no alcohol but tastes just as good. They may have a drink with alcohol at party or dinner, but they want their second drink to be just as delicious but alcohol-free for many reasons: they have to drive, work the next day, don't want to feel hungover, or are watching their health."

In the last five years, the non-alcoholic options in restaurants and bars have skyrocketed. Non-alcoholic beer and wine have become a huge category in beverage sales worldwide. Most of the big brands are offering options and the small boutique companies are delivering delicious award-winning products.

I've enjoyed some non-alcoholic spirits myself and am consistently happy with those offerings in restaurants and bars. Servers and bartenders should lean into this option, as it's a great offering to any guest and not bad way to upsell a delicious drink for someone who isn't in the mood for alcohol. Many in the industry have seen this as an added avenue for after-dinner drinks and pairing options with meals and desserts.

Food

Most new hires will have some training shifts with the runner or expo (expeditor). This is my favorite introduction to any restaurant and a part of training that is immensely valuable. This allows a new employee to get the vibe of the kitchen, see the food coming through the pass, and observe the dishes being picked up and taken out to the tables. New hires should be encouraged to ask questions and get a feel for how this kitchen works. The expectation is that they will learn the food more quickly by seeing it.

Also, stay aware of all the movement around you. Make it easy for people to move by you and be aware of *your* movements. Hug the line a bit and keep a path open. In the kitchen, people are carrying hot plates, trays of dishes and sharp objects, and everyone needs to stay attentive and aware.

Every kitchen is different. Successful managers know that new hires need this time to watch the pass while teamed with a seasoned runner or expo.

Jumping in to Help

This really will depend on the style of training that the restaurant wants to give new employees. Hard workers want to jump in and help. I appreciate that and it's a great instinct, but it's not going to help on the first day. Proper time is essential to have new hires see how this specific kitchen's communication works, how the food is presented on the plates and placed in the pass. I came up in the business following a simple rule: you don't touch a plate until you complete a strict menu test. They wouldn't even let you put your hand on a dish until you could explain all the elements on it.

It's crucial for new employees to understand a restaurant's systems so they can see how they fit into those systems. You can do this by watching, listening, and asking questions. Keep this in mind when you want to jump in and help on Day One. Your intention is excellent, but for the moment stick to the plan: observe and learn. Of course, this is only a recommendation—if a leader tells you to throw down your notepad, pick up a dish, and follow them on the floor, you do it. Some restaurants have a different framework and style of training. If your leader wants you to jump in and go, you go. Good luck!

The Floor

Even before learning the menu, it's vital to memorize the table numbers and seat numbers of the restaurant. A seating chart should be one of the first items a new hire receives when being onboarded. It's difficult to drive the car if you don't know where you are going. You ever see someone wandering around a restaurant looking for place to put a dish? They pass by your table three times only to find you on the fourth try, three minutes later, and place a lukewarm ribeye in front of you. That's never a great indicator of good team communication.

After learning the food on the line with the runner or expeditor, the next step will most likely be running food with them. This is a great way for anyone to train. It's the fastest and most thorough way to learn how the kitchen and the floor work together. Through this process, new servers and managers will see how the movement on the floor and operations of the sections work before they start training in those specific areas with managers, servers and the rest of the front of house team.

Seat Numbers

Seat numbers are very common in upscale restaurants. It's rare that someone should be coming over to the table calling out food like they're hawking peanuts at a Dodgers game. If the restaurant has the technology handy and seat numbers can be put in with food orders, then the correct dish should be placed in front of the person who ordered it and announced correctly.

This means that a runner or anyone running food should be prepared in the kitchen when they are grabbing a plate. They should know what seat the plate in their right hand is going to and what seat the plate in their left hand is going to. Take a moment, briefly, visualize the table and the seat, and then grab the plate. This one-to-two-second pause will set that runner up for success when they walk up to the table and place the correct dish in front of the correct guest.

Shadowing a Server

If you are new to a restaurant, managers and servers will most likely shadow a seasoned server before they are given their own small section. Ideally, before the shadowing happens, a few details should be directly addressed with the new employee:

- Stay close enough to your server/trainer that you can hear what they say to the table.

- While you may be familiar with serving tables, try to listen to everything your trainer has to say without being defensive or stating, "Yeah, I know that already." The idea is to learn how all these things are done at *this* restaurant.

- Be aware of the flow of traffic around you; you are an extra person on the floor that the team isn't used to.

- If you have a question, write it down and ask your server/trainer when you are off the floor or in an area where you can have a moment.

- While you may be well intentioned, the restaurant policy may be to have you watch service, not participate in it. Don't grab dishes and start clearing tables. There will be time for that. Watch how it's done. Observe the team that is there. (That said, if a manager or your trainer asks you to do something, you do it. Every restaurant has its own style of onboarding and training.)

- Most likely you will have more time for questions and answers at the end of the shift, while people are doing side work.

Be Prepared

One of the topics I address the most in any hospitality job or position is being prepared. We talk about how we get prepared, both physically and mentally. I look at preparation as something that is completely in my control. As leaders, it's important to have employees understand what they need to do to be ready at the start of the shift. Expectations should be set, but this is also a subject that will always need some reminding and care. Do I wish everyone would start their shift completely prepared in uniform, attentive, and mentally focused to accomplish the goals of the team and restaurant? Sure. Tall order? You bet. The more a conversation can happen around this idea, and the more leaders can help their employees answer questions surrounding preparedness, the better off the team will be. Each person should ask:

- What is your mindset when you walk in the door to work?
- How are you dressed and groomed?
- Are you prepared to lead or support your team?
- What specific element of service are you going to improve on during this shift?
- How can you communicate to your team or managers the help you need in preparing?

Grooming Standards

You should always have a clean uniform. If you can have a backup clean shirt in the car or somewhere, that is always good. There are a few small, inexpensive items that can help with a quick brush up.

- A shoe polisher
- A lint roller
- A Tide pen, or something similar

- A wrinkle-free spray

I usually find mine at the dollar store. Pro tip: don't use the lint roller from there. It can make your shirts tacky.

While I present this list in Part 1: Casual, it warrants repeating. A general rule for grooming standards may be:

- Uniform cleaned and pressed, no stains
- Apron is clean without stains or spots
- Shoes are clean and in good condition, polished if applicable
- Hair pulled back (if long)
- Facial hair groomed so it doesn't look too unkempt
- Fingernails trimmed and clean
- No excessive perfumes or colognes
- Nametag on, if applicable

These standards can vary depending on the style and look the restaurant wants its employees to have. I've eaten at some great restaurants where they are very lax with some of the items I listed above. I don't need a server or a manager in a fancy dress or a bowtie and suit jacket. If the standard set by the restaurant is servers wearing flip flops and a tank top, with Metallica blaring out of the speakers in the background, that is fine by me! Enter Sandman, but make sure you provide good service: connect with the guests, be knowledgeable about your food and drinks, and provide quick, pleasant, inspired service.

A person's grooming should be a choice, though intentional. It shouldn't look like a server didn't have time to stop home and get changed for work. When a restaurant has a lax dress code, it can be a slippery slope. It can easily become unmanageable, to where the staff doesn't look professional. Leaders and employees should always be paying attention to their team's grooming standards and everyone ought to check themselves before they step on the service floor.

Mise En Place

This is a chef's process in which items are organized and prepared before cooking. The FOH always refers to this as the items you should have on you in preparation for the evening. Every restaurant will have a list of mise en place that specific employees should have on their person. While always required of servers, I'm a firm believer that all supervisors and managers should also have these items on them at all times. An example may be:

- 2 pens
- 1 wine key (opener)
- 1 Point of Sale key card
- 1 lighter (for candles, although many are now battery operated)
- 1 pad of paper

Setting Up the Room

This is a repeat from the previous section, but essential in any restaurant. It's always important to have the dining room set up for breakfast, lunch or dinner service. There will usually be a standard as to how everything should look. A general rule of thumb is you want it to look clean and aligned, ready for your guests. Depending on the room, some general standards may be:

- Align the tables.
- Ensure the tables don't wobble and the chairs are sturdy.
- Clean the chairs so they are free of dust, crumbs, and anything else.
- Make sure the floor is clean and free of debris.
- Check that artwork is straight and free of dust and debris.

- Check that all lamps and lights have working lightbulbs.

- Light all candles (before service starts).

- If using battery-operated candles, ensure you have backups in case they go out during service.

- Fill water pitchers and set for service.

Setting the Table

I was probably predisposed to set the table correctly because it was one of my favorite tasks to do when my parents had people over for dinner. I liked pulling out the nice plates and silverware, the special glasses. It was a rare occasion and required a simple shift in mindset. Two things: be spotless. And make everything match. I had a good leader and enforcer in my mom. "Make each place setting identical and be sure to polish each item." She had an eagle eye when it came to the details. This approach includes when a table is reset. The table should look just as good after being reset during service as it did when the restaurant opened. Here are a few general notes on a properly set table.

- Tabletop is clean and free of debris.

- If using a tablecloth, it's clean and pressed, placed with seams face down, and hanging evenly over the table.

- All flatware (term means the same as utensils, cutlery, or silver) are polished and clean, free of food particles, stains, and chips/cracks.

- Utensils should be handled by its base, glassware by its stem or base, plateware by its edge.

- All glassware should be checked to be free of stains or water spots.

- Vase, candle holder, or any other table accessory is clean and free of debris.

- Utensils should be aligned. One inch from the edge of the table is a good standard.

- Utensils, glassware, and plateware is set to match each of the other tables in the dining room. No matter the setup, uniformity and alignment should be consistent across the floor.

- If napkins are pre-placed, they are folded evenly and placed at identical positions around the table.

Line-Up

Sometimes referred to as stand-up, briefing, or the huddle-up. This is a pre-shift meeting lasting anywhere from three to ten minutes. Line-up is a time to focus for the shift and cross-check some information. It usually involves the staff, manager, and chef, but can be as few as two people. This is an ideal time to prepare for service, inspire the team and each other, and clarify any vital information needed.

Information discussed may include:

- Position assignments for the shift, how many sections, and which section

- Items still on the menu that are not available that shift, requiring a verbal warning to the guests *before* they look at the menu

- Any items that have a low count (meaning only a few more exist and will most likely run out during the shift)

- Items that are being substituted for dishes or ingredients that are unavailable

- New menu items and their descriptions

- Specific points of service to focus on during the shift

- Announcing sales goals for the shift and sharing selling tactics

- Sharing positive notes, quotes, or feedback with the team

- Sharing constructive feedback from guests or ownership with the team

- Notification of any equipment that is out of service and will affect the team and guests

- If short-staffed, discussion of how the team will manage with fewer employees on the floor and how that will affect service.

Personally, I think line-ups are essential at any job. It's great to connect with each other, formulate a plan for the shift, present ideas, or ask/answer any questions. It's an ideal moment for supervisors and managers to inspire their teams and all employees to switch gears and move into a service mindset for the shift.

Two common issues can weaken line-ups: one is that employees sit down and it dissipates the energy in the room. Some restaurants call it "Stand-Up" for that very reason. Everyone should stand, stay attentive, and keep the energy focused. Another issue is that employees like to skip out of line-up because they are setting up their section, bar, or busy with another task. While this may happen on a rare occasion, managers should require everyone to attend line-up and stay focused. Do you ever see a professional sports team huddled up for the pep talk/review with the coach before the game, while one player is still doing warm up exercises? No, you don't. There is a reason for that.

Line-Up (Shift) Board

For restaurants that have a lot of staggered shifts or only a couple of employees, a line-up or shift board is a great option to have for those employees who miss line-up. Management can post necessary line-up information here. Oftentimes there will be a sign-in sheet on the board to ensure all employees that missed line-up read the information, sign the sheet, and are prepared for service. I always feel bad for a server who presents a great tableside explanation of their favorite items on the menu, only to return to the table with their head hung down, informing the guest they are out of that item. Having a way to pass on the information at line-up is essential.

Steps of Service

How do your steps of service differ from a casual restaurant? The steps of service increase for you and the team as you aim to provide more upscale, detailed service for guests. Some points of service may include:

- Hosts and managers, having reviewed any reservation notes, should greet guests by name, take them to their table, and notify the server of special occasions or food allergies. The host or manager should present menus and a wine list, if available.

- Server greets the table. They may give a more in-depth introduction to the restaurant and the chef's style or menu. They introduce the courses and sizes, explaining if it's a shared-plate restaurant. They will certainly provide a more in-depth description of the curated cocktails and wines by the glass and bottle.

- If the restaurant has a sommelier, the sommelier will introduce themselves to a table interested in a bottle of wine. Provide wine service if needed.

- Server will have a deeper knowledge about menu items, be familiar with guest preference notes in the reservation system and use those notes to add a touch of personal anticipatory service.

- If bread service is offered, it will usually happen at this point in the service.

- Server puts the order in the computer, ensuring courses and seat numbers are correct. If plates are being shared by the table, server selects which course they should be a part of, usually according to chef recommendation and/or table preference, ALWAYS double checking before hitting enter/send.

- Server checks back with the table to offer cocktails, refill wine or other beverages.

- Runner or server brings first course to the table and ensures they have any additions they may need *before* walking away from the table.

- If it's a shared-plate experience, each person should have a clean, empty plate in front of them before the first-course shared appetizers or smaller-portion sizes are placed on the table with shared utensils (*no one should have to ask a server or runner for sharing utensils in this style of restaurant*).

- Servers should check back with the table a couple of minutes later (people always miss this one!) to see if anyone needs anything.

- A floor manager, if able, should stop by and engage with a table at some point during the meal. Check in with the guests and introduce themselves. It's a nice upscale touch.

- A note about the shared-plate experiences: Shared plates are often brought out at the whim of the kitchen. You will need to ensure there is space on the table each time a shared dish is brought out. *Do not get in the habit of asking your guests to move items around the table for you. This is your job. They are here to enjoy each other's company, not participate in the steps of service.* This is an extra task that comes with executing this type of experience. For more information see the essay, Shared Plates, further along in this section on page 126.

- Server checks back again, offering cocktails and wine and refilling water throughout the meal.

- Servers, runners, and bussers clear the dishes promptly when the first course is finished at the table.

- Server, runner or busser resets the table with new utensils and clean, shared plates if needed.

- Repeat this process per number of courses.

- Server, runner, or busser clears the last course and ensures the table is clean and maintained.

- Server should offer an after-dinner drink from the bar, coffee, and/or dessert.

- If applicable, table should be marked for coffee and/or dessert.

- Bring the coffee immediately. If it can be in sync with the dessert, great, but you also need to be conscious of time, so the quicker this last course happens, the quicker you can move the table if a turn is involved.

- After dessert is finished, a server, runner or busser should clear the table one last time.

- Server should ask if they may bring anything else out to the table.

- A floor manager, if able, should stop by toward the end of the meal or shortly after and ask the guests how their meal/experience was. Thank them for dining at the restaurant. This provides a nice button and closing connection with the guest.

- Server brings a check to the table.

- Server collects payment, processes it, and gives it back to the table. (This can all be done at the table if the restaurant uses handheld POS systems.)

- If the table is splitting the check with multiple cards, have a system where the server can remember which guest, at which seat, handed them their card. This saves the server from calling the guests' names out loud like a carnival barker. Servers can use the guest's name a little more privately when they hand them their check. This is a nice opportunity to say thank you while using their name and clarifying that it is indeed their card/check.

- If possible, there should be a pen for each person who is signing a check. They shouldn't have to wait around because the server only brought one pen for six people to share.

- The server should thank the guests for dining and tell them to have a good day, afternoon, night.

- Every restaurant is going to have a different method for this, but I like cards closed out as soon as possible instead of waiting until the end of the shift. There are many reasons for this, but closing the table immediately on the POS is important.

Additions to the Steps of Service may include:

- An amuse-bouche course (a taste of something from the chef)

- Wine list consultation from the manager, server, or a sommelier

- A detailed explanation of specials or menu style

- Additional food courses ordered

- A presentation of dessert menu and detailed explanation of desserts

- A tableside explanation and/or presentation of more complex coffee orders (which may need to be made tableside)

- A tableside explanation of after-dinner wine or liqueur options (which may need to be made tableside)

Greeting and Seating

Just as more is expected of an upscale restaurant, more is expected of the host seating guests. Restaurateur and hospitality expert Elizabeth Blau told me, "One of the most valuable jobs I ever had, coming out of graduate school, from Cornell, armed with my master's degree, was going to work at the original LaCirque. And they had me work the door and I was the hostess. And I was like, 'Are you kidding me, I have a graduate degree and I'm standing at the door?' It didn't take long for me to see that that was the heart, the center of the restaurant. How people were greeted and seated, watching the room and which people wanted this table over that table. It took a skilled person ... and it was a great lesson."

I mentioned the basics of greeting and seating in Part 1: Casual, on page 16. Adding to that list may be a few more detailed upscale items.

- The host should be able to enter and adjust items in the reservation system and know the details of seating the room.

- The host may be expected to greet guests within a certain amount of time as they enter the restaurant. 30 seconds is a good guestimate.

- While maintaining a friendly manner, the host should attempt to use the guest's name, if known.

- If the host learns any details about the guests (anniversary, birthday, dietary restrictions), they should be able to enter those into the reservation system and/or keep a running notepad and enter the information when there is time to do so.

- The host may be asked to take drink orders if the guests are waiting for a while

- The host should *ask* the guests if they would like to follow the host to the table.

- If applicable, the host should know how to present the menus and wine/cocktail list at the table and give a brief introduction if the server is delayed.

Printable Chits/Communication

Most reservation systems have the ability to print a chit, a small piece of paper with guest information on it. This gives the guest's name, assigned table, special occasion, guest preferences and special dietary information. Chits are currently the most efficient way to get the guests' information from the host into the hands of the manager or server.

The guest information is from either the person that took the reservation or the guest that put the information in the system themselves while they were making the reservation. Often, if it's predetermined what tables guests may sit at during the beginning of the shift, chits can be handed out to servers, so they have a little head start studying who may be sitting at the table. The whole point of the chit is to enhance personalized service. If no one uses the information on the chit, it becomes somewhat pointless. If you have the guest's name, servers and managers should use it. If a guest has stated it's their birthday or anniversary, that should be recognized at some point. If a guest has a dietary restriction, the server should clarify that with the guest when they approach the table or are explaining the menu.

If a restaurant has regulars, items that guests really like are often listed in the guest notes. Guest notes become part of the restaurant's permanent profile of the guest. Reservation notes are those taken specifically for that reservation. These are all ways to customize and personalize the experience for the guest. Communication is key and the chit is a great way to share that information.

Table Presence

There is a difference between friendly service and great service. Great service is a combination of needing to be friendly, while maintaining professionalism. This doesn't mean employees have to be stiff at the table, but it's necessary to address people in a respectful way. Instead of saying, "Hey guys," employees might use the time of day in the greeting, "Good morning, afternoon, evening." Everyone should be aware of how they are speaking to a table. It needs to be sincere, but respectful. Authentic, but professional. In upscale restaurants the presence needs to feel a bit more refined than in a casual restaurant or how someone may address their friends and family. Taking time to do skills exercises, role playing introductions and conversations that are common at tables, is a great way for teams to refine their verbiage and focus on offering a more upscale experience.

Higher Quality Alternatives (Upselling)

We have the ability to upsell almost anything in a restaurant. When I first started out, it made me nervous to offer a more expensive item than the one the guest was initially asking about. I was younger, didn't have much money myself, and I thought it was taking advantage of the guest. Once I realized I was simply offering something of higher quality to them, to enhance their choices, my view and confidence shifted. It wasn't about the money, it was about the product itself, and most importantly, the guest experience.

Of course, it is called the hospitality *business*, and that means all of us should be concerned with generating and improving sales. That's a vital part of business. How leaders frame the offering of alternatives, or upselling, can really help employees lean into it. Skills exercises at line-up will demystify this for employees. Have veteran servers or bartenders share how they offer alternatives that are at a higher price point. Practice on each other, learn from one another. Remember to keep it natural and authentic and focused on improving the guest dining experience.

Taking the Order

I touch on the basics about taking the guest's order in the previous section, Part 1: Casual, on page 18. Clarifying orders before servers walk away from the table and *double checking that order* in the P.O.S. before it's sent to the kitchen will alleviate a lot of miscommunication.

Who at the table gets to order first? That depends on the restaurant. At restaurants that would prefer to have women order first, follow these directions.

- Determine who is the head of the table; usually it's the person that has the reservation in their name. They will be the last to order. Move clockwise and select the first woman to their left and that will be the person to start with. Continue clockwise taking the orders of the rest of the women at the table. After the women have ordered, skip past the head of the table and take the order from the next person at the table, working clockwise again, until you arrive at the host, who will be the final person to give their order to the server.

- Some restaurants may prefer that a server start with the most senior woman at the table. The above directions would apply, starting with the order of the most senior woman sitting clockwise from the designated head of the table and continuing from there.

Allergies, Dietary Restrictions, and Preferences

In an upscale restaurant with access to reservation notes, it's a nice touch to bring up a note while taking the order, "You prefer no garlic on the vegetables, correct?" "I notice there was a mention of a gluten allergy, would you like something instead of the side of pasta?" Preferences are a great way to connect with guests and to anticipate other needs. This shows guests they are cared for and listened to. It's great service.

Delivering Food to the Table

The task of delivering food to the table is a special moment that can easily become washed over and muddled. This is the main event; it's why the guests are here. The kitchen pours their hearts into dishes and along comes a runner who just clanks it on the table and hurries away in a desperate rush to get back to the pass. There are two reasons to announce the food: One, it's a nice touch to have a quick explanation as the guest is looking at this beautiful plate of food. The guests heard about it in theory from the server, saw some words on a menu, and now this moment is the payoff. On the flip side, the guests doesn't need a dissertation on the history and creation of the dish while it gets cold in front of them. This is a moment, a moment to connect, so take it. Two, I have a short memory and with all the amazing things we are eating and drinking in a restaurant, a guest may need to be reminded of a few of the elements on the dish. They may remember they ordered the branzino, the ribeye, and the oxtail pasta...but they may not remember what comes with those dishes. So, punch it up a bit. Name the main and one or two other elements and *then* hightail it back to the pass.

Back Handing

It's important that the server/runner create space between themselves and the guest when they are dropping food or drinks off at the table. By using the proper hand when placing the item in front of the guest, the server/runner avoids showing the guest the back of their hand, while making space between themselves and the guest. The phrase heard from most managers is, "Watch your backhanding." You can find the detailed explanation of backhanding earlier in the book, in Part 1: Casual section, on page 21.

Table Maintenance

"Please watch your tables people, please detail your tables." "Water levels, servers!" "Utensils down BEFORE the food." The list goes on. I apologize to all the managers who had to remind me over and over, night after night. It eventually became second nature to me. Managers and servers should always be watching for table maintenance. This is part of coaching during service. It gets repetitive, but the more the team understands it's part of the process, the culture of executing great service at a high level, the less it becomes about wrongness and more about developing the team's attention to detail and consistently meeting those service standards.

Managers and leaders will get frustrated about constantly harping on table maintenance. Rather than allowing it to dictate your mood, accept that reminding the team about table maintenance is part of a leader's role in shift service. The same as a chef saying, "Order up" or "Need hands!"

In a job interview, I was once asked, "Do you mind reminding people over and over about fulfilling specific tasks?" I said, "I don't mind." He paused, "I mean reminding them a lot, over and over, without getting frustrated?" I said, "Yes, I can do that. I don't mind." He smiled with a look that said, "Remember this, your patience will be tested." And it was. A couple of months in, I was mumbling to myself, "I can't believe these people. I can't believe how many times I have to remind them of this or that. These are adults! This is crazy, blah, blah, blah." I fell for it. I was using up unnecessary space in my brain having this conversation with myself, working myself into a frustrated mess about how unfair and annoying it was.

I share this because we are all human and having to remind people over and over about anything is frustrating. But when I was able to accept that this was part of my role, as the interviewer had wisely warned me, I was able to view it from a different perspective. I was able to move past the frustration, realize I was wasting a lot of energy and acknowledge this was a way I am useful to the team. Accepting this allowed me stay positive. This adjustment changed my tone and my approach. It improved my relationship with the role, the conversations in my head, and my relationship with our team.

Here is a reminder of those table maintenance details:

- Refill water in glasses when one-half full. This may vary depending on size of water glasses at the table. It should never go below 1/3 full without the guest being asked if they would like a refill.

- Refill iced teas, sodas, and wine. Inquire about reorders (cocktails and wine).

- Clear any empty glasses, used paper napkins, dirty utensils or dishware.

- An employee should always *ask* if an empty cocktail glass can be removed *before* they reach for it. And always offer to order another drink for the guest.

- Ensure that candles/electric candles remain lit *throughout* the meal.

- Ensure the table is completely set (marked) for the upcoming course with correct utensils *before* the food is brought to the table.

- If plates are shared, ensure space is available for those plates to be placed on the table. (Avoid asking guests to move plateware and glassware so the food can be placed down. This requires pre-planning on the service team's part.)

Water Service

When greeting the table, say hello, introduce yourself, and ask for a water order. See if the guests would like bottled water—sparkling or still (some people say flat, means the same)—or if they would like tap water. Some guests prefer bottled water, and it's a great opportunity for the server to sell a product and make the guest happy. Servers should always offer tap water as well, as some guests are conscious of cost and others of their carbon footprint. On that same note, some restaurants produce their own still and sparkling water in-house, so be prepared to offer these.

I hate to interrupt a guest to ask what water they are *already* having. A good system is to write down what type of water each guest is having as soon as it's poured the first time. A quick jot in a server notebook. This ensures that the server does not need to interrupt the guest, while keeping their waters full. It also gives the server the option to communicate and delegate to others if they need assistance at their table. This will come in handy between the server, a runner, a busser and other servers that may be assisting in the section. Some restaurants use certain coasters and other signs to convey type of water to the team. It's good to have a tight communication system.

Bread Service

I have had this experience two times in the last few months: we ordered bread and it was dropped off to the table in a pastry bag, like you would place a doughnut or small item in. At one restaurant, the bread was not announced, just casually slid onto the table. Two pieces in the bag for 3 people. The other time, a runner muttered, "Your bread," and walked away.

If the restaurant is going to put in the effort of offering bread to the table and then deliver it — in a basket, on a plate, or in a bag — the server or runner should take a moment to announce it. Tell the table what kinds of bread are in the bag. And if butter, oil, or a spread is offered, ensure the guests know what that is as well. It doesn't have to be a huge presentation, but it should be pointed out to the table. Certainly, if the bread is from a local purveyor or house-made, it should be stated.

Managing the Pace of Your Table

Everyone needs to understand time management in a restaurant that is dependent on multiple seatings. It's crucial for every position to understand how reliant they are on each other when it comes to time. I mention later in the book that a table is kind of like real estate. It will generate a certain amount of money, and then you need to reset the space and have it produce more money. Time takes on value for the restaurant and employees. And managing that time and maximizing the value is a major objective for managers and servers.

Get the Order In

The general rule is: take the order and get the order in as fast as possible. If a server can stay aware of how the kitchen is keeping up, that is always good. I've held tickets to give the kitchen a little time, but some chefs will insist that you get the orders in ASAP and the expeditor and kitchen team will manage it from there. I always roll with the chef's wishes. I've also gotten burned as a server and manager by holding tickets and then forgetting that I held them, wondering where the food was, only realizing twenty-five minutes later that I never put it in. This is an awful feeling. This reinforces my idea that servers should have a little checklist per table and make sure they are hitting all of their steps. If an employee's mental checklist is wavering, they can/should revert to the old pen and pad.

Prep Times

Managers and servers should make it a point to understand the difference in preparation times in relation to the guest flow in the restaurant. Knowing the general amount of time each dish takes to cook will come in handy. A great expeditor and runner will know this information too. A dish that takes ten minutes to prepare at the beginning of the night in a semi-full restaurant, when the restaurant is a little slower, may take less time to prepare than at 8:30 p.m. when the restaurant is packed and the kitchen is slammed.

Courses

Keep your courses tight, but not too tight. Here's what I mean: you want a slight wait between courses before the next one is placed down. This isn't the town crab boil where you drop another bucket on the table as soon as the first one is empty. Give the table a moment to enjoy what they just had. Three minutes, five minutes, eight minutes. It's up to the restaurant. I like five minutes at least. This is where a server can do some table maintenance: clear the table, clean the table, mark the table, refill beverages. Now it's ready. It's a built-in break.

Three or More

You may have a table having three courses or more. That's great—these are people who love food. It's awesome that they want to have more courses, but this can affect the flow of the kitchen, the timing of the meal, and the table turn time. If an extra course is ordered and not expected, it should be communicated quickly to the manager and kitchen so adjustments can be made. Communication is key.

The timing for firing multiple courses requires a server to pay very close attention and maintain a good balance of space/time between those courses. The second course shouldn't arrive *as* the starters are being cleared. Just as important, there shouldn't be a huge lull between courses. These issues almost always come from the course not being fired on time. It takes practice and great places have managers, servers, and bartenders that understand firing times well. It's never going to be perfect, but that doesn't mean perfection shouldn't be the goal every night.

As I mentioned before, it's likely this style of restaurant will add a runner. Regardless, a server will have to fire multiple courses for all of their tables. If the expeditor or runner is put in charge of firing courses for the tables in the restaurant, a server should still understand how and when to do this. Servers are in charge of their sections. Communication is paramount between these positions, regardless of who may be firing the actual courses.

Marking

Marking means placing correct and clean utensils down in front of the guests *prior* to the next course being set down. In upscale restaurants, it's possible that the server is marking every course at the table. But you could be getting assistance from a back server, a runner, or even a busser. Marking, plausing, silvering, and putting down the flatware or utensils all mean the same thing. Different restaurants use different terms. Common sentences you may hear:

- "Did you *mark* 63, seat 2 for the ribeye?"

- "Can you make sure table 5 is *marked* for entrees, they are plating it right now."

- "I've *plaused* 105 for soup and the table is ready for course two."

The clean utensils should always be brought on a CLEAN tray. Many restaurants will use a clean cloth napkin that is folded and pressed on a tray or plate and lay the utensils on that.

Used Utensils

Some restaurants that specialize in a shared-plate experience do not feel the need to replace the used utensils with clean utensils. Don't be surprised; it may be the style they are going for or justifying ("Hey, people don't mind. They don't want their conversations bothered with servers putting down clean utensils"). Or, frankly, there may not be enough utensils in the restaurant to mark for multiple courses. **If a server, runner or employee is asked to leave used utensils on the table, and they must move them to make space for a new course, it is best to not to touch any part of the utensils that might touch the diner's food.**

Use a Tray

The standard used to be "Always use a tray." I see hipster servers casually walking across the floor carrying a glass of riesling, lightly swinging their arm. It doesn't bother me at more casual restaurants. My preference, but certainly not the rule, is when picking up or putting down any glassware on a table, employees should use a tray. Small trays are great for an item or two. Again, if the boss says, "Trays are out of fashion and we are going for an 'old school,' before-trays-existed, casual vibe," then by all means, use your hands. Listen to the boss.

Do a Lap

Similar to the ongoing reminders of consistent table maintenance, managers and seasoned servers are always encouraging team members to get out of their sections and see how they can help co-workers in other sections. "Do a lap!" It makes the team feel supported, provides more attention to details, and always makes guests feel taken care of.

Clearing a Table

If the team is clearing a table throughout service, the table should never look cluttered with used and empty items. As mentioned earlier, the restaurant policy may be to clear the plate if a guest is finished or to wait until every guest at the table is finished with the course. This doesn't mean empty shared plates or glasses don't need to be cleared during the course.

I've listed these tips again, as I did in Part 1: Casual, because this is a vital step in the dining experience. It's important for all employees to be on the same page about when and how they decide to clear a table.

- Ask the guest if you may take their dish away *before* you start to take it away.

- If a guest has pushed their plate away from themselves, it can be cleared.

- Be careful placing your hands or arms too close to guests' faces.

- Minimize the clinking of utensils as you place them on plates you are clearing from the table. This can create a lot of unnecessary noise in the room.

- Do not scrape food from one plate to another in front of guests.

- Try to not stack plates, although in high-volume restaurants this may be unavoidable.

- If you are stacking plates, don't stack too high. And be conscious of utensils sliding off the plate onto the floor or hitting guests.

- If two guests are quite close to each other or conversing, a good rule is to not put your arm in between them. Clear from either side.

- Your clearing tray should look orderly when you are walking back past tables headed to the kitchen.

- While items on a table may be difficult to reach, avoid asking guests to hand items to you.

Dessert

Managing the dessert course is the crucial bookend to finishing the meal. There can be a wide range of dessert preparation in upscale restaurants. A cook may be doing dual duty (salads and dessert), or you may have a dedicated pastry chef in the kitchen, solely focused on the dessert courses. Knowing the general amount of preparation time for each dessert to be made or assembled and delivered to the table can be critical as the server manages the last portion of the guest's restaurant experience. Knowing this information will always come in handy when the team needs to turn a table a little more quickly or assist a server who needs a quick dessert on the fly.

I was always a fan of being able to describe the desserts so well that I had the option to skip presenting a dessert menu to the table. It minimized the time it would take to get the menus, hand them out, give the table time to look them over, and come back to take the order. This verbal offering may not work with some restaurant service styles or with larger dessert menus. A server should always offer the option of a menu, so any guest has the opportunity to read it.

When it comes to special occasions, the dessert plate is a great way to add a cost-effective celebratory item. A candle, a topper pick, or if the kitchen can write with decorator icing or cake drizzle on a plate, "Happy Birthday" or "Happy Anniversary," is a very nice way to recognize a special meal. To go above and beyond, making it more personal, adding the person's name, the couple's names, or shared last name is a generous way to add to their celebration.

After-Dinner Drink Offerings

After-dinner drinks are an opportunity to enhance the dining experience at the end of the meal. Depending on the style of restaurant and selection of after-dinner liquors available, it should be seen as a great additional offering. "May I offer you an after-dinner drink with your dessert? Perhaps something from the bar or wine list? We have an amazing selection of bourbons and scotches, etc." This part of the dinner is often overlooked for improved sales and is also a great way to extend the guest's dining experience.

That said, staying aware of table turn times is also essential at this point in the meal. While these offerings provide an upscale experience, they do extend the table time. If the table is needed back quickly, be aware of what you are offering the guest at this critical time.

The Dishwashing Station

While this too is a repeat from earlier in the book, there is a reason for it. It's one of those things that will always need repeating, no matter the style of restaurant. We celebrate redundancy. Be conscious of helping in this area because everyone is responsible for this high-traffic station. Respect the station and the dishwasher. Help the dishwashing station stay organized:

- Employees should not leave a bunch of food on the plates when they place them in the station.

- Put the correct glassware in the correct glass container at the dishwashing station.

- Be careful to not accidentally toss utensils into the food waste bin. (Happens a lot!)

- If placing a very hot plate in the dishwashing station, notify the dishwasher so they are aware and don't burn themselves.

- Be conscious of the system that the dishwasher has set up and be helpful to that person and their role. They are focused on getting all those items cleaned and back to the team as quickly as possible.

Hardworking dishwashers will greatly appreciate this kind of help from the team.

Dropping the Check

Ideally, a server should make sure the guest is done before dropping the check at the table. This may differ with expedited breakfast or lunch service if it's noticed that a guest may want to leave quickly. "May I get anything else for you this morning/afternoon/evening?" is a pretty standard line to use. The server should be checking in to make certain the guest is satisfied and ensure they had the opportunity to have everything they wanted. A few points about who should get the check:

- If a server is not sure who is paying for the check, place it in the middle of the table.

- If a guest says to the server, "I'll take the check," the server should give it to that guest.

- If the guest says, "*We* will take the check," play it safe and leave it in the middle of the table.

People split checks a lot. The server should inspect the credit card slip before they approach the table so that the correct debit/credit card is paired with the correct slip. DOUBLE-CHECK THE NUMBERS! A server can also reduce the guest's wait time by ensuring each debit/credit card gets its own pen.

The server should say thank you and make eye contact when they drop the billfold/tray, and again when they see the guests getting up to leave the table. This is part of the bookending I talked about in the opening of this chapter and it's essential to the guests' dining experience. A guest should *never* leave a table after paying their bill without some member of the team saying thank you and goodbye to them. Don't assume the person at the host stand is going to do it, as they may be busy with another guest. The best-case scenario is a few people (manager, server, busser, or other servers) thank the guests and say "Have a good afternoon" or "Goodnight. Thank you!" on their way out the door.

Cleanliness and Reset

In an upscale restaurant, dirty tables should always be cleaned quickly and reset. In addition to the list from the cleanliness and reset section in Part 1: Casual, on page 27, here are a few tips:

- Make the least amount of noise possible. A tray should be used, and a bus tub should rarely be seen in this style of restaurant.

- As always, be aware that people are in the dining room and guests can see you as you clean.

- No one should ever put fingers in glasses and carry them away from the table.

- Food should not be scraped from one plate to another while there are guests in the restaurant.

- Everyone should be aware of clanking of utensils and dishes. This creates unnecessary noise.

- Tables should be reset as quickly as possible, and everyone that is able should participate. A vacant, unset table looks almost as bad as an empty, dirty table.

Award winning chef Stuart Brioza, whose chefs participated in front of house service, told me, "In the beginning, the environment of State Bird Provisions was so cool and team-driven, intense. A cook would see a waiter clearing a table, with another waiter ready for the wipe down of the table and all of the sudden, that cook is standing right there with set-ups in their hand ready to reset the table. We call it a "swarm." There is not one waiter who ever clears, wipes, and resets a table on his or her own. The swarm is super-key. Now everyone is totally involved in the restaurant. They are not just kitchen, they are not just waiters."

Side Work

An earlier list of side work can be found in Part 1: Casual section on page 29. Please reference this section if you need guidance in this area. Additional side work you may find in an upscale restaurant may include:

- Polishing utensils/ flatware/ silverware (these words are interchangeable)

- Assisting with cleaning and placing of wine decanters.

- Pre-setting polished wine buckets on the floor, filling those with ice, if necessary.

- Assisting with pre-setting wine bottles used during tableside service, to pour wines by the glass.

- Changing out water or flowers in table vases.

THE GREETING

THE STRENGTH OF THE HOST

I've had the great pleasure of knowing some amazing hosts and maître d's. To watch the great ones is kind of awe-inspiring. My friend Joe Herrschaft was one of the best in the business. He'd control the books, set the plan for the evening, greet the guests, circle the room, checking back and engaging with tables. Joe was big on reservation notes and ensuring that his servers had all the information on the guests,. Even before the reservation systems of OpenTable, Resy, SevenRooms, and others, he would remember birthdays and anniversaries, favorite tables, drinks, dietary restrictions, even sing songs. (I've seen him lock down a dining room and sing a huge "Happy birthday" song...even run across the Sonoma Square to sing a song at another restaurant because they called him and said one of his regulars was eating at their place.) It didn't faze him. He was about the guest experience; whether in his restaurant or another's, his goal was to enhance that experience.

On the flip side, there is a maître d' in the movie *Ferris Bueller's Day Off* that is played ridiculously well by the actor Jonathon Schmock. His take on the character is this off-putting, judgmental person who greets guests at the host stand with facial expressions that are delightfully pompous and superior. This is the exact opposite of how someone would greet a guest. In the majority of my interviews for both my books on restaurant service, this is the area where most professionals thought the ball was dropped. Whether it be the phone interaction with guests, the initial warm and friendly greeting, or explaining why a table isn't ready yet, this is an area that requires attention and consistent monitoring.

At the host stand, the person(s) working is usually wearing a few different hats. They are:

- Saying hi to the guests on the phone, answering questions, and navigating those conversations

- Constantly updating the book or reservation system and reservation/guest notes

- Welcoming guests as they arrive

- Monitoring the waiting area and ensuring it isn't overcrowded or uncomfortable

- Managing guests who may be frustrated and irritated while waiting

- Ensuring the table is properly set and seating the guests

- Paying attention to specific requests of incoming guests (preferred tables, servers, etc.)

- Navigating the restaurant book and floor plan and evenly sitting each table in servers' sections

I actually heard a manager once say, "Just put a pretty face there and they will figure it out. All they have to do is be nice and take people to their seats." I've seen this plenty of times in L.A., and it's a massive mistake. If this is the only thing a host/hostess is doing in a restaurant, you may need to revisit the role and its value to the restaurant team. I've seen this position make or break the restaurant. This is a vital role in executing the strategy of management and the team.

First Impressions

The host stand is where most guests will get their first impression of the restaurant, either in person or on the phone with a host.

So why not spend some quality time training and learning this position? I've seen this this role trained so well that they are unflappable and pretty amazing improvisors. My friend, hospitality veteran and regular maitre 'd on "Hell's

Kitchen," Marino Monferrato, told me, "Every member on the staff needs to know menu items to a certain degree. A hostess/host needs to know each item, the certain ingredients, and what is gluten free, etc. A hostess/host is a great tool to filter lots of questions and to help guests to make the decision while they are on the phone or the stand. This allows the guest to find out the information right there and then. If the hostess/host has to spend extra minutes on the phone explaining the menu and how it works, it's better there than when the guest arrives at their table. The host/hostess just saved the server from a guest asking tons of questions at the table. That phone conversation just had an impact on the floor service for the night. It's a team effort."

Every so often I hear a young person say, "Oh, I have a job at a restaurant, I'm just a working as a host." *Just?* I don't think so. I'm quick to remind them that with a great attitude, they are going to learn some amazing people skills and be challenged, but also rewarded with a fast schooling on listening, time management, and improvisation.

Here are some quick skills exercises for everyone - hosts, servers, managers, runners, and bussers. If you are a manager or host, gather the team around and try one. Practice how you want to play.

Pre-Shift Skills Exercises

- **Phone Call:** Guest inquiring about vegan, gluten-free, and eco-friendly dishes. Practice your phone voice, lighter/friendlier tone. It should be intentional and warm but not like you are answering your phone on your couch.

- **Bully guest:** A guest who does not appear to have a reservation but thinks they did and are being adamant that they be seated in the restaurant.

- **Annoyed guest:** A guest who is not happy with the table they are being seated at.

- **Figuring out a name:** Welcoming a guest and trying to ascertain their name, so you can find it in the reservation system. Explore a few different ways you can ask the guest for their name.

- **Good evening/Goodbye:** Three ways you could welcome a guest. Three ways you could say goodbye. Role-play it. Someone be the host; someone be the guest. (*You can pick names from guests already in the reservation system if you'd like.*)

- **Bored Bill/Barbara:** This is fun. Imitate all the ways you could look bored to a guest while you are at the stand. The more hosts get used to recognizing non-verbal communication, the more anticipatory their service will become.

- **The Book:** This is a scheduling-the-room exercise. Open the reservation system to a night way down the road and use it as a booking exercise for a new host to learn about seating arrangements and turn times.

13

DOUG WASHINGTON

Principle/Creative Director at Doug Washington Design

Formal to Fun

It isn't only the service that changed. The atmosphere, the delivery, and vibe have changed the most! At the end of the day, we had the same farms, purveyors, and level of server knowledge. We were grinding servers to know every wine on the list and where it was from. We had the same silverware and plates. We had the same technical service: you didn't take a drink out without a tray; the pre-set silver went in the right place and was set before the food went down. We followed the same rules, but what changed was *how are we delivering it?*

Instead of the crappy music we were listening to for years, we changed it up. Blues music with southern food. I don't want it to be quiet. I don't want it to be so loud you can't talk, but I want it up a notch. We didn't want tablecloths, so away those went. We didn't want stuffy uniforms. Let's loosen it up a bit—so we went with jeans instead of black pants and told the staff to wear a nice shirt.

Techniques of Service

The technical side hasn't really been made less casual. If I take a glass of wine to a table without a tray, a manager or sommelier will come over and emphatically say, "Hey, you have to put those on a tray!" And I'm the owner.

But they are right. They are upset because you are now breaking a technical service expertise point. It doesn't have anything to do with casual dining or fine dining.

If you get a plate and your steak is at 3 o'clock, instead of 6 o'clock, unless it's plated that way because it was intentionally designed that way, then it's just a mistake. If the coffee cup is placed with the handle is at 9 o'clock instead of 3 o'clock, and the spoon is backwards, that's not more casual, it's wrong. If you get your soup and you must wait for your spoon or the soup is up on the edge of the rim of the bowl—it's not more casual, it's just wrong. I think there is a clear delineation between things being right and wrong or more casual and more fun vs. stuffy.

Confidence

In more casual fine dining, everybody still wants the same level of product and purveyors and wants servers to have the same level of knowledge. When you ask the server about the wine, they don't say, "Let me find someone who can answer that for you," but can themselves answer, "I've had that, it's a Rhone style, it's spicy, it's got good body, and it goes well with these dishes."

The Details

It's the little things. A good server is so sharp, they pick up that someone is looking around, searching for something—the restroom or a different table. Could be you are one-third or halfway through your entrée and the person with you has finished theirs. And that server walks up and asks, "I need to ask, is everything okay with that?" To me, I'm blown away. And I would respond, "Oh god, yes, I'm just eating slow or talking too much." And they say, "Okay, great, I just wanted to check." But they noticed and sincerely cared. Are people hunting for things that could be wrong, and are they hunting for ways that could make your evening?

Awareness

The whole thing about service is "Are you aware?" Are you aware of your surroundings? Are you aware of people? Are you aware of how they feel?

It isn't always a good thing. Sometimes I wish I could relax and not be concerned with how people feel all the time, are they happy and all the rest of it. The flip side is I learned to care. I learned that hospitality isn't just looking and being nice. It's about being aware.

14

DESCRIBING FOOD

Bringing the Menu Off the Page

Kirsten and I were recently at a restaurant in Echo Park, Donna's. We've been many times now. The first time we were there, our server, Michael, approached the table and introduced himself. He was very relaxed, present, and excited to hear we had not eaten there before. When we jumped into the menu with a few questions, his responses made us put our menus down immediately and just listen. His descriptions made the dishes sound so delicious! He brought it off the page. This is essential. It doesn't have to be more than a few sentences. We could tell Michael was describing something he truly knew. His word choice, his feeling, and his confidence. As he continued to describe different dishes, we knew we were in great hands. A pro is a pro. Without even talking to each other, we knew we were going to go all in on Michael's recommendations.

Diners have become savvy and the dialogue has changed at the table. Of course, a server still needs to read the table and determine how much information a guest may need or want. A return guest may not need the full description, but if they have brought friends who have never dined there before, the server needs to be able to read that and deliver the full explanation. Regardless, a server should never be just listing or repeating the words exactly as they are on the menu. It risks coming across as uninspired.

Describing, not Telling

Servers should go through the menu and work on some *descriptions of dishes*, not simply listing the ingredients. Practice. I used to practice on my friends and family. Managers should use skills exercises to have the team share their descriptions. Try using descriptive words that speak to texture, cooking techniques, and flavors. These are all different from simply listing ingredients. Now, I say this with a caveat: you don't want servers to automatically over-describe; that may drive a chef a little batty. Keep it in check. But work with the team on moving them gracefully from telling to describing, and it may make for a more engaging experience with your guests.

A Few Options

Have a couple of different ways to describe the same dish. I say this because you want it to be authentic. The server might say to you, "The branzino is absolutely amazing. It's grilled on the almond wood fire, with a touch of olive oil, Celtic sea salt, and squeeze of Meyer lemon. It's one of my favorites." And you think, that sounds amazing. We must have that! And then ten minutes later the same server is at the table next to you and says verbatim, "The branzino is absolutely amazing. It's grilled on the almond wood fire, with a touch of olive oil, Celtic sea salt, and a squeeze of Meyer lemon. It's one of my favorites." Suddenly the dish feels a little less special to you. And then, five minutes after that, you hear the same server at the table across from you say, "The branzino is absolutely amazing. It's grilled on the almond wood fire, with a touch of olive oil, Celtic sea salt and a squeeze of Meyer lemon. It's one of my favorites." And you think, "Good grief, they are really pushing that branzino. Is this the last day before it goes bad and starts smelling fishy?" Or "Are they running a contest to see who can hawk the most branzino tonight?" Managers should stay aware of servers making the experience fresh and authentic for the guest. It's good to have some alternate descriptions in your back pocket for small rooms and close tables.

15

ADAM COLE

Chef, Consultant

Components of a Dish

When training runners, the most important thing is to get them interested and excited about ingredients going into each dish. I start them with the verbiage that is on the menu. So, at the very least, they can take a dish to the table and describe the dish correctly.

Once they have the basic description down, as [the] chef wrote it:

- They are going through the details of learning each of the components on the dish.

- They will then need to identify each component on the dish, for every dish on the menu.

- The third level of knowledge training is breaking down each of those components into individual ingredients and learning what each ingredient is and hopefully why.

You can teach a runner an awful lot about basic cooking methods and skills by getting them to understand what goes into each dish and why. If a guest has any question about anything on a dish, the runner must have that knowledge and [be] ready to address ANY point—so they can go into a lot of description if that is what the guest would like. You might have a person ask, "Where is the sea bass from?" The runner should be able to answer that on the spot.

"*It's also called loup de mer. It's another name for the fish, its farm raised in the Mediterranean, off the coast of Greece. We get it every other day.*" Knowing all this blows people away. It's a free component to creating good service.

Food Methods/Knowledge

It's important for runners to know about ingredients and cooking methods because the diner keeps getting more intelligent about what they are eating and what the cooking methods are. Servers, runners, and everyone in the front of the house needs to understand the food methods better than the average diner. If the average diner is getting smarter—then the front of the house needs to continue to do the same.

Over-Describing

I truly believe that diners' brains shut off after hearing about the third thing on the plate. Over-describing a dish at a table is one of the ways in which restaurants fail all the time. Don't over-describe.

16

CREATING TIME

Efficiency, Time Blocks and Linking Tasks

Anyone that knows me, knows I can talk. When I was moving into upscale and elevated dining rooms, I was slow on learning the nuances of firing courses, needed to improve working a few steps ahead, and LOVED to talk with my tables. All of these together had me running behind on tasks, slow on firing times, and creating long table turns. I had to find a balance: connect with the guests and provide a good experience but get all my tasks done in a timely manner. My time management needed improvement. When I first started at Capo, Max, the GM, timed me at a table and gave me some really constructive feedback about how to shorten my intro and not get too caught up at the table. Capo had such fast service that I started to break my steps of service into time blocks, including my opening and closing side work. Feedback from Max and some of the veteran servers made me realize I needed a different mindset to execute this style of service. Be efficient with the time I have. Also…I was wasting money by not being able to turn my tables and get out of my section to help the team.

This was great coaching by management and other servers. Once I started paying close attention to time blocks, timing myself, and improving my efficiency, I was able to free up space to do all the other things to help the team. I was creating time. This reduced my server stress incredibly, and I was able to contribute more. With extra time a server can:

- Ensure their section and tables are maintained and clean

- Get out of their section and assist other servers by doing a lap and checking other tables and sections

- Assist the runner with dropping food to a table
- Run drinks from the bar
- Tidy up the server stations
- Replenish marking trays
- Assist the host with seating guests
- Participate in completing side-work
- Check the bathrooms for cleanliness
- Connect more with guests
- Be more present with a less frenetic energy

Re-evaluate your Process

I often hear servers say, "I don't have any time. I need to focus on my section." But to get to the root of why they don't have time, they may need to break it down. They may need a little coaching from management to do this. Assist them by giving them details on where they can be more efficient, instead of generalizing and repeating phrases like, "We need to go faster." Break it down. I was lucky I had Max and others that worked with me at Capo when I was struggling with the demands of a new style of service. Managers should jump at the opportunity to help servers tighten up service blocks (a few steps of service combined or task combinations) and fine tune their process. Assisting employees to link certain steps and tasks can create time that will be needed elsewhere. Here are some examples:

- When an employee drops food at a table, they should scan for anything on the table that they can pick up and take away (dirty cocktail napkins, empty cocktail or beer glasses, bread and butter plates, dirty plates).
- Anytime an employee fills water at the table they should be checking

all other glasses to see if they can offer refills on beverages, propose another glass of wine or cocktail, or pour their bottled wine.

- When an employee clears a table of dirty plates, use that same time to scan the table to see what, if any, utensils may need to be reset for the next course.

- When an employee is at the tea or coffee station and have that extra minute while the tea steeps or the coffee brews, tidy it up, clean off the spilled grounds, restock the teabags, etc.

17

MARVIN WELLS

Director of Hospitality, FAO Hospitality

Hiring

Everyone who sits down for an interview is extremely nervous, and you can tell. You can make them more comfortable by asking questions like, "So what do you do? What am I not going to find on your resume? Do you jump out of airplanes, or what else do you do?" They are always disarmed by that, and a more relaxed conversation ensues, and I feel like you get a good read about people when you can talk to them about things other than "What's the worst situation you've been in at a table?"

You get more when you can talk to people, put them at ease and then they just start talking. Can they hold a conversation? Because guests, a greater percentage of guests, want to talk about whatever—the last movie you saw or things of that nature.

Learn Names

Names [are] always a big thing for me. By learning people's names, whether it be in the front of the house or back on the house, that endears that person to you and they are more willing to help you.

Be Encouraging

I always try to be honest with the employee. There are going to be times when you want to run out of here screaming and yelling because you feel it's too much. You're going to have some days where everybody gives you a high-five. There are going to be some days where it's just overwhelming, and those moments, whether it be good or bad, you have to go back to who you are. You were picked out of a lot of different people for this job, so you're not here "just because." You are here because we all believe in you. You're here because we think that you can do this. We are also here to help you get there. We are not here to have you fail tests; we're here to have you pass those tests.

Selling vs. Describing

Being able to communicate what an item is by *description* is one thing, but being able to *sell* it to somebody is completely different. You can describe a burger: it's on a bun, it's got mayonnaise, mustard, pickles, and the guest is now falling asleep. OR you can say it's our own baked sesame seed bun, we [grind] our chuck every day, grill it to your temperature, it's topped with our traditional burger toppings, all brought out with our crispy potatoes. You're going to *sell* it differently than you are going to *describe* it.

18

MANAGING AND MONEY

Navigating the Areas of Costs

I had a sobering but enlightening conversation with Brian Borowski, the Director of Operations of Edible Eats restaurant group in Denver. He told me that, given the challenges in restaurants in recent years, it's difficult to separate the financial conversation from the service conversation. You need to understand both. "Our management has to have as much awareness of their administrative responsibilities as they do about their service presence. Ten or 15 years ago the only thing we really stressed about was how was your guest and staff? How was your guest experience tonight? How was your staff experience tonight? Regardless of which environment you are working in; - casual, upscale, elevated - now there has to be a dialogue around fiscal responsibility and fiscal awareness. This impacts our service because we staff less people than we used to staff on our floors and because we are more careful, intentional, and thoughtful about how we order and what we spend on supplies. This responsibility impacts our service because it's influencing the way we can handle improvements, repairs, and other projects in the restaurant. So, on the financial side we talk to our teams about this - taking care of the materials and supplies they use, being mindful of the amount of time they spend on the clock as they wind down at the end of service. These are active dialogues we are having daily with our hourly staff; it's not just a dialogue with management and leadership."

A few administrative and management areas managers should stay on top of include:

Finances

It's very important, truly vital, for all managers to have a grasp on the restaurant operations and polices that affect the finances of the restaurant. Everything affects the finances: hiring, labor costs, food costs, utilities, rent, laundering, cleaning crews, reservation platform subscription fees, etc. Being able to read a profit and loss sheet will make you stronger and more proficient as a leader. Lean into understanding these financial tools and learn to pivot quickly when the numbers indicate a need to do so.

Scheduling

Smart scheduling is vital to any restaurant and ties directly to revenue and balancing projected business demands. Understanding proper staffing levels and business flow can minimize overtime costs, optimize labor costs and improve staff satisfaction. Many scheduling software platforms may work directly with projected restaurant volume, labor tracking, and payroll. Some systems may allow employees to directly request time or swap shifts with other employees. Most managers will need to learn the restaurant's scheduling process and software and how to use it effectively.

Attendance, Rest and Meal Breaks

I can't tell you how many headaches are created from late punches and missed or late rest break and meal punches. This is one of those issues that managers are constantly reminding employees about. It needs repeating because it drastically affects payroll and the restaurant expenses. A few minutes here and a few minutes there, per person, can create meal penalties and unnecessary overtime pay. Managers can save the restaurant a lot of money if they create positive dialogue and communication with staff about attendance policies and punching in and out at the correct times.

Correcting time punches digitally and manually to ensure employees are being compensated for hours worked is going to be a part of management duties. Some restaurants may have a payroll person assisting with this area. Keeping a keen eye on correct dates, hours worked, and other vital information on these forms is very important for any manager.

Gratuity and Distribution

Another administrative task that is important to understand in a restaurant is how the gratuity/tip system works. Is it tip pooling or tip sharing? Tip pooling is when there is a collective pool and an agreed-upon distribution policy among eligible employees. Tip sharing is when server or bartender keeps their own portion and shares a portion or percentage of that amount with other employees. Regardless of the system, managers have to understand the system in the event that they need to record the numbers, check a spreadsheet to ensure consistency, or upload numbers for tax purposes.

HR Policies

Aside from attendance and time-punch policies, there may be a lot of other policies and procedures for a new manager to master. The depth of the progressive discipline framework will depend on the restaurant and it's important to get a clear understanding of this as soon as possible. If the GM is not available or the restaurant does not have an available HR representative, managers will have to handle disciplinary issues themselves. When handling any disciplinary actions, managers should ensure and double check vital information, dates, and times that they record on forms. Ideally, this is part of their training and the stronger a manager's understanding of the restaurant policies and procedures, the quicker they will be able to support the team and restaurant operations.

19

CAROLINE STYNE

President and Wine Director- The Lucques Group

Smoke and Mirrors

I love the smoke and mirrors of a restaurant. I love the whole idea where the guest doesn't need to know anything about how the restaurant operates. It makes me a little crazy when I hear the host or runner say the table number out loud. The guests don't need to know that the tables have a number. They don't need to know anything that turns it into a transaction instead of an experience. They only need to know they are being seated at a lovely table, in the corner, looked after by warm and caring people, and all this stuff just happens around them, seamlessly.

Allowing Failure

I try very hard not to micro-manage people because when I do micro-manage, I feel like the person never feels at ease or is able to be themselves in the role. They are feeling constantly watched. I definitely check in and I am consistently talking with them, but it's important to let them do their thing. As difficult as it is, learning through making mistakes can be the best way to learn because the learner experiences the fallout and consequences of the error. I'm a parent and I just so badly want to keep my kids from making mistakes and guide them to the right answer. But the wrong answer is sometimes just as important. Not that I want mistakes to be happening, but if you don't allow a person to do things on their own, to find their way, then how are they going to learn?

Feedback

I used to get more nervous about feedback because I'm kind of a non-confrontational person. But at a certain point I realized, "Wait it's not a confrontation, it's an education." So, when managers or employees step into a new role, I just say from the very outset: "I'm going to be giving you feedback and it's not a criticism of you or of your thought process, it's just guidance as to how we want things to be done here. It doesn't mean that you've made a bad decision or that you are wrong, I'm just going to be guiding you, and I hope you can be open to that."

I usually try to keep the feedback very concise and intact. I will pull somebody aside after the fact, away from anybody that can hear, and I'll have a diplomatic conversation about what I witnessed and what I would prefer to happen in the future. "I just want to talk about what I saw a few minutes ago, when I saw A, B, C, and D. I'd love to know what your thought process was behind that. Can you take me though it?" And then I let that person speak and usually I'll respond with, "OK, well what I would have done is…"

Wine Support

Whenever I put a new wine on our wine list, we give the staff an information sheet about each wine and it says: what it tastes like, who makes it, and what region it's from. We keep an iPad of all that information available. We talk with the staff about flavor profiles and similarities that each wine has to other wines. We talk with them through the concepts of which wines pair with which dishes on the menu, so that they have that information when somebody's ordering. They can then reference that feedback and say to a guest, "This Chablis will work really well with that sea bass because it has high acid, beautiful minerality and citrus." If you arm your employees with understandable information that they can apply to their steps of service, then it at least gives them enough information to be able to accurately and confidently sell a bottle wine to somebody. You've given them the sales tool to build up their check and actually give the guest the experience they are looking for.

20

THE GREAT DELEGATOR

Prioritizing and Communicating with Teams

Watching someone delegate tasks well and execute a plan with many different moving parts is one of my favorite things. It's what makes a great coach, an exceptional filmmaker, an amazing chef, or an effective manager. It's a skill that is learned over time, and if you have the chance to work with one of these people, hopefully you will get to learn the skill and how to use it. It is rare to see someone who is able to juggle many tasks, under a lot of pressure, and delegate in a concise and calm way to multiple people and teams. I'm not talking about the people who do this while having meltdowns and screaming at people. I'm talking about the people who do it well.

On the line, you will see a chef cooking while giving direction to other cooks, controlling the timing to a tee so that each plate on a ticket, every element on it, is ready to go at a precise time. And they do this repeatedly, all shifts. I've had the advantage of working with some great service directors who had incredible vision (not to be confused with eyesight): they could see the whole floor, take in each section, each table at the same time and conduct service, while coaching a team in a calm, composed fashion all night long. These are the individuals you want to learn from.

My first big lessons in delegation was when I worked at The Dining Room. The front servers were the leads on the floor, sometimes known at captains. As leaders executing this particular style of service, we were to stay on the floor the whole time. That meant I had to adjust my processes from all the restaurants I had worked in before. I had been used to leaving my section to fire courses, run food, check in on the kitchen. This wasn't allowed. I was to always stay on the floor. I had to rely on my back server and server assistant (busser) to do tasks that required leaving the floor.

This was an adjustment, took a lot of trust, and required me to improve my communication skills as a delegator. I had to figure out how to verbalize the things I needed done with the assistance of my co-workers. If I had 14 items running through my brain, I needed to find a way to categorize and prioritize them so I could take care of each one. But just as importantly, I needed to be able to clearly communicate these tasks to the rest to my team when I needed help.

I've seen servers who don't learn this skill and it is always apparent when they are in "the weeds." Someone will come up and ask what they can do for the server, who is already on the verge of a breakdown, and they can't verbalize what they need in a concise, well-formed way. The offer to help them just stresses them out more. Often, this will lead that server to say, "Forget it, I'll just do it myself." I get it, I've been that server, bartender, and leader. **Once I learned how to delegate, stay calm in the pocket, and use a good tracking system for my tasks, my section became more efficient.**

Often a manager or maître d' is giving direction to hosts, seating guests, ensuring servers are hitting their sequence of service while turning their tables, and communicating with somms and the kitchen about timing of courses and the flow of the room. They are looking at the whole picture to make sure everything is running smoothly. This role of delegator requires a tremendous amount of multitasking, foresight, and gracefulness - all while hungry guests are waiting. It's a very difficult job to do well.

When a manager or server is a little stressed and overwhelmed, it's also really important that the team doesn't take on that energy. Sometimes the frenetic energy a stressed person exudes can rub off on the team. That can shift the energy of the room quickly. Employees should maintain awareness. Take on the tasks and importance of the moment but avoid taking on the frenetic energy. Communication is vital here and leadership has an opportunity to work with individual team members on ways to help them feel more comfortable, less stressed, in those moments. Help isolate the triggers and work through those moments, so they don't become habitual.

21

JOSH GOLDMAN

Hospitality & Beverage Consultant

The Deal

The guest is the star. They showed up, decided to spend money. By their participation, they are paying the bills, keeping the restaurant open, and allowing us to take care of them. And now we have to fulfill our side of the deal. We need make sure they have a great time. They came into our house, like someone coming into your own house. If you don't want company, you shouldn't open your doors. But if you do, you have to treat them right, treat everyone the way you would treat the most important person in your life.

Product Knowledge

A server who has been trained can be highly useful to a business and can be a sales advocate. They are your sales force. It's retail like anything else. Information, product knowledge, having the knowledge to be a productive sales associate is incredibly important. If everybody knows all about the product, the guest wins. That's the goal. If you have no idea about the product you are selling, it's going to be really awkward. The more information the team has and knows about the product, the more confidence the team will have.

Practice and Speed

Practice makes perfect. It's like using a peeler. Somebody always cuts themselves. You must develop the muscle memory in practice, so you are ready for the game. Get a bag of oranges, go home, and practice. Speed trials—competition for bartenders to learn through. Head-to-head and timed. Stress test. You train for getting packed immediately and you train hard to find your stride in training, instead of finding your stride when you open a restaurant on Day One.

22

ATMOSPHERE

MAINTAINING GREAT SERVICE IN LIVELY ROOMS

I was at a hip, new restaurant recently and it was fun: great lighting, cool artwork on the walls, loud music, somewhat chaotic, lots of people moving around. A busy hotspot. Plates were coming, plates were disappearing, some plates had utensils, some did not. People were pouring wine across the table, spilling some drops, servers yelling across the room...like I said, chaos. Fun. Loud. The friend I was with leaned into me and said, "They go for a dinner party vibe here." Oh...is that what they call it? I was thinking, "What the heck is going on here?" Don't get me wrong, I liked the vibe, the music, atmosphere, but that's where the control of the experience looked like it ended for the management team. It didn't flow into the service provided. It didn't seem intentional all the way through.

I've seen this at a lot of restaurants over the last 30 years. It's when atmosphere takes precedent over service and caring for the guest experience. Form over function, whatever you want to call it. I've also seen a few places do this really well. Intentionally. When I've seen this type of high volume, atmosphere-centric restaurant work, with great service, it's completely magical and awe inspiring. It's an amazing balancing act of *appearing* chaotic and very fun but actually being in control and having intention. The experience is still of value and memorable to the guest.

The Attitude

I used to joke with a friend when we would go to clubs in Hollywood, in our twenties, "Do they do a training where they tell everyone not to smile? Is this a requirement?" Do you have to be model hot and have a frowny, Zoolanderish face to get hired here? It's probably why we preferred pubs to clubs. There was more of a connection made. I get that at a club the music is super loud, people are there to dance, have fun, and it's hard to hear people even order their drinks over the bumping bassline. But looking like a bored, uninterested host, bartender, or server standing around with your arms crossed isn't going to add to the desired atmosphere. It's painful when I walk into a restaurant and see employees that look like they'd rather be somewhere else. Unengaged. Managers and veteran servers should always keep the team inspired and engaged. Coaching on perception, optics and non-verbal communication, when necessary, should help support a good team skillset and attitude.

Balance

I want to be in a fun restaurant. I love loud, vibrant restaurants. When it works. I recently ate at a super lively restaurant, Ribalta, near Union Square, in New York City. It was busy, it was fast, it was happening. No matter how busy and loud it was, we always felt taken care of. We didn't feel like we were unattended or forgotten. Our server was gracious, loud enough to hear, paying attention to tone, not just volume. Key in a loud restaurant. We had very fun evening with friends. That's not rocket science. That was just attention to detail. The staff was in control the whole time, servers and managers guiding us through the experience. It can't be left to happenstance and open to inconsistency. Consistency matters, and if you aren't in some control of the wild, fun vibe you are trying to give guests, you may run the risk of losing return customers.

23

ROBIN KIRBY

Operations leadership team- Kokkari and Evvia.

Consistency

One thing you have to establish in a restaurant to maintain your identity and your following, is consistency in service. The hallmark of every successful restaurant is the consistency in the level of hospitality and service. People expect a certain level of hospitality, and they get it every time they come. It's day-to-day dedication to keep that. There is consistency in cultural and hospitality philosophy. That makes a difference for restaurants that are successful long term. It's easy to be a restaurant that is successful for two or three years; that happens all the time.

Hiring

We hire based on personality and that ability that people have to connect with people. That gift to light up the table, to turn people around, that genuine interest in the people connection.

Guest Details

One of our biggest strengths is taking care of our repeat guests. We take notes: where they like to sit, who they like to serve them, their likes and dislikes, their favorite dishes. We are good at maintaining that file for our regulars. Going out of our way to give them their favorite table or taking the time to note their number 2 table. Definitely calling our guests by their name. We have notes that we hand to the servers: names, significant other's names, birthdays, anniversaries, and quirks regulars may have which we want to accommodate.

Patience, Perseverance, Kindness

Whenever someone comes at me in my personal life, I remind myself to take a deep breath, stay calm and be the person I want to be. Don't let someone else dictate your behavior. I had to learn that. When I was younger, I was much more defensive. One thing that I have learned is that patience and perseverance, with kindness, trumps most behavior. Meaning: if you can stick your ground and be kind and maintain calm, most of the time you can bring someone on board with you. If you can take the higher road, maintain openness and kindness, it will win nine times out of ten.

24

SHARED PLATES

The Challenges of Upscale Family Style

I love eating family style. I used to hate it because I'm a twin. And if you're a twin, you understand you have to share everything. And it can become irritating for both of you. So, by the time I moved out of the house, I was ready to take on the world and not share anything! I'm exaggerating a bit here. I do think my ability to compromise and find group solutions is rooted in a childhood of having another human being right next to me, but when it came to food and splitting dishes or sharing, I was ready to commit to the notion of, "I'll stay in my lane, you stay in yours." This entrée is mine! Now, many relationships later, and many offers of, "Are you sure you don't want to try mine?" (a known gimmick to make me offer some of my dish), I have greatly improved my ability to share my appetizer and entrée with a dining companion.

Many years ago, when I was working in restaurants, I witnessed this shift in upscale dining to a popular "shared plate" experience. This wasn't at your casual Italian restaurant or chain restaurant, and they didn't market it as "family style"; it was happening at much more upscale and pricier restaurants.

When this style was coming into fashion, I noticed that it allowed chef-driven restaurants to serve their dishes the way *they* wanted. Meals coursed the way *they* wanted it, served hot and not sitting in the pass for any length of time. I like the concept, and the places that crush this style do it well; it's fun, it's like doing a shared group tasting menu with your whole table. I also simply like the innovation of providing an upscale dining experience that has a family-style-esque vibe, sharing dishes, connecting through amazing food, and it's awesome...when it works.

Prepare Your Team

To pull off this style of dining service requires greater communication and an orchestration that is much more complex than your traditional sit-down experience. It's not easier, it's more difficult. It requires *extra* steps of service. I think this is what people who experience challenges pulling off this type of service don't understand. You run the risk of providing a bad guest experience if you haven't trained your staff well and considered a whole new set of questions to accompany a "shared plate" dining style. For instance:

- Have your guests dined in this type of restaurant before? Servers should have a quick, detailed explanation of the style of service and what the guest may expect. Don't assume people know.

- Servers should be able to suggest a general number of shared plates and portion sizes for the number of people at the table.

- Oftentimes a server will say, "The kitchen will course this and send it out." This puts the timing in the hands of the kitchen, but issues may arise from this:

    - If the kitchen is putting up plates as they see fit, are they aware of what's happening at the table? Are they in constant communication with the server and runner, so the table is prepared — has space, is marked, and ready for those dishes?

    - If the table is stacked with three items and the kitchen is pushing more out, is the guest going to watch the seared scallops get cold on the table as they try to enjoy the steak tartar, not wanting to cross flavor profiles? Are they going to watch the light dressing soak into the salad course because they are a slower eater? Don't create an issue for the guest, anticipate the issue before it happens and solve it.

- How often is the server offering new plates? Is it the chef's desire that their food flavors cross? Should the sea bream with citrus yuzu be plated on the remnants of a piquillo sauce from a different dish? Is it intentional?

- Are there enough shared utensils, so people feel comfortable plating their own food with another person at the table? Is the server leaving it up to the guest to ask for a serving spoon? Is the guest expected to put the fork that has already been in their mouth into the shared dish to put some food on their plate?

Make Space

One of the biggest challenges in a shared-plates-style restaurant is for the runners who are dropping dishes off. From personal experience, it was always a bad look when I showed up at a table with two plates in my hands and didn't have any room at the table to place them. Having to ask the guest to stop enjoying their meal and move some plates around the table is a failure. The guest's job is to enjoy the meal and pay for it, not assist in setting the table, making room for shared plates, pouring water, refilling their wine, asking the server for extra utensils. This is the job of the restaurant and its employees: **beat the guest to the request.**

GARRETT HARKER

Restaurateur- Eastern Standard, Standard Italian, Equal Measure

The Guest Perspective

Guests generally come to a restaurant with varied agendas. In this day and age, in general, the guest is looking for a very personalized experience. And people use restaurants for much more varied reasons: Someone may opt in for a tasting menu; others oysters and a glass of wine. It may be food-centric, cocktail-centric, or wine-centric. It creates its own challenge for conventional service ideas. We used to script the way our service was. When people use the word "fine dining," I think, "That's a chef, they are creating an experience. It generally lasts for a certain amount of time; the service is generally choreographed a little more." Now, it's more personal and about connection with the server and the server helping fit the agenda of the diner in a much more interactive way.

It's critical to the success of Eastern Standard that the service staff be very flexible, use their imagination, and be in the moment. You can't go on automatic pilot at any restaurant anymore. The servers have to be responsive. The most successful servers we have are extremely empathetic, very motivated. It's really about a complete experience and the connection with the guest, which means we really rely on a talented, motivated service staff to help us be successful.

Hiring

We look for people that have a passionate interest in something that, maybe on the surface, doesn't appear to be connected with the restaurant industry or appreciation for food and dining. Someone who is curious, has an active mind, and a lot of interests.

Ten or fifteen years ago I remember writing this quiz that we would use to vet candidates: *How would you garnish a Gibson? What is a beurre blanc?* Just to see how much exposure they had to food. We don't do that anymore. We vet candidates on whether they are engaging. Are they interesting? Maybe have they traveled, participated in a team environment. Are they charming and warm somewhere in their core?

Education

Some of the education initiatives at Eastern Standard were lessons about the founding fathers and what the Constitution was, lessons about different cities around the country—they were not necessarily based strictly on food and beverage. We were thinking knowledge for knowledge's sake, education for education's sake. Creating that environment where every moment is an opportunity to learn and an opportunity to teach. I want students and teachers front-facing in my restaurants, and I think the guests will come away with a very positive service experience.

Our staff is not walking away everyday with knowledge they are going to drop on the table and blow people away with it. But that enriched environment we create for our staff lets them let down their guard and feel like, "These people are taking care of me, investing in my future, they are committed to an environment where I can be the best at my job."

The millennial generation are used to access to anything they want to learn about. They like a very high-stimulus environment. Chances are, [considering] the nature of the modern workplace, wherever they go, they are going to have that type of environment. And so, we think, "How can we create a really rich, working environment that at a basic level satisfies and inspires them?" I've absolutely seen it. Most of them do not enter the restaurant business with a notion that this is how they are going to dedicate their lives, but whether they are with us for a year, five years, or ten years, I think when they are under the fire of a busy Thursday night, they forge a confidence in themselves.

We take our employees on field trips to see how craft beer is made, how an oyster farm operates, what a wine distribution center looks like. It's a romantic approach to the business, but it's also a clinical, thought-out approach. I want that kid that ends up in front of you to feel so proud of their restaurant, their career, and the industry that they represent.

Empathy

The superstars that have worked for us in a restaurant setting, I call them hyper-empaths. Their ability to put themselves in your shoes and connect with you is absolutely an evolutionary gift. It's so natural and effortless, it's a beautiful gift. I can't teach that. What I can do is take someone that might not be as socially gifted and give them confidence and try to connect them to the basic reflexive pleasure from taking care of someone. From delighting them. From surprising them.

Self-Education

I think servers can seek out like-minded individuals. Even on a team and in a restaurant that might not have education initiatives, there are people they are working with that are like them: curious about this business, fascinated by the winemakers and the oyster farmers and the people growing food. Seek out those people. Part of hanging out together should be experiencing things together. Go out to a restaurant that you've heard about that has some interesting approach and do it together. Do a lot of stuff on your own. Read websites. Read *Eater*. Immerse yourself in travel books and wine books. That's all in the same family of what we do day in and day out in a restaurant.

It's information that may not inform the next guest's dining experience, but it gives you confidence. And if that comes through just by eye contact, by posture, a sort of natural grace and elegance, then that's worth all the initiatives that we do to spark a love for this business and a cultural appreciation for anything in the world that is happening around you.

Improving

You look back at the end of the night, and you think, "This is what we did well, and this is what we could have done better." You get up the next day and try to take one little step toward improving. I love that process. It gets me out of bed every morning. I can't wait to come in and see what these kids are up to. There is no winning in this business, just the pursuit of the unattainable. That perfect Saturday night doesn't exist, but you keep at it.

26

TURN AND BURN

The Real Estate of a Dining Room

My dear friend and a great hospitality guy, Frank Jakubka, once said to me, "You need to think of your table as real estate! That is a place to make money. You have to know how to turn and burn." I love this phrase.

What I like about managers and servers seeing a table as real estate—a rental, if you will—is we have a responsibility to ownership to try get the most out of a table. It's a simple concept.

- One, try to sell great food and beverage items to the table and get the check average high.

- Two, try to turn the table in the allotted time so the team can perform the task as many times in a night as possible.

- Three, do it while offering great service that entices the guests to return to the restaurant.

A Balancing Act

I'm not going to lie; I've had some managers and owners yelling at me to turn my tables. Max would get pretty frustrated at me when I first started at Capo. I had come from a three-hour "dining experience" Michelin-starred restaurant with 24 tables. Capo was intimate, and those 16 tables had to turn. It can be very stressful, but we should all understand that a table generates money. It's really important to know how a server can move their table along quickly and, most important ...without them feeling rushed. This is the server's and manager's dilemma.

If a server can figure out how to consistently turn their table and have pretty high check averages, while delivering top-notch service, they are going to be golden in the eyes of leadership. If a manager can coach their team to do this, gradually building each server's skillset and confidence, it's going to be a win for everyone. How can servers move a table more efficiently? Here are a few tips:

- Greet the table as quickly as possible.

- Set the pace by recommending a delicious beverage or special to start before they look over the drink menu.

- Drop two dessert hints when you mention the specials or off-menu items.

- Get your orders in early.

- Stay on top of your table maintenance.

- Keep your firing times tight.

- When the entrée course is finished, clear and clean as much of the table as possible.

- If possible, verbally list desserts before you hand guests the dessert menus and then see if they prefer to see the menus.

- Get your after-dinner drinks (coffee, beverage) in before you get the dessert order. This is essential. Timing is important on this course. It's ideal for the coffee order or after-dinner drinks to be placed at the table right before the dessert course. If they order a drink *after* dessert, the table may end up staying an extra 15-20 minutes.

- Drop the check promptly, but not too soon.

- Pick up the check when it's signed. You want the table to be as clean/cleared as possible.

- If a valet service is available, offer to have the valet bring their car up "so they don't have to wait." This allows the server to return to the table to let them know their car is waiting for them when they are ready.

- Even if the valet is a third party, it's important that the hosts have great communication with the valets. The guests will mostly assume they work for the restaurant. The valets should try to use the guest's name and thank the guests for dining with the restaurant.

JACKSON CANNON

Beverage Director- Eastern Standard, Standard Italian, Equal Measure

The only reason I ever wanted to make a better drink was to service someone. In this work, to make an analogy to a musician, I'm not one that was motivated and gratified by playing scales. It's about making music, playing with people, being in a band and getting people to dance to that band. There are a lot of cerebral layers on top of this essentially hospitable act of saying hello to someone, welcoming them in, and pouring them a drink. And I would do that if there were no craft cocktails. I love it so.

Figure Them Out

You should love to figure out what people are all about and love to listen. With that comes the basic framed questions: Would you like something with a little citrus in it, or no? Do you prefer drinks that are boozier? What's your favorite color? All the questions. You have to hear what they don't say: profile to a certain extent. Generally, when people say not too sweet, agree with them, but do not change your recipe until they have had a sip of one of your sours. Often, the guests are bringing a frame of reference that has nothing to do with a well-crafted drink. You have to create context with the guest. If you want a job doing that, that should sound cool to you. You should love to figure out what people are all about and love to listen.

Education, Retention, Burnout

If we can keep the educational part active and alive, I find that people are a lot less likely to get burnt out. We learn by reading and doing, but we really learn something when we teach it. So, the best thing I can do to somebody who may be feeling a little burnt out is to guide them in leading a tasting, a presentation, or briefing or something of that kind.

There are even opportunities to shake it up in place and sell an opportunity like that: not just asking a bartender to stand up in front of a briefing but booking them as the bartender for a class on X kinds of cocktails. Sell tickets to the thing and put them in front of an audience, working off a table bar in another room at a restaurant. It's a kind of a completely different experience, and that keeps you on your toes, engaged, and energized. Those are some of the things we try to do.

28

EVOLVING TECHNOLOGY

Embracing Innovations

I don't think I've ever worked at a restaurant or hotel where someone didn't have issues with the Point-of-Sale system. Somebody is always frustrated about how old, slow, or bad the P.O.S. system is in the restaurant. Or, if there is a change to a new system, how much worse this system is than the old one. I've found myself mumbling for many hours about how challenging a system can be. In retrospect, my complaining was a waste of time, and my energy could have been put toward the solution of making it work and accepting the present circumstances rather than turning into Mr. Mumbles.

So, how can we worry less about lag times and the lack of customizable buttons and focus on communicating as clearly as we can with the system we do have? And how can we put our best foot forward when new technology is introduced to the restaurant and team?

With the way technology is advancing, restaurant teams will most likely be asked to adjust on a more regular basis to new technologies. There have been massive shifts in the last ten years with multiple P.O.S. systems that are more accessible, mobile, and user friendly. I'm sure more are coming.

AI and Us

AI is rapidly changing technology and the way we use it. As I've seen the technological enhancements in restaurants over the last 25 years, I'm sure that aspects of AI will help streamline restaurant operations, lower costs, improve communications, and enhance the guest experience. Users will engage AI to find a restaurant they are guaranteed to like, dishes they may enjoy based on uploaded flavor profiles and their own order history, dynamic-priced reservations, and so many other smart strategies.

I've often been asked if I'm worried about AI replacing all of us in hospitality. For the most part, no, I don't think so. I have seen robotics and machines rolled out in Fast Food and Fast Casual restaurants replacing some frontline workers, lowering labor costs, and at the same time giving guests the opportunity to order quicker and engage in the ordering process in another way. I've seen QR codes multiply in some casual sit-down restaurants, so the first interaction with a human is when the drinks are brought to the table. I've seen kiosks added into hotel lobbies to quicken the check-in time for those guests who prefer that option.

But when it comes to sit-down restaurants, bars, and this book, specifically, they key to success is making human connections with the guests and providing an experience. The AI enhancements only punch up and give weight to the need for us to connect with each other. I love hospitality for exactly this reason: we should be finding that moment to connect with our fellows, our guests. If, as a collective, we are leaning into technology to do more of the work, then we have a great opportunity to make human interaction feel that much more special. We are built for this moment. We've been doing it. I don't think an AI can read the dining room the way we do, evaluate the look in a guest's eyes, shift direction because I picked up on a slight pause in the guest's sentence, comment on the color of a scarf, and anticipate needs based on the feeling I'm picking up as a professional. Sam Altman, the CEO of Open AI, mentioned on a recent podcast, *This Past Weekend*, "In this world that we're heading to of like crazy sci-fi technology becoming reality, the sort of deeply human things will become the most precious, sacred, valued things and they will really care about like the human experience more than ever."

It can be scary to make this change. My advice: Say yes. If the owners of the restaurant want to try something new and feel like it's going to make a difference, the best thing a manager or server can do is offer support and try their best with the introduction and rollout of the new system. It's always rocky for everyone involved in the onboarding of a new system, so prepare for some bumps and stay positive. My experience, most of the time, has been that after a while, efficiency improves and so does the guest experience. Encouragement and patience are paramount for the leaders as they help an often-frustrated team get more familiar with the system.

Reservation System

- Plus: Can be used to forecast the shift and schedule the room well, leading to tables being turned quicker. I like that you can list guest preferences, specific reservation notes, long-term guest notes (allergies, dietary restrictions), and can help ensure that both the back of the house and front of house don't get slammed. These systems are beneficial for the business that uses the information to be better informed about guests, their needs, and their shopping history. Guests may also use some of these system's websites or apps when searching for very specific dining options.

- Minus: These can be expensive for the restaurant to use. And they are often not used to their full potential. They should be updated by managers or staff swiftly during service, building profiles and limiting no-shows to avoid losing money. These systems are built to assist and maximize the potential of the restaurant.

Text When Ready

Simply asking guests for their phone number.

- Plus: It's an easy way to disperse the crowd waiting for tables, giving them the option to take a walk or explore the area around the restaurant. It gives the restaurant the option to let the guest know when their table is ready without investing in a pager system.

- Minus: Guest has to share their phone number, and the host needs to dial a number or text a number. Always double-check that the number is correct and ensure you are aware how loudly you read their number back to them. Privacy is important.

Restaurant Paging Systems

Used frequently in high-volume casual restaurants that accept a lot of walk-ins and are able to accommodate.

- Plus: It's an easy way to dissipate the crowd waiting for tables, allowing the guest to take a walk or see something in the area as they wait for their buzzer to alert them.

- Minus: They take up space, they don't look amazing, they need to be cleaned, and you have to make sure they are charged and ready to go.

QR Codes

- Plus: Can be great for turn times as the guests can start looking at the menu immediately and be ready with questions or orders sooner.

- Minus: If the QR Code is not clear to scan it can become quickly frustrating for a guest. Their stands, frames, or plastic coverings should be examined and cleaned when the table is re-set.

- Minus: If the QR Code directs the guest to a page that is not mobile-optimized and simply has a PDF, where a guest must zoom in and around to see, it can become very frustrating. The information on these pages needs to be updated regularly. The same for website/ menu information.

- Minus: QR codes can feel a little impersonal and affect the initial introduction of the restaurant and menu. Ensure it's an intentional and well-thought-out decision.

Taking an Order with a Handheld Device

- Plus: This is very efficient, will save time by skipping the step of going to the computer P.O.S. station, and gets the order into the kitchen quickly.

- Minus: Makes it easier for a server to forget to make eye contact and engage with the guest. The server should be aware they don't just start typing away and forget to engage with the guest.

Paying with Handheld Device

- Plus: Again, this is more efficient and quicker for the restaurant and server.

- Minus: Give the person space and time. Not everyone can read a small screen on a device well. Don't hover over them as they figure out how to give a tip, adjust a tip, or read the bill on the device; they may need a moment. You could do a quick sweep of the nearby tables or, if you are instructed to not leave the table, you could either step to the side or engage with another guest at the table.

Headsets

- Plus: Great for communication in large restaurants.

- Minus: You want to ensure the guest in front of you knows when you are talking with them and when you are talking to a team member on your headset. Ideally you should step away, as you would answering a call, and speak briefly into the headset. Awareness is key. You don't want to give off the vibe you're running through Costco speaking loudly into your headset, asking a team member which isle the giant cans of jalapenos are in. Be graceful and aware of the guest experience.

29

MICHAEL VOLTAGGIO

Chef, Author, and Restaurateur

Social Media

People research the restaurant and they do it visually, looking at the social activity, that day's menu, and what's happening in a restaurant right now, at this moment. And you have to pay closer attention to what you want people to perceive as they are coming in the door. Because they are doing research like that before they walk into the restaurant. And I think you have a harder job surprising them because they have seen what they can expect to experience *before* they set foot in the restaurant. So now, you have to do something above and beyond what they have seen visually on social media.

Food Knowledge

Now that guests have as much knowledge of food, if not more, than people in the work force, people are interested in things above and beyond the filet mignon, the mashed potato, and the asparagus. They know cooking processes, modern ingredients, they are hip to where the food is coming from now. "I love salmon, where is the salmon from?" As opposed to "What kind of salmon are you serving?" People want to know more about how responsibly you are sourcing your ingredients and what the level of quality is.

Inspiration

I'm trying to employ and use this phrase myself: "Inspiration instead of intimidation." It's like the Ritz-Carlton one, "We are ladies and gentlemen, serving ladies and gentlemen." It's having the level of maturity to recognize the fact that after you are done speaking to a server or a chef or anyone that works there, the next person they talk to, or encounter could be a guest. How do you want them feeling when they are communicating with a guest in your restaurant? You have to talk to your team the way you want them to talk to your guest. If you wouldn't say it to the guest, then you shouldn't say it to your team. You must make sure there is a genuine feeling of positivity and hospitality.

30

WHAC-A-MOLE

Smarter, Not Faster

If you've ever been to an arcade, you've probably come across the Whac-A-Mole game. This is the game where the player has a mallet in their hands and they slam it down on the puppet head that pops out of one of nine holes. The goal is to whack each puppet's head as it pops up at various speeds. So, in the heat of the game, you are whacking different puppets' heads as they pop up in each of the holes. It's fast, it's fun, and it should stay at the game house or the midway. I have often thought of this game as I've worked in very busy restaurants and bars. During my first few years in restaurants, Kirsten would ask me how my night was, and I would say, "Whac-A-Mole all night. Awful."

I was having a difficult time keeping up the pace and sustaining it. In retrospect, it was because I was treating it as a Whac-A-Mole game and not figuring out how to view the situation and group of tasks a different way. I was playing for speed, not efficiency. I was trying to get quicker, which is important, but at a certain point, isn't going to help and will hinder innovation and exploring a different approach. Efficiency requires you to ask, "How can I accomplish this job with the least expenditure of time and effort?

Play Smarter

If you are going to lead a team of restaurant employees or a section on the floor, you have to put the speed-obsessed task manager in the back seat so you can evaluate options of improvement and efficiency. Pause. Look up. See the room. See the big picture. Make space to ask yourself: Is there a better way?

While playing for speed may have been a great asset for a long time, you may need to pause that tempo, slow down and explore delegating some tasks to people you trust. Play smarter. If you don't, you will be constantly swamped and worn out, leaving you less time to wisely guide the ship in the right direction. Eventually, you will burn out.

Find a New Way

The flip side to Whac-a-Moling could be turning into a hyper-micromanager: sit back and tell people what to do. "Did you do this? Did you do that? I would do it this way." This type of leadership can be a little controlling and the opposite of empowering. I think there is a space and time for this management style, but it should be brief and intentional. Delegation alone will not build leaders.

If you are a Whac-A-Moler, give yourself time to step back and examine your current process. Restaurants move so fast that it's easy to forget to do this. We always feel like we have no time. Make it a point— scrutinize your tactics, re-evaluate them, see if there is a better way to get what you want.

Talk about your systems, communications, how you lead teams, and hold yourselves accountable. Reviewing and fine-tuning skillsets promotes personal innovation. Keeping a learning mindset and staying open to new ideas, regardless of time served, is vital to growing as a leader. If you make a habit of this re-evaluation process, you'll find your results will improve.

31

DAVIS CAMPBELL

Founder- Wines Together

Practice

It's frustrating to watch a server open a wine bottle and they rest it on their knee and cut themselves on the foil because they don't know how to use the knife on the wine key. In a restaurant you have this bar that has all these wines that need to be opened every shift—all the wines by the glass—and there is no reason a server can't take five or ten minutes a day, go in and say, "Hey my friendly bartender, would you let me open those bottles of wine so I can get better at it?" That's what I did when I started, because I knew it would help me get better.

Knowledge

When I was a server, my whole approach to wine was: if I'm better at this, I will make more money. Not just because I can sell more expensive bottles, but because those diners are going to appreciate the service much more since I'm able to give them the detailed knowledge about something they want to know about. You can give them facts, it's entertaining, and people love stories.

Just by taking five minutes a day, looking at a wine list, and saying, "Here's two wines here, let me look up these vineyards. Oh, you know what's really cool is that it's a brother and sister who opened this vineyard because they were tired of the rat race of San Francisco, so they ponied up all their money, got some investors, and bought fifteen acres." And then you are telling people this—and they are pulled in, they are interested. It connects them to their wine and it makes for an interesting dining experience. And that's what not only raises your check average but raises your tips.

Missed Selling Opportunity

In terms of sales, I think most of the time a bottle of wine is going to help you out. I think the missed art of wine sales is once you sell a bottle of wine and your customers drink it; there are always wines by the glass that can be sold after that bottle of wine is finished. Servers always offer another bottle, and the guests say no because they are eating dessert. But one more glass of wine for customers is pretty exciting. It's that little thing that can boost their experience.

What Wine Do They Want?

It's okay to ask people, "What are your favorites?" "What do you like?" And if you can get some generalities from the guests then you can make it much more specific for them. That is a great way to sell wine. Ask them a few questions and narrow it down to what they like, apply your knowledge, then make it specific -and if that bottle fits in there, you can, with confidence, recommend it.

Three Wines, Three Price Points

You can get a pretty good idea of what somebody wants to spend as you are asking them questions. Let's take pinot for example. You open up the list and there are ten pinot noirs on the list. One of my first questions is always: have you had any of these before? And if they have, they say, yes, and let's say it's the highest-priced wine on the list. So now you know they have had that before, so they understand the flavor and complexity of an expensive wine. It's easy to go and recommend something like that when you know they have had it before.

If they point to the lowest price on the list, then maybe it's not the best idea to start them at the most expensive price. Range toward the middle and see how they feel about it. Look at their face when you ask them what they are looking for. Look at their face when they point to things on the menu they have had before and sometimes, they will just flat-out tell you they don't want to spend that much and that makes it much easier. I would go to where they were comfortable, but I would push it a little bit.

It's really all about the presentation and how you talk to people. If you are kind of snobby, they are not going to be so apt to spend a whole bunch of money. If you are nice and accommodating, generally, they may take the suggestion you have. And it's easy to suggest a few different types of bottles.

When you are reading people it's always smart to have a high-end bottle, a mid-range, and a low-range bottle. And if you have that confidence and you go for the high-end bottle and you think it didn't go that well, it's easy to slide down to the middle bottle, give a little pause, and see how they are feeling there. I think a pause is a good way to gauge people while you are selling them wine. I think it's really important to not push, but listen. It comes down to reading people, and to do that you have to really be able to listen.

Clarify Price

I think it is important for people to know exactly what they are spending on their bottle. You don't want to say, "This is an amazing bottle, it's one of my favorites." And they say, "Great, bring it!" And then you bring them their bill and it's $300 more than they wanted to spend and then you have some very upset guests. You want to make sure you have them look at it again and double check that price. It may be as simple as, "You are having this 99 Marcassin Pinot, here," and maybe give a tap on the menu so they look down at exactly what it is.

32

THE CHALLENGING FOLKS

Professionalism and the Search for Similarities

You don't have to like someone to work well with them. Sure, I could spend a bunch of time telling you how to learn to love everyone, build true connections with people, and develop empathy and compassion for high-functioning narcissistic sociopaths, but we shall skip that lesson! Somebody else wrote that book. You are going to have to work with and serve some people who are difficult or may have opposite viewpoints and values than you do. So, let's talk about it.

The good news is you don't really need to like or dislike a guest to give them good service. And the same can be said for working with a fellow co-worker. Sure, our behavior is sometimes shaped by our feelings, but personally liking someone shouldn't determine whether we give good service or not. We don't have to feel one way or the other to do our job. We are professionals. We should be able to do it regardless of how we feel about someone.

What's in My Control?

I had an experience with an investor of a restaurant where I worked. I was not a fan. He was more of a non-involved investor than the operational type, but he was always seated in my section, and he was very rude to people. For whatever reason, he was kind to me, but you could tell he was the type to pick and choose who he would like and who he wouldn't. He didn't understand—or worse, didn't care - about showing favoritism and putting on different faces for different people. Kind to the customers, awful to the staff. That type of person.

Here's the thing. I have one thing I can control: the service I provide as a professional. I'm the one that determines what professionalism is and my ability or inability to consistently offer that at a high level. While all of these judgments I'm making about the investor of the restaurant or some other guest may be true, they shouldn't really affect the way I'm able to do my job and fulfill my goal of providing good service. If I can't do my job well in this situation, that's on me. It's not the other person's fault. Our co-workers and guests may come and go, but we need to root down and be able to focus on our job, our professionalism, regardless.

Okay to Not Align

If everyone was the same, I'd be bored. My ideas and values may not align with a co-worker's or guest's, but I can still take care of my side of the street, do what's in my control. We are asked to do our jobs all the time when we aren't feeling super passionate, engaged, or inspired. If you are tired, you are still expected to show up and work. I've heard managers say, "If you aren't feeling it, act 'as if.' Act like you are feeling it." It's our job. We have to find a way to still make some connection, regardless of our feelings.

Room for Doubt

When I was bartending, I realized that 95 percent of the time, if I can ask someone five questions, I will find I have something in common with them: a connection. I had many years to test this, and it was true. I tried it at dinner parties, cocktail events, places I didn't know anyone. It's tempting to draw a bunch of judgments from the first and second questions and decide to bail. Leave the conversation. "Oh, this person is a bore." Or "This person isn't like me." Or "This person isn't the type of person I would enjoy talking with." But this doesn't leave room for curiosity. What if you are wrong? Doubt isn't necessarily bad; leave yourself a little more time to make a better-informed decision.

Next time you find yourself in this situation with a co-worker or guest and you are hung up on the differences, ask yourself a few questions about making that little connection:

- Are there two storylines here that I can separate? Is one dependent on the other?

- Do we have any similarities? Is there some minor way I can find to connect with this person even though we may have some differences?

- If I decide I don't like this person, can I find a way to still achieve our goals and objectives?

- If a guest is challenging, is there a way I can provide good service while paying less attention to the negative storyline I may be building in my head?

33

RECOVERY SITUATIONS

Winning the Guest Back

My best moments have been in recovery situations. You are going to have guests who find themselves upset or annoyed for myriad reasons. Oftentimes it may not have anything to do with you, but that's not really important, because everyone has an opportunity to fix the issue and ensure the guest is happy as quickly as possible. We don't want to join in the blame game; we want to move to resolution.

I've always found I've had to challenge myself to learn, grow, and connect deeper with people in these moments. The biggest gift I've received from these moments is learning how to pause, take a breath, and check my ego. Not easy for me. But creating that brief pause has done wonders. The plus side of recovery moments is this can be a moment to go big, win the guest back. On the negative side, it's easy to make a bad situation worse.

The Magic Mistake

My wife Kirsten, who is an amazing improviser, calls this moment of opportunity "The Magic Mistake." Actor Michael Caine likes to say about these issues, "Use the difficulty." I've heard it referred to as a "Golden Opportunity." Everyone has their way about it.

I have found that my ability to be quick on my feet, with empathy, has turned trainwreck situations into huge wins that keep bringing those guests back to the restaurant. If you and your team can see these situations as an opportunity to connect with the guest and move into solution, you can have some amazing outcomes.

Michael Bauer, the former restaurant critic for the San Francisco Chronicle mentioned to me, "People can have a bad experience with food, but if the staff takes care of it, apologizes, they can turn a bad experience into good. What the guest remembers is not that they had bad food, or the order got mixed up, but that it was handled professionally."

Making a Bad Situation Worse

I learned a few things the hard way. Here are a few suggestions for dealing with an upset guest.

- Making them repeat themselves over and over will only get them more frustrated. Try not to pass them off to others.

- When they are telling you what they are upset about, don't interrupt them. Listen until they are completely finished.

- "I'm so sorry you feel that way" is not taking ownership of the situation.

- Do your best to resolve the issue there and then.

- Know when it's out of your control and you should bring in someone higher in seniority or the general manager.

- Communicate any issue, even a resolved one, to leadership so they can follow up.

Win Them Back

At The Dining Room, if there had been a previous issue with incoming guest, our Director of Service, Robert, would assign me the table. At first, to be honest, it was kind of frustrating. What am I, the fixer? Often in hotels, you need to fix an issue with a guest, and one of the many ways is to offer a complimentary dinner at the hotel restaurant. In this case, it was dinner at our Michelin-starred restaurant. It's pretty amazing to have a nationally recognized restaurant as a tool for recovering a guest.

We were an answer to fixing many guest complaints or issues that arose during a guest's stay. And I slowly fell in love with being the fixer, leaning into the difficulty, trying win people back. It was rewarding to focus on them having a great experience — so great that they would forget about the past issues and we would have our valuable, return guests back in the mix and happier than before.

We were lucky; The Langham Huntington Hotel in Pasadena is a stunning property built in 1905 by Henry Huntington. Only months before my arrival it had been The Ritz-Carlton, Pasadena. A beautiful property with great service values and a rich history of going above and beyond for guests. Plus, when you work with great chefs, amazing food will solve a whole lot of issues.

At line-up, Robert would say, "Josh, you will have the Wilsons in at 7:30 p.m. They previously stayed at the hotel and had issues with noise and no hot water. The hotel has invited them back to enjoy the weekend and are comping dinner. Win them back!"

Treat the table the same as any other table, except turn up the service. A few ways to do this may be:

- Be super-spot-on, very detail oriented; create an amazing experience and evening for them.

- The whole team should know this is a table we are winning back.

- Ensure an amuse bouche arrives at the table. If this happens as a part of normal service, is there a slight adjustment that can make it more special?

- Have the sommelier introduce themselves and pour a little taste of something special with an explanation of what it is.

- Ensure the GM or leading manager comes by and introduces themselves.

- Send the chef out to say hi and introduce themselves between courses.

- Have the pastry chef bring dessert to the table.

These are little moments that can help win those guests back. A frustrated guest is in a moment of vulnerability. And that is an open door to swoop in and really make a difference. Enhance the experience. It's the magic mistake that can lead to an opportunity to win over a guest that will return again and again.

34

GARY OBLIGACION

Former Director of Operations- The Alinea Group

A More Casual Service

Casual does not mean sloppy. At Roister, it is still imperative that the servers know every single ingredient on every single dish, so that their knowledge base allows them to provide service and be experts in that restaurant. They have a confidence level that you don't often find in restaurants that *look* like that. It's closer to a regular restaurant where they have a side towel they bring out to wipe down the table, instead of using a serviette and a metal crumber [as you would] if you had tablecloths.

Making It Personal

One of things we pride ourselves on at Alinea, our flagship, Michelin three-star restaurant, is telling our teams to make it personal, use humor, knock down that wall—and make it accessible. It's amazing how often you will find tables laughing at Alinea, along with our servers. It's necessary.

Table Talk

The description that you have on a given dish, you can use that **one** time per room. So, if you are going to describe a dish here, you can't use that on every table because they can all hear you. You have to have different approaches to every single dish. You have to make it personal to that table.

Details of the Room

You go in [the dining room] and you say, "What is the temperature like? Is it a little too cold, too hot, too humid? Is the music to high or low? Are the tables straight, clean? Are the flowers fresh and alive or are they looking a little tired? Are there aromas that aren't supposed to be there?" It's all of that. Do you have a party disturbing the ambiance, and does that affect someone else's ability to enjoy it, and what do you do about it? Seeing the room allows you to play all of these factors against one another, mitigate any problems, accentuate anything that is positive, and allow yourself to maintain control.

Continually Refining

The only standards that matter are ours. The awards are just an indication that somebody else has noticed that we met our own standards or gotten close to it. We know when we do it right and we know when we miss. And it's up to us to acknowledge every single one of those times and figure out, "Why did we miss? How do we prevent ourselves from missing again? We attack every single day and we, as a service team, we sit there at Alinea and we invite everyone into that conversation—the entire front of house. And we will say, "Okay, let's talk about last night. What came up?" It can be good; it can be bad. It could be somebody saying, "I was watching how we did the presentation of whatever on table 22 last night and I think we should approach it a different way." Something that small. Where we are continually refining and rethinking everything we do. But it's not about awards; those may happen as a by-product of our doing it the way we know we are supposed to do it.

35

LEARNING TOGETHER

Creating a Culture of Becoming Better

One of my favorite aspects of working in hospitality is how much we all share our information. It's a craft. And as craftspeople we follow the unwritten code that you should "pass it down." Pass down the information you've learned to the next generation. I learned this working at our family lumber yard. Different guys took pride on bringing the new people along. You could always find someone who would show you the ropes, the shortcuts, the details. Personally, I always try to make time for someone who's asking for advice or guidance. I feel it's part of the job, our hospitality industry, our code, to teach each other not just to do something, but to do it well. To do it *well*. To help someone become great, even extraordinary at something.

The Precious Problem

I have had moments of frustration with people who don't want to share information in our industry. They want to keep the knowledge to themselves. Food, beer, wine, experiences eating at other restaurants. All of it. Our collective success is based on our ability to learn, grow, share with each other and our guests. It also takes a team. Not sharing information just seems like a short-sighted, selfish act.

I've had trying moments with precious sommeliers who protected their wine notes like they were getting ready to deliver the news of who won Best Picture at the Oscars. Maybe from growing up in a wine region, I was accustomed to people talking about wine in a relaxed way, without pretense, simply sharing what they were excited about. Managers and teams should be sharing about the process of winemaking, tasting notes, story of the vineyard or a winemaking family... whatever. The idea is to excite each other and that energy and knowledge will get passed along into the guest experience.

Keep It Real

I had a few gigs in high school. I worked at a gas station, a racetrack, a couple of restaurants, a farm, on a construction crew, our family lumberyard and on a bottling line at a winery. That bottling line made me realize how complicated the process of making wine is. And messy! (Side note: The sticky glue from the wine labels takes forever to get off your hands!) Mind you, I didn't start learning the real intricacies of wine until I was in my late twenties. But growing up around the industry, with working owners and farmers, there is an inherent salt-of-the-earth feeling when you are actually at the winery or in the vineyards for other reasons than an Instagram op.

Working as a busboy at The Swiss Hotel, I remember celebrated winemaker Sam Sebastiani would come in the restaurant, oftentimes in dirty jeans, with dusty hands and filthy boots—his work clothes. Back then, most of the winery owners were like this. To me, they just seemed like working people. My dad looked the same when he would come in from the lumberyard. That's the wine country I grew up in. It didn't feel precious. Keep it simple. Share information in the hopes that maybe it sparks a conversation, maybe it ignites some curiosity and excitement in the new kid, a colleague, or a guest.

Wine and Capo

My wife and I were excited to become sommeliers for one reason and one reason only: our frustration with a couple of the sommeliers in our past who wouldn't share information with us. Bye! That's it. When I got a job at Capo in Santa Monica and was introduced to a wine list that had over 2,500 bottles on it, I knew I was in for a ride. At my interview I remember Max (Marder) and Davis (Campbell) telling me, "We don't have a full-time, regular sommelier during service here, the wine sales are on each server, so start studying." This made me happy and very nervous.

I was very excited to delve further into learning more about wine. And the expectation was high. It could be stressful when you sell $600 in wine one night and the server in the section next to you sells $3,700. I am competitive by nature, so it got me studying even more. I loved learning more about geography, weather patterns, soil, pruning, and all the things surrounding the taste of the wine. I loved the story of the vineyard or winemakers. Story made it easier to connect to. Sure, I could explain a flavor profile and why it was dynamic or not, but my love was in the whole story of wine. Finding this trigger turned my curiosity into knowledge and made me better at selling wine.

Capo was a clinic on sharing knowledge: every person on that team would share info about winemakers, great vintages, tasting notes. Justin Prairie, the wine buyer for Capo at the time, curated the list and was very generous with his knowledge and sharing of information with the servers. We tasted a lot, and everyone seemed to have a very strong area...usually the region that made the wine they loved the most. We would share videos of winemakers talking, books, reviews of wines, podcasts, films, anything that sparked an interest. I'm reminded of winemaker and author, Raj Parr telling me about his experience in restaurants and creating a learning culture: "Most restaurants I've worked at had weekly or biweekly tastings. I always encouraged everyone to come, to taste with me before or after service, if I'm doing that. Up to 70 percent of our staff would come to those tastings. I offered them books that I have, but in many cases, we had a small library of books in the restaurant and I'd really encourage them to read those. And now, it's so easy with the internet, it's all there. Do your research, come back and ask me questions, and make an effort to develop your knowledge."

What I liked the most was how approachable everyone was; the room and the people at Capo weren't pretentious. We were selling big wines, but there was an effortlessness and joy in it. Each person on that Capo team taught me a lot about wine with their humble attitudes and graciousness. It was an amazing way to get introduced into wine and it culminated with me and my wife Kirsten eventually achieving our Level One and Two sommelier certifications.

36

HERE TO SERVE ME

Ego, Status, and the Words We Choose

I was working at the Hotel Bel Air as a caterer for weddings when I was in my early twenties. It was a great gig! Two weddings a day in summer, I was an on-call guy, as it was a pretty sought-after catering job. I was out in the garden for a pre-ceremony cocktail hour in the signature uniform: black pants, tuxedo shirt, white coat, bowtie. I was standing there, holding a porcelain platter with a beautiful shrimp cocktail setup (shrimp cocktail in a center crystal bowl—fresh jumbo shrimp surrounding the bowl) in one hand and a stack of napkins in the other.

A well-dressed lady in a designer gown came toward me. "Good afternoon, would you like to try the shrimp cocktail?" I spoke. She didn't reply or even look at me. I offered a napkin for her to take, which she did. And she picked a large shrimp, dipped it in the cocktail, bit into the shrimp and ate it in front of me. Still no eye contact. She stood there for a moment, put the shrimp tail in a napkin and looked at the tray I was holding. Seeing a nice trash receptacle behind her, I mentioned, "There is a receptacle behind you, ma'am, if you would like to discard the napkin." Another pause—still without looking me in the eye. She then glanced down at my hand holding the napkins, reached toward my sleeve. She took the finger on her left hand and put it in between my tuxedo shirt sleeve and skin on my wrist, pulled down lightly to make a gap, and with her right hand she stuffed the napkin in between my shirt and my wrist and walked away.

I just stood there. I'm usually one for a quick comeback, but I had no idea what to say. I watched her meander over to the next server with the chicken satay on a platter while I stood there in shock. In retrospect, I should have yelled out to the other server to look out that they don't get stuck in the wrist with the large satay skewer if she tried to discard it up their sleeve. I immediately headed back to the kitchen, discarded her trash from inside my shirt, tidied my platter, and headed back out to the party. Professional. Humiliated, but professional.

I still think of her. There was zero regard for me. Nothing. I've had quite few guests like this in my career. Not to that level of offense, but close. It was hard for me to accept that I was just kind of looked through. If you are in hospitality, we are built to be the complete opposite. We look for opportunity to help, to read a guest, consider others. But this disregard will present itself—and it's okay. I've learned not to take it personally and control what I can: to be of service. This wasn't going to stop me from doing my job.

The toughest guests for my ego are the ones who simply treat me as if I am their personal servant. Everything is determined on their terms, and they can be short, rude, and demanding. I'm pretty sure it drives all of us nuts—because it goes directly to our ego. The guest that doesn't make eye contact, won't acknowledge you when you are standing there, and will cut you off mid-sentence. It's very challenging, but if the guest is treating you this way, I have to assume that's the guest experience they want.

I've learned, with a lot of ego checking, to just go to the other side, control my part of the situation and let them do their thing, as long as it's not harming me. I lean into it. But guests do cross the line, and a manager should always step in if any employee feels that a guest's behavior is getting abusive. A well-thought-out and quick response is best delivered by the manager.

I'm lucky that I've worked with some very appreciative managers, not many who felt I was just there to serve their needs. I've heard stories of employees dealing with managers who also treat them as if they don't exist, are a pawn in the game, and are easily replaceable. A manager will never become a great leader if they are treating employees this way.

One of the best managers I had was skilled at making us feel like we mattered. He was quick with acknowledgments, fair with criticism, and was all about connecting with us as employees and individuals. He maintained an amazing balance, making you feel like you were the only one in the room with him while also inspiring the whole team to something greater. He was determined to build the team and balance its strengths.

Here to Serve Me behavior can show up in how a server will treat a back waiter, server assistant, or a busser. This needs to be a healthy relationship that can sustain clear direction and delegation, but oftentimes the culprit is tone—how it's said. It's important that servers are aware of how they ask someone to do something. Maintain awareness of volume, intensity, and attitude, the same as they would with a guest. Sometimes a slight adjustment in word choice can do wonders. "Will you?" sounds better than "You need to...." "If you have a moment can you..." sounds better than "I told you, you need to...." Managers should be on the lookout for how these interactions are occurring.

There is always room for improvement in this area. I work on this to this day. This quick Thumbs Up, Thumbs Down skills exercise at line-up may raise awareness and offer alternatives. Try these:

- Thumbs Up, Thumbs Down. Ask the servers or anyone at line-up to give a good example and a bad example of asking for something from a co-worker. Ask the group to silently give a thumbs up if they like it or thumbs down if they don't. Ask someone to explain any of the examples that happen.

- Thumbs Up, Thumbs Down. Get more specific and ask servers or any other employees to use different volumes with the same sentence. Whisper to loud. Ask questions such as, "Does it feel warmer, colder, enthusiastic, standoffish, approachable, robotic, authentic?"

These exercises are useful to create awareness or when problems need to be addressed. They should be practiced on a regular basis as a brush-up on considerate culture. We all know it can be rough at 8:30pm on a Saturday night. Communication can be brisk. That will happen, but these exercises may be useful if there are issues arising in the team. As a leader, whether a manager or server, it should be understood that your colleagues work with you, not for you. Stay focused on positive communication. This is a good perspective. Balancing this well, while giving direction and leading your team will make the experience much more rewarding and engaging for everyone involved.

37

PASCALINE LEPELTIER

Master Sommelier

Curiosity Mindset

Ideally, [candidates would walk in] for an interview knowing the most important wine regions of the world and the basic grape varietals of the world. But the minimum requirements in terms of factual knowledge [were] not as important as the curiosity. I thought it was better for me to hire people with not as high a level of knowledge, but with the right mindset, a good memory, and an open-mindedness. And then it was my job to provide them with the education material I want them to know. So, we created the beverage bible with my team. That is what we were using to train everyone that was coming in. I always thought that education was a crucial part of my responsibility.

Criticism

I want the ability to talk to my team and say, you know guys, you did great, or what did we do wrong? Or what can we improve? I want a staff that is willing to understand criticism, to move forward and to learn. It goes so far. Rather than somebody that reacts and says, "This is the way things need to be done and I'm not going to change." We are looking for someone to adapt, so I was looking for a person with that type of personality.

Proactive Education

If you are a server and you are into the wines and things like that, you can put yourself in a tasting group. Get some people together and start to do some tastings on your own. Get some money together, $100 bucks a week. What can we buy for four or five of us and taste together? Do that. Use all the resources of where you can taste wine. If you are curious, look at your local wine shop and see if they are doing tastings. Go and taste there.

Sharing Knowledge

If you like something and you like to sell it and it's a thing that you are really into, I would highly recommend that you should be able to teach it to the staff. You are going to learn way more by sharing your knowledge than by keeping it for yourself. Teaching it to someone really forces you to express it and see exactly what you know. This what I tell my staff— "The more you share with us and the more I share with you, the better we are all going to be as a team."

38

EFFORTLESSNESS

Practice, Repetition, and Confidence

These are some comments I've heard in reference to professional athletes or gifted musicians.

- "He is amazing! It's like there is no effort involved."

- "She was born to do it."

- "So gifted. They are absolutely gifted."

About seven years ago, I was driving with friends from Salt Lake City to Park City, and as we were coming into Park City, we saw what looked like enormous slides pressed up against the majestic mountains. I asked my friend, a local, what the deal was. He told me that those were the ramps for the Olympic ski jumpers. As he mentioned this, I noticed a dot at the top of a ramp, and then a person raced downward and disappeared. I was confused. It was late May and there was no snow anywhere.

My friend explained that even when it's not winter, they still use the jumping hills to train, falling into pools filled with water. It's how they can make all of their mistakes without getting hurt. Wow, that made total sense. I just had never thought of it. Of course, they have to have a safe place to practice, and they probably fall most of the time they are trying new feats. Same applied to snowboarders, gymnasts, and a slew of other athletes. Practice makes perfect and so does failing.

Practice and Repetition

Greatness is boring. I'm reminded of the routines of so many great athletes: Kobe Bryant's routine of taking 900 shots every morning, seven days a week, at five a.m. with a trainer. Lionel Messi arriving hours early for practice to perfect his footwork. Venus Williams practicing visualization. When we tune in to see these people perform on TV, they look great. Phenomenal. They make it look effortless. They actually APPEAR effortless. But you know that it requires a lot of effort and time to appear that effortless. They put the work in. It's what elite athletes do.

In his book, *Outliers*, Malcolm Gladwell notes that it takes 10,000 hours until you master something. Now, don't worry, I'm not going to tell you it takes 10,000 hours to master managing a restaurant or serving tables. But I will say that practice is needed to make what you and your teams do seem effortless. As you take on more tasks and move faster, and more efficiently, in front of guests and with your teams, you will need to make yourself look effortless. Your guests expect that of you, and even when a server is overseeing eight tables, are in the weeds, and think their head is going to explode, they will still need to appear in control, relaxed, and confident.

If you or your team feel uncomfortable about any of your skills, I suggest isolating the issues and practice, practice, practice. Daily. When I worked at The Dining Room, we had these crisp white tablecloths on top of huge round tables. The far part of the table was oftentimes inaccessible, which meant the server would have to reach across the table to the seats on the other side and pour wine with their arm fully extended. A drip was unacceptable, and there was no way to quickly dab the top of the bottle in your opposite hand. If I saw a drip, because it would fall before I could pull the wine back across the table, it was a clear failure. Everyone could see the drip on the table. The only way to perfect this was training. Practice. Repetition. Practice.

Skills Exercise

I brought empty bottles home, and I filled them with water and cranberry juice. I bought some used white sheets at the thrift store and threw them over a table in my apartment. I'd practice for hours pouring wine into glasses with my arms fully extended until I didn't spill a drop. Believe me, it required a lot of effort. But when the time came on a Saturday night during the rush and my section was full, I could calmly take that bottle and pour the wine for the entire table, regardless of accessibility, without thinking twice about spilling.

Fileting fish tableside was something I had to practice at home, too. My wife loved it. Steaming milk to perfect my latte foam, shaving truffles, carrying a full tray of full wine glasses with my left hand, when I had only ever used my right. We practiced these at work together - but I practiced at home too.

Isolating these tasks and learning to do them really well will help your service team execute them effortlessly. They will be able to have an easy conversation with guests while they do it. Practice will lead to confidence. It's how any team member can get better at juggling multiple tasks. Managers and leaders should be looking for moments to have your team practice. Set up a table before the shift and create a group skills exercise around aspects of table service.

ALICE WATERS

Chef, Author, Restaurateur- Chez Panisse

Service and Hospitality

I expect the same courteous informed service from somebody who serves someone upstairs at our café as I do for downstairs in the restaurant. I expect a certain decorum, and I expect the chefs to be equally professional. Whether they are cooking something very simply or whether they are doing it in a more studied way. I think that kind of hospitality is equally critical.

This is the place where you communicate with each other and pass on a set of values to your children, to your friends. And it doesn't matter how fancy that place is. It could be a three-star restaurant or a coffee house; that gathering place is powerful and important. It gives punctuation to the day. For me it always gives meaning to my morning when I sit down and eat breakfast and drink my tea. And I love it when somebody cooks my breakfast and brings it to me. It's a big picture of hospitality.

Anticipation

We are talking about care, empathy, and anticipating people's needs and desires before they ever ask you. I always thought I was a great waitress. I loved the challenge. I loved being able to bring something to someone before they even knew they wanted it. It's a thrill that you can make someone really happy. It's such a gift.

Knowledge

Food knowledge is critical. We want people who really appreciate a taste of something to know that that taste is connected to sustainable farming. And that's why we write it at the bottom of the menu. *["The food we serve comes from farms, orchards, ranches, and fisheries guided by principles of sustainability."]* That everything we serve is part of that commitment. The waiters need to be informed about it. I don't want a superficial answer. I want a waiter to say to me this is an organic chicken, and they are grown locally, there. **The more informed the restaurateur, the more informed the waiter, the more informed the customer. It's about trust, relationship, and telling the truth.**

Connections

I love it when you can have a little rapport with the guest, they can get to know you a little bit, in terms of personality. Not that you are trying to tell them what to eat, but maybe you have a story about the farm and you get an opportunity to talk about it. Just some little thing that makes them feel more connected to the restaurant.

Constructive Feedback

I always talk about it right away when I am hiring somebody. This restaurant has always operated on a constant critique, and nobody can take that personally. You cannot take it personally. It's not about that. We are just trying to get better at what we do. If you are too sensitive, it really doesn't work. We collaborate and are trying to solve the problems together. But if you are too sensitive about it, it's not a good place for you to be working. There have been people that are too sensitive and can't hear what we are saying. I always want everybody's opinion. And I think that came from my father. He was a business psychologist and always gave people positive feedback and he gave them negative feedback and then...gave them a way of improving.

Burnout

That's something you have to be aware of, you constantly have to be a good manager and talk to people, and if they aren't improving or changing you have to step up and say, "Maybe you need to do something else." I switch people around in a lot of different jobs; it's something I like to do. I'm always trying to see where people's talents lie. Somebody who is amazing answering phones in the office with a big smile, I say "Oh my god, they need to be in the dining room, what are they doing in the office? They are so vivacious."

PART 3: ELEVATED RESTAURANTS

40

THE RUNDOWN

Elevated Restaurants

Elevated restaurants have quite a range of dining experience and styles. Often the style of service will be decided by the chef and/or restaurateur, and it's done this way to complement the food. Food is king. Sometimes referred to as Fine Dining, I use the word "Elevated" because there are now so many styles and ways to offer a Fine Dining experience that I didn't want to limit this style to white tablecloths, fancy silver, and cloches.

Team

Elevated service requires a lot of attention in the kitchen and on the floor. To execute this style, additional roles may be needed and/or more team members may be added to the roles already mentioned in this book. Some *additional* roles may include:

- Captains: the definition of this position can shift a bit from restaurant to restaurant. Traditionally, a captain will run a section of the dining room. The captain, who may also be referred to as a front server, will have a back server that reports to them in their section. I've also seen captains assigned half of a restaurant, almost as if they were a floor manager, with multiple front servers reporting to them and then back servers reporting to front servers.

- Runners: there will tend to be additional runners in restaurants that are specializing in tasting menus with multiple courses. Tasting menus mean more courses per table. However, back servers and front servers may also be involved in the running of food, depending on the style of service the restaurant provides.

- Back servers: this is a common role added in elevated dining, with the shift to more steps of service and details required to deliver this experience. Reporting to the captain/front server, they often split tasks with the front server and together they have a clear understanding of which position is covering which tasks in their section.

- Sommelier: if a restaurant has a wine program with a much larger list, they will likely have a wine expert or sommelier on staff. The sommelier (and sommelier team, if needed) will engage with guests about wine and tasting menus involving wine pairings.

- Wine Director: a person overseeing multiple sommeliers and the entire wine program. They will be the curator of the wine list, execute ordering of wine, and facilitate wine education for the staff.

- Beverage Director: a person overseeing the cocktail program of the restaurant and/or multiple bars and bar managers. Often, they will design drinks, order specific liquors, and facilitate cocktail education for the staff. May also oversee the wine director duties.

BOH

- Polisher: most restaurants will have all FOH employees participate in the polishing of glassware. I've worked in a couple of places that had a specific polisher. They may be used in elevated dining to ensure that every glass (water, wine, and cocktail) is immaculate, with no water spots on it. They are relied on heavily in restaurants that specialize in wine, requiring the use of many wine glasses.

- Cooks: there may be many more prep cooks and line cooks in elevated dining. Since the food is much more complex, creating, designing, plating, and timing for multiple courses requires more cooks. These cooks will be placed in kitchen areas that need their expertise in specific disciplines.

- Expeditor: head chef or sous-chef will most likely fulfill this role.

- Sous-chef: multiple sous-chefs may be required, depending on the size of the restaurant. These chefs will be overseeing areas of the kitchen and the cooks that report directly to them.

- Pastry chef: a chef solely dedicated to the dessert and/or baked goods for the restaurant.

- Executive Sous-Chef: This role may oversee all sous-chefs and assist with managerial operations of the kitchen including purchasing, payroll, and scheduling.

- Chef de Cuisine: a chef de cuisine (CDC) is in charge of the entire kitchen. Oftentimes, this is a position in restaurants owned and operated by a restaurant group or celebrity chef/restaurateur. CDCs may have the ability to change the menu. The CDC will directly report to the owner and/or Executive chef.

- Executive Chef: this can be the chef de cuisine as well. Creates the menu concept and dishes, oversees purchasing and labor costs, and oversees the business decisions of the kitchen and staff.

Upper Management/Owners

- General Manager: in charge of daily operations, they coordinate front and back of house operations. They are usually very involved with the FOH staff, service, and guests.

- Director of Operations: this position usually oversees the operations of multiple restaurants, with GMs reporting directly to them.

- Owner: person or group that owns the restaurant.

- Investor: person or persons who have invested capital in the restaurant and receive "shares" in return.

In hotels you may come across various titles when it comes to management. Oftentimes you will see the person overseeing all food and beverage operations (including "outlets" such as restaurants, bars, in-room dining, F&B pool service, etc.) hold the title of director of food & beverage. They will traditionally report to the director of operations or the general manager of the hotel. Reporting to the director of food and beverage may be director of outlets, senior operations managers, or restaurant general manager.

Training

In an Elevated style restaurant, employees are expected to come through the door with a high level of service and food knowledge. Moving from upscale to elevated means offering premium food and beverages and enhanced service. As the cost goes up for the guest, the restaurant must offer additional value to justify those costs. It's paramount for management and leaders to ensure employees are trained well and can answer *all* questions of guests seeking a special experience they can't find anywhere else. This type of restaurant should be the best! It requires massive attention to detail and the team must always focus on the guest experience.

Point of Sale

I go into detail about Point-of-Sale systems in Part 1: Casual, on page 5. Please reference this section if you need guidance in this area.

Management Duties

If you haven't read the detailed section on management duties in the previous section, Part 2: Upscale, you can find those on page 62. A few additional management duties may be:

- Stay aware of and in-tune with service standards of companies that may possibly give ratings to your restaurant. (Forbes, Michelin, etc.)

- Receive linens or cloth napkins that are delivered daily and ensure those items are in consistently good condition.

Cocktails

One of my favorite developments in elevated restaurants is that delightfully custom-crafted cocktails have become a vibrant part of the guest dining experience. Mixologists are having conversations with chefs to craft drinks that enhance the dishes being served. I've seen cocktails paired with tasting menus and recently witnessed an amazing offering of agaves and tequilas selected to specifically pair with dishes. This was not always the case. Wine was boss for a long time. We will get to wine, but knowledge of spirits and understanding flavor profiles are now must-haves in an elevated restaurant.

When the managers, sommeliers, and servers engage in improving their knowledge of craft cocktails, they can enhance the guest experience. They can also upsell. A strong cocktail and liquor program director can educate staff, and anyone looking to learn more or refresh their enthusiasm can find many available sources online. A few classic cocktail and liquor books I've used as references are:

- *Death & Co: Modern Classic Cocktails*
- *Difford's Guide to Cocktails*
- *Whiskey* by Michael Jackson

Wine

I grew up in wine country, but I don't think I really understood the impact of wine until I worked in a restaurant that specialized in wine pairings. It's not like I didn't enjoy sipping on wine, but when that perfect wine was selected for a specific dish, something special happened. It elevated my culinary experience.

As a manager or server in a restaurant, it's important to be able to guide a guest through selecting the "right" glass of wine they may enjoy with a specific dish. If you have a wine geek or sommelier on staff, hopefully there is a cheat sheet on which wines by the glass pair best with which dish. It's important in an elevated restaurant that not only the sommeliers know the wines, but the managers and servers as well. This is part of the service value being offered. Each person touching the table is able to engage about the wine. This immediately makes a more dynamic experience for the guest.

If a manager or server has the knowledge and skills to recommend an excellent wine by the glass, this will free up the sommelier to execute wine pairings for dishes and focus on selling bottles of wine. Wine education is great way to keep servers engaged and line-up is a perfect place to speak about wine by the glass or bottle. It's a good space to quiz the team on tasting notes, or have them quiz each other in a collaborative, constructive way. This builds the culture around the beverage program. At Capo, we were always asking each other to explain a wine. While setting up the room, you would hear servers asking each other how they describe this brunello or that Barolo to a table. Why Sonoma Coast pinot noirs taste differently than those from the Carneros region. I've learned a lot by simply listening to other veteran servers being able to describe an excellent wine. A couple of quick examples would be:

- "I like this wine because it's low in acid, has a silky, smooth finish, and the bright flavors of currant and plum will really compliment the branzino."

- "This is a light refreshing wine, unoaked, with chalky minerality that will play off the oyster well. The winemaker named the wine after her great-grandmother who grew up in the farmhouse where the winery tasting room now stands."

You can build a confident team quickly when you offer more education and discussions on wine. Focus on brief tasting notes and/or a quick story about the winery, winemaker, or their special process. Learning should be fun, and it should be all about the guest. Employees need to read the table, knowing if the guest needs a 10-second description or would like a 45-second description. Some ways managers could practice these descriptions at a line-up may be:

- In elevated dining, after-dinner ports, dessert wines, brandies, and other spirits are excellent ways to enhance the experience. Pick a few random options from the list and have employees describe them. Knowing one that pairs particularly well with each dessert is a great way to upsell. Be an expert.

Pairings

Suggesting wine pairings for the guest elevates their experience and shows the value of your expertise. It is a great way to connect with guests. Rote memorization of varietals and regions was never an effective way for me to learn about wine, but when I tasted how a wine or other beverage could bring out the flavors of food, it inspired me.

There is an old saying about choosing the right wine for your meal, "If it grows with it, it goes with it." Traveling through Italy and France on my honeymoon brought this phrase to life for me. I could taste it: the local style wine brought out the flavor of the food. It made every bite and sip better.

Pour an ounce or two of any wine or beer and taste it with a piece of melon, lightly dressed salad, smoked trout, or prosciutto. The sweet, acidic, salty, fat, or spicy dynamics of food engage with the different levels of tannin, body, acid, and alcohol level and spark a huge difference in flavor profile of your food.

For practice, and certainly fun, Kirsten and I would pick up some inexpensive wines and little portions of food at our Trader Joe's and play around, experiencing the different combinations. This type of exercise was my biggest, quickest, jump in understanding how food and beverage work together.

Don't dismiss non-alcoholic options in beer, wine, and mocktails. That field is growing, and your ability to pair those options should, too.

There are a lot of resources available to improve knowledge around pairings: books, podcasts, social media reels from sommeliers and wine lovers. For many, many years, my favorite book about food and beverage pairings has been "What to Drink with What you Eat," by Andrew Dornenburg and Karen Page. Two newer books I highly recommend about food and wine pairing are:

- *Wine Simple: Perfect Pairings by Aldo Sohm with Christine Muhlke*
- *Wine Pairing for the People by Cha Mccoy with Layla Schlack*

Food

Learning details of dishes and ingredients was a steep hill for me to climb when I moved into elevated restaurants. It wasn't that every guest wanted to know every single ingredient on the dish, but that *I had to know* every ingredient if a guest asked. This is the expectation at this level. What is chervil? Does micro-sage taste like regular sage? What's the difference between Italian parsley and curly parsley? Why does lamb from New Zealand taste different than lamb from Colorado? Can I explain the difference in taste and heat between espelette and cayenne peppers to a guest? See? It's already more detailed than upscale restaurants. Everyone that is touching a table is expected to be an expert. This knowledge creates value for the guest and keeps employees engaged.

Early in my elevated dining career, I started to visit the farmers market in my neighborhood. This quick trip would put me in the world of the food before it arrived at a restaurant. It was fun to talk to the farmers and vendors about their fruits and vegetables. If anyone knows how to describe a farm product, it's a farmer! I worked on a farm, The Patch, one summer when I was in high school. Hoeing rows of corn at 5:30 a.m. taught me a lot of respect for the effort and dedication it takes to raise the food we put on our plates.

At the farmers market, in plum season, there aren't just one or two types of plum like you see at the grocery store, but four or five (Satsuma, Black Amber, Shiro, Burgundy, Golden Nectars). I got used to seeing what fruits and vegetables were in season and these seasonal offerings would be reflected in our menu changes. The details mattered: why was one farmer's potato better than another's? What was the difference between varieties? Why did we choose this tomato? What species of salmon? What farm is the pork chop from? Learning the specifics about our ingredients allowed me to go deeper into the role required of me at this level of restaurant. If I'm claiming to be able to create experiences and connections for guests through specialized food and beverage offerings, I had to hone those skills. The farmers market trips really enhanced my ability to guide guests on a culinary journey.

I was always provided a very detailed, up to date, menu description when I was hired at an elevated restaurant. I was tested by management before I could even walk on the floor. The most successful restaurants are consistent in these first steps. Before I could place my hand on a dish, I had to be "off book," with all dishes memorized *and* able to eloquently *describe* the dish. This type of testing never ended, not even for veteran servers. Managers and other employees were always asking "newbies" or each other to describe a dish for them. They were protecting the culture of the restaurant and were setting the service expectation for new hires. Working in elevated restaurants required a lot of me, but I bought in completely and loved learning about the details of food and beverage. This also made me a better cook at home and more appreciative of the meals I had when dining out. Win-Win.

The Pass

As mentioned earlier, the pass is the area where the expeditor is handing plates off to the runners and/or servers. It's really important for a new employee to have time to learn how the pass works. Watching the timing, presentation of plates, and communication at the pass will help develop that employee quickly. The intricacies of every pass are different, as they are tailored to that specific restaurant. A few tips:

- The pass should be kept clean and organized at all times.

- A clean, damp towel should always be available to wipe drips or touch up the sides of dishes.

- If used, printer tape should be checked and a back-up roll readily available. You don't want to run out of paper on a busy night.

- If monitors are used, ensure they are clean and easy to read.

- Shared utensils for shared plates may be stored at the pass and intentionally positioned on the plate just prior to the plate leaving the kitchen. Some restaurants may opt to place shared utensils on the plates at the table.

- Plates are hot, be careful.

- Keep voices low at the pass because a lot of communication, movement, and direction is happening.

- Write down questions, as there may not be an opportunity to ask in the speed of service. Find those answers when service has calmed down.

- Understanding the details of the pass is essential to new supervisors and managers as it's the key connection point for the front and back of house.

Communication at the pass is important and it's vital to understand that this is where the FOH and BOH meet. There will be different rules for every kitchen and restaurant. Chef Josh Even, of Fossetta, Restaurant Daniel, and John Dory, in NYC, mentioned to me, "During service I feel that the front of house should only address the kitchen by going through the expeditor (the point person). Don't talk across the pass; don't ask the cooks something. And try to make your questions happen when service is not in full motion. You can't have the distractions. The front of the house is always in a somewhat social mode because that is part of their job. When that bleeds into the kitchen, it can cause problems because social mode is not the mode they [the kitchen] are in. They are in the mode of multitasking and juggling a lot of direction." Stay aware that there are many areas of focus at the pass.

Restaurants divide the floor into sections for various purposes. If a restaurant has a staff that includes captains, front servers, back servers, and bussers, the floor may be divided differently than if it had a traditional breakdown of servers/runners/bussers. If it's a slow night and it's decided to run with 3 servers instead of 4, that will require a different layout for the floor. The layout is chosen from the combination of how many employees are working and what the cover count requires. Great restaurants know how to pivot quickly and run a different offense, adjusting employee count, without compromising service.

Seat Numbers

Almost all restaurants at this level use seat numbers as a way to anticipate needs and be able to deliver personalized service. This ensures that no one is "auctioning off" food at the table or placing the wrong items in front of the wrong person. (This can be a serious problem because of dietary restrictions.) I love the seat button numbers in point-of-sale systems. Using seat number buttons enables the team to be very specific about allergies and dietary restrictions, as well as honoring special occasions.

At The Langham, our chef, Craig Strong, would see a birthday listed on a ticket with the correct seat number and arrive at the table just to say, "Happy Birthday." This always delighted guests when the chef walked directly to that person and addressed the person by name, "Happy Birthday, Allison!" It still would have been good if he walked up to the table and said, "I understand it's someone's birthday tonight." But he wasn't interested in good, he wanted to be great. So, we got more specific. Personalized, elevated service for the win.

Seat numbers must be used by everyone on the team constantly. Details elevate. When a runner can say to a server, "Seat 2 needs a touch up on wine and seat 4 may need another cocktail," that is much better than, "Table 23 needs some wine and a cocktail." It's more efficient, and it will be noticed by guests.

Tasting Menus

I love tasting menus! They offer delightfully unique dining experiences with many courses, flavors, and creations of the chef. There are many ways to do a tasting menu, which is a series of courses (average 3, 7, or 12). The course count could go up to 20 or more. A few styles of tasting menus in restaurants may include:

- A tasting menu that is always offered as a menu option, alongside the regular ala carte dishes.

- A tasting menu that is the only option. The restaurant does not offer ala carte dishes.

- A tasting menu that offers, at an extra cost, wine pairings with each course.

- A tasting menu where the guest can pick from a certain number of items on the menu to build their own, 3-course, 5-course, or 7-course meal.

- A special occasion tasting menu that is offered only on specific holidays (Valentine's Day, New Year's Eve, Mother's Day, etc.)

- A tasting menu that is offered as a pescatarian, vegan, or vegetarian option.

- A dessert tasting menu that includes a variety of small dessert courses.

I was introduced to tasting menus when I first worked at Blue Velvet with Kris Morningstar. It was fun as a server to be able to offer this special menu, this elevated experience, to guests. Not just on a special holiday, but nightly. From a service standpoint, I liked the idea of a set menu. I liked the structure and the wine pairings that could further the experience. Of course, when every table is ordering wine pairings with tasting menus, that can complicate timing issues with the whole team. The more a team works together in this environment, rising to the challenge, the easier that rhythm and timing falls into place.

Be Prepared

I like to get to work with a little time to reflect before I start my shift. This was not always the case; I learned it in elevated dining. I realized that taking just five minutes to sit in my car, refocus my energy or clear my mind, helped me center and prepare for the shift ahead. I needed to mentally shift from my personal life into my restaurant mindset. Here are a few things I would do:

- Review the restaurant menus

- Do a five-minute breathing exercise to help relax and bring me into the present

- Assign myself one element of service to really perfect during my upcoming shift (maintaining water levels, pulling chairs, guest name usage, saying goodbye to tables, greeting guests within two minutes, etc.)

- Rehearse a new way to greet a table, explain a dish, or greet a guest at the door

- Read an online article about a new restaurant or event in the area
- Look up a definition, farming process, or food prep for a new ingredient that has been introduced on our menu or will be soon

These are just a few ways you can set yourself up for good shift.

Grooming Standards

In elevated restaurants, you will find higher standards when it comes to grooming. With peak price points, employees will most likely have a uniform, whereas management may be required to wear their own clothes. Whatever the case, everyone's clothing needs to be impeccable. Management should be checking to ensure everyone is in a clean, tailored, fresh uniform.

I don't mind if a restaurant is going for a specific look that *intentionally* may be more edgy and give off a deliberately hip vibe. This doesn't mean the clothes can't still be clean, free of odor and fit well.

The same is true with the person. I don't mind what someone's hair looks like, tattoos, jewelry, etc. as long as it's not interfering with the guest's dining experience. The guideline is determined by the restaurant and what it expects from its staff. I think jewelry should be minimal for safety's sake and clean hands and nails are always a must. Creating a habit of thinking, "How may the guest see this?" is a good check. Always take a moment to step out of your role in the situation and look at it from the guest's point of view and how they may perceive the interaction. Please review the list of grooming guidelines in Part 2: Upscale on page 71 for a refresher.

Mise En Place

Along with pens, wine key, point of sale card, and a pad of paper, service staff may be asked to have a table crumber in a restaurant that uses tablecloths. This is a small device used to scrape or scoop crumbs up off a table with a quick movement of the hand across the tablecloth. I was recently at a restaurant where we had a server approach with a lot of items on them. Multiple pens visible on their apron pocket, pocket looked overstuffed with maybe a pad of paper, phone, wallet, who knows. This is not an elevated look.

Employees shouldn't look like a walking desk drawer. They should have *a few* essential items on them.

Setting the Room

When I first started working at The Dining Room, I was shocked at the attention to detail expected in a Michelin-starred restaurant. The hotel had just shifted from The Ritz-Carlton to The Langham, but the employees and GM were the same and the expectations were clearly The Ritz-Carlton all the way. I was confused when, upon being hired, my schedule had my in-time listed as two hours before the restaurant opened. At previous restaurants I would show up 30 minutes, maybe an hour before a shift started, quickly set up the room, have a line-up and start service.

What the heck were all of us going to be doing for 2 hours? I found out: details! We set up the room, from scratch, every shift. Since we had a cleaning crew come in overnight to clean all floors and surfaces, we had to move *everything* back into place. We placed items to match, exactly. Uniformity of the room was paramount. When items match and there is an exactness to how the tables are presented as guests walk into the room, it sends the message: we are ready to receive you. Everything is set perfectly, glasses polished, utensils intentionally aligned with each other. Subconsciously, it sends messages to the guest; "You are cared for," and "We are ready to be of service." The dining room is set, and we are prepared for the two most important elements in the experience: the guests and the food. In Part 2: Upscale, I provided a very detailed list for setting up the room on page 73. Here are some vital additions to that list:

The Room

Alignment of everything is important. In an elevated restaurant, you want to ensure every table is aligned, balanced, and clean. Anything that can be seen by the guest's eye should be pristine.

- Floors and carpets immaculate.

- Table undersides should be checked.

- Chairs should be checked to ensure they are in good shape and if they need a touch-up, it's attended to. (We always had stain pens for our wood furniture and a tool box with necessary tools to fix items in the restaurant.)

- Artwork or items on walls should be even and all light bulbs in the room in working condition.

- Flowers or plants need to look fresh and presentable, and water changed in glass vases if it looks slightly unclear. Be aware of the smell of the water in the vases too: this can greatly affect the guest experience.

- Any server stations that are visible to the guests should be clean, items for service aligned, and should remain so during service. Avoid clutter in these areas.

- Water pitchers filled and set for service.

- Personal items should be put away, not visible from any guest's perspective.

Setting the Table

Working at The Dining Room was my first introduction to what true attention to detail meant. It was above and beyond. There is a detailed list about setting the table provided in Part 2: Upscale on page 74. Added tasks to that list in elevated restaurants may be:

- Tablecloths may need to be steamed and ironed so they are pristine, free of creases, falling over the tableside and hanging even on all sides.

- Utensils should be polished and placed on a table and at the exact measurement from the lip of the table to the bottom of the utensil. Measurements from the side of the charger plate or set napkin to the first placed utensil should match as well.

- Pre-set water and wine glasses checked for any water spots.

- Back-up glassware should be checked for water spots prior to service, so less polishing needs to happen during service.

- At The Dining Room, a very long string was used ensure all the tables were lined up. Everything was measured with the string. Old school. Two servers took an end and were the last to go through the room, double checking that *each item on each table* was aligned.

- Seat cushions are checked for any crumbs. If the restaurant has an overnight cleaning crew, these areas should still be checked.

- If a charger (pre-positioned) plate is used, they should be in flawless condition.

- Cloth napkins should be pre-set and folded *exactly* like the others. This can be an issue when the teams are folding napkins after the shift. They may be tired, their attention waning. This requires paying close attention or someone has to refold the next day. Ideally, a task should only be done once. Each napkin should match the next in style, cleanliness, and exact fold. I punch this up because it's frustrating to see all the work that goes into detailing a dining room and then to see four napkins on the table that each look just a little bit different from each other. Details matter.

Line-Up

I've detailed ideas about line-ups in both, Part 1: Casual on page 13 and in Part 2: Upscale on page 75. Please reference these sections if you need guidance in this area.

Steps of Service

How do the steps of service differ from an upscale restaurant? Simply, there are more. If the reader hasn't read the steps of service in Part 2: Upscale, please consult the Steps of Service list on page 77. It is very detailed, and this next section builds on that.

The steps of service increase for the team as the elevated experience aims to provide more personalized and detailed service for guests. This will be as in-depth and detailed as the restaurant operations team determines. As I mentioned at the top of this chapter, every person on the restaurant team should be creating value by finding moments to offer luxury touches to the guest experience.

The brand Hermes uses the phrase, "quiet luxury." I've always loved this. It doesn't reek of excess and grandeur but is found in the details and personalization of the product or experience. Luxury can mean much more than flash or pomp. Luxury can be executed through service in many creative ways without breaking the bank. The goal is that guests feel they can only have this rare experience in your restaurant, feel completely cared for and want to be guided by an expert through this special meal. Steps of service are the navigation tool we use to create this experience. Great managers and leaders are able to coach on these steps throughout service, always working with their team to improve steps and ensure the standards are being met.

At The Dining Room, we had 128 steps of service our team had to hit from the moment a guest walked through the door to the time they exited. We compiled all the service standards from different auditing companies we knew would be rating our hotel and dining room and combined those standards with ours into a master list we could use. With this, we created our steps of service. Granted, we split the list up, so certain roles fulfilled specific duties. Robert Hartstein championed this project. My job as a front server/captain was to know all of them. Since we were the leaders in the room, we had to be able to perform every step in the event that someone else missed one. We tracked everything. This was crucial for the type of experience we were offering guests.

A detailed steps of service list is vital to the success of the team. It sets the expectations and provides employees a map to creating exceptional experiences. The steps of service help supervisors and managers with coaching and holding the team accountable. I want to be clear though: this steps of service list is not what made us semi-finalists for the James Beard Award for Outstanding Service in the United States. It's not why we were listed as one of the top 50 restaurants for service in the country from OpenTable. The reason we were on those lists was our team's ability to enjoy themselves *within* the structure of the steps of service we created; to emotionally engage and interact with guests. They had to go hand-in-hand. We had employees that practiced the steps so much and knew them so well, they could connect authentically with guests while creating a unique, elevated experience. They never looked stiff or robotic. They made it all look effortless.

Knowledge creates confidence. It takes consistent work to get to that point and maintain it. There are good reasons million-dollar major-league baseball players are still taking batting practice and fielding groundballs before their games. Why professional hockey players are practicing short shots on the goal two hours before game time. Practicing the fundamentals before the game allows players to be more present when they are actually playing the game. Great restaurant employees are able to forget about the steps because they become second nature, and then they can remain focused on the interactions with guests. If we want to be the best restaurant in town, in the state, in the world, shouldn't we be consistently practicing the basics as well? This is why I like brushing up and improving skill sets through daily exercises and role plays. Regardless of awards and lines out the door, we celebrate redundancy.

Greeting and Seating

In elevated restaurants, the host position takes on a more critical role in the guest experience. The host stand is the key information hub. An expanded team can provide more support, answer and return calls and emails, flag special occasions and dietary restrictions and compile extra details in guest's profiles. Extra details may include special notes about the guests' wine preferences, dishes they loved, dishes they did not enjoy, a reminder of where they live - anything that can help the team anticipate the guests' needs. These responsibilities are added to greeting and seating the restaurant and managing the flow of the room.

The elevated experience requires us to make the communication of this information seamless and non-repetitive for guests. That's part of the magic. Ideally, the guest should be *asked only once* in their communication with a restaurant about dietary restrictions or special occasions. This is a great test for the team in elevated restaurants. It seems extraordinary to the guest when each person to touch the table "magically" knows this information. Communication is paramount to pull it off.

The Maître 'd

At this level of restaurant, the maître 'd is usually acting as the front of house leader and may well be the general manager. They may be the one that is absolutely in charge and depending on the size of the restaurant, there may be a couple of hosts working with them. They are delegating a lot of the tasks for the evening. They will be finalizing the menu with the chef, the section assignments for the team, reviewing the entire guest log for V.I.P.s, special occasions, and specific requests and notes about guests that will be coming in. Oftentimes, it takes multiple people to execute all of this well and communicate it to the rest of the service team.

Printable Chits

Chits are one of the most underutilized aspects offered in a restaurant POS system. I think they should be used in any style restaurant that has the option, but I see them mostly used in an elevated restaurant experience. Chits are currently the most efficient way to get guest information into the hands of the manager or server. Getting the correct guest information on the chit is usually handled by the reservation team or anyone updating information in the reservation system. Using the information on the chit is up to the service team. Let's get into it.

For example, when a guest comes into a restaurant where they have *already* made a reservation and that host asks, "Are you celebrating anything this evening?" and the guest says, "Yes, it's our anniversary" — that's good communication. But if the guest was *already asked that* when they made the reservation via phone or computer, they are now being asked it *again* from a member of the same team. This is a breakdown in communication. This can get a little worse when their server walks up to the table and asks, "Are you celebrating anything this evening?" and the guest now says for the *third time*, "Yes, it's our anniversary." Let's keep going down the spiral. The manager walks up to the table in between courses and makes conversation with the table, "How did you come to dine with us this evening?" The guest answers, for the *fourth time*, "It's our anniversary." Yes, I'm happy that the team is asking a vital question, but they aren't using the system that is set up for them to hit this moment out of the park. The question *should be asked once* and relayed to the team. That's the goal.

Let's look at this guest experience a different way. I walk in and introduce myself, "Good evening, we are the Farrells. We have a reservation for 7 p.m." The host, making eye contact with a smile, says, "Good evening, Mr. and Mrs. Farrell, welcome and happy 18th Anniversary. We are so excited you are joining us." Kirsten and I look at each other and smile. The host takes us to a quiet table they know we would like, because I had typed it in the reservation notes when I made an online reservation. The host hands our menus to us and says, "Annabelle will be right with you. My understanding is Mrs. Farrell has a seafood allergy, is that correct?" Kirsten nods her head. "The only items you won't be able to have are the langoustines, the lobster risotto and the vongole. We do have some excellent specials this evening that Annabelle will share with you. Enjoy your meal and Happy Anniversary!"

A minute later Annabelle approaches the table and says, "Happy Anniversary Mr. and Mrs. Farrell; I'm Annabelle." Annabelle has on her tray two short pours of bubbly in champagne flutes. She places one in front of Kirsten and another in front of me. "Mr. Farrell, I noticed you prefer a non-alcoholic option, so I poured you a taste of our new 100% non-alcoholic sparkling rosé wine from TOST. And a taste of the Jay Sparkling Rosé for you, Mrs. Farrell. Please enjoy this gift from us to you as we begin your anniversary dinner."

Eventually, when Annabelle specials us, telling us about the menu, she may mention — again, without prompting from us — "Mrs. Farrell, I understand you have a shellfish allergy, but if you had your eye on risotto this evening, we have a porcini risotto on our specials with fresh porcinis from the Willamette Valley." Anabelle is anticipating Kirsten's needs before Kirsten has to ask about non-shellfish options. At this point, I hope you get it. Annabelle may have already reviewed this information having access to that information beforehand: either a chit in her pocket before service or a chit given to her by the host after we were seated. Key information in the notes and *using those across* the team can completely elevate the guest experience. Clearly, this is a much better way to start the first 20 minutes of a dining experience than the previous example I gave.

Communication! Gather information, communicate it to the team, and everyone should use those clues to anticipate needs. This should always be a priority of leaders, hosts, servers, and the team. Bits of information lead to specific details about guests and they feel the restaurant is tailoring the experience specifically to them when an employee uses and recalls that information.

Remember:

- Gather the information
- Communicate it to the team
- Use that information to anticipate the guest's needs

Important information that could be listed on a chit:

- Special occasions
- Dietary restrictions
- Preferred seating
- Beverage preference
- Frequent menu items ordered
- Preferred server
- Special notes on past experiences

Table Presence

I have a lot of experience waiting on very wealthy, famous people. I even had the pleasure of serving the President of the United States. The first time I waited on a very famous billionaire, I was shocked that the whole six-top just stopped talking when I approached the table, giving me their undivided attention. The billionaire asked me what I thought of the menu, my favorites, what I liked about the chef. I simply answered and gave them my spiel about the restaurant and seasonal menu. He nodded and took my exact advice.

They all did. I left a little stunned. *Good god, this billionaire just did what I told him to do. He's treating me like I own the place.* Later when I was speaking with Kirsten, we were breaking down the interaction and a few things came out. She said, "Well, you realize you have the status at the table, don't you?" I said, "He's a billionaire." She said, "It doesn't really matter. Money alone can't dictate status. Status is given, not taken. You are the expert in that situation. You know the restaurant better than they do, you are wearing a vest with a tie, and you are standing and they are sitting. You have the height. They are literally looking up at you. They are going to give you the status, because you have the answers they need to make their experience great." Here's the point: guests at an elevated restaurant want to know they are in good hands, that the server and leaders of the restaurant are in control and that they don't have to worry about a thing. They can just show up and enjoy.

Table presence is vital in elevated service. How do you hold yourself? Your posture, your uniform, your knowledge, how you speak, and most importantly, what you have to say. Being able to convey that in a warm, inviting, vibrant way and making it seem authentic, not robotic — are all elements that managers should be working on with staff. We can train on it.

Table presence doesn't need to be over the top. We aren't the stars; the interaction between the guests at the table is the whole point. We are elevating that relationship with amazing food and great service. Beware of making it too much about the service. Some warning signs of over-service may be:

- Hovering around the table in a distracting manner.

- Filling up water too often. Just do it when it's necessary and the levels demand.

- Staring at the one person that hasn't finished their dish at the table so they hurry up and you can mark the table before the next course arrives.

- Long explanations about dishes. Explanations should be intentional and based on reading the needs of the guest and experience they desire.

Guests want you to have the answers. They want you to lead them on a wonderful journey. They want to be taken care of and feel this is a unique experience. Confidence is key at this level. When people feel whoever is driving the experience is confident, it allows those guests to relax, connect with each other, and enjoy a meal together. That should be the goal of every restaurant employee. **Knowledge creates confidence.**

Higher Quality Alternatives (Upselling)

I addressed this topic in Part 2: Upscale on page 82. I think the biggest area of upselling in elevated dining is in wine. I address this further on in this section when I speak about "Selling an Experience" on page 228. I think knowledge is vital to what we sell in restaurants. But you need to read the table. I've seen servers get burned on trying to oversell a table or worse, being very pushy about an item — white truffles, Louis VIII cognac — or overselling so many dishes to a table that they walk out the door with to-go bags looking like they just spent six hours shopping at Nordstrom. You don't want to burn the guest. But you also don't want to rob them of an experience they may want to have. Practice! Work with your teams. Have them practice offering higher-quality alternatives to each other in skills exercises. The best sales people can read a guest well and know when to quickly shift in the sell. I say alternatives because it's important to have options in few price points ready, so the server can meet the guest where they are. The goal is of course to go big and have a super happy guest feel like they just had one of the best experiences of their life, but you also want that type of guest to return. To feel the value of the experience and tell all their friends about it. You want to build trust with the guest so the next time they come in, they put themselves in your hands, allowing you to guide them through another experience.

Taking the Order

I explain taking the order in detail in Part 1: Casual on page 18 and in Part 2: Upscale on page 83. Please reference these sections if you need guidance in this area. At this level of restaurant, anyone taking a food order needs to be a complete subject matter expert on the menu and wines by the glass. Of course, if a sommelier is needed, they can be summoned, but a great server should be able to confidently guide the guests through the menu, recommend pairings and create a special experience for the guests.

Allergies and Dietary Restrictions

As I mentioned above, the team should know about any allergies, preferences, or dietary restrictions at the table prior to the guests arriving at the restaurant. This would be available from the guest's own notes in their online reservation or noted when they spoke with a reservationist. In the case of tasting menus, this information should be checked with the chef prior to the reservation to ensure adjustments can be made to the menu. Ideally, the reservationist would know what types of adjustments are allowed for a chef's tasting menu.

That said, a brief acknowledgement about allergies and preferences still needs to happen. It's either inquiring because no one has asked the question yet or confirming the information that already exists in the reservation notes. This confirmation may happen at the host stand or from the server at the table. It will depend on the restaurant policy. Personal guest details and tailored explanations while taking guests' allergies, dietary restrictions, and preferences into account is a genuine touch of elevated service.

Delivering Food to the Table

A rule at The Dining Room was that the front servers would not leave the floor. They would always be floating in their sections, consistently available to guests. When the runners and back servers would place the plates at the table, the front server would step in as soon as the plates were placed and explain the dishes to the table. This allowed the runners and back servers to tend to more running or other duties and the server, the main guide of the meal, could quickly describe the dishes that were placed on the table. This made the moment a little more special. And it should feel special; this is the main event: the food! If the front server was busy at another table, the back server could stay after the plates were placed and describe the dishes for the guest. The third option was the runner was still able to deliver just as good an explanation.

Synchronized Service

I'm a fan of synchronized service. Synchronized service is when two employees walk up to a four-top table with a dish in each hand and place the one in the left hand on the left side, in front of guests sitting opposite of each other at a table, move clockwise a seat, while moving the remaining dish in their right hand to the left hand, and simultaneously place the next dishes in front of the remaining two guests. This is an underused style of service that creates a touch of elegance. It's clearly coordinated, and it shows the guests there is care and thoughtfulness in the presentation of the course. Why don't more restaurants do this? An excuse I often hear is, "We don't have time for that." It doesn't take more time; it takes a commitment to better efficiency and communication. It takes coordination. And I think it saves time. Either someone is making two trips, which means someone is sitting at the table with food and the other guests aren't, or one trip with all plates being placed together.

At The Dining Room, weren't allowed to leave the pass with more than two dishes in our hands and our rule was the whole table had to be served at once. This forced us, to adjust our table approach and communicate really well. I have to give credit to the head runner, Alex Tabish. The runner has to gather whomever they need to participate in taking the food to the table, together. It can be difficult.

This needed a "Say yes" culture from the team. So, anyone that was asked to assist with running a course had to do their best to make time to run food. Anyone and everyone. No one was allowed to opt out. Sommelier, director of service, anyone that could: we were all committed to the whole table getting the course at the same time. We repeated this synchronized effort for clearing tables as well.

Great communication, eye contact with each other, each of us looking for that slight nod across the room from a fellow team member, letting others know they were going to need help delivering or clearing, made it a joint task.

Running a skills exercise before service with empty plates can provide a quick reminder to pay attention to each other's movements. This is a rehearsal: walk the team in unison, plates in hand, and place them at a table. Let the team match strides, pay attention to the level they hold their plates, find a rhythm and align with each other. If you match each other, whether delivering food or picking up used plates, it looks coordinated and special. The more practice, the more natural it becomes, the more effortless it looks. It doesn't have to be precious. Soon it flows. It reaches a point where team members aren't even thinking about it. This style of service adds tonality and atmosphere to the room. It elevates the experience. It matters.

Table Maintenance

If, as a leader, you are feeling frustrated reminding your team about table maintenance at your restaurant, please read my section about finding value in that aspect of leadership on page 85. Timing is key for table maintenance in elevated dining. So many moments of the evening are orchestrated that servers and team members should all be communicating well and ensuring all steps of service are taking place at the correct time. There isn't room for common mistakes at this level of service, so ensure:

- Proper utensils are placed at the table *before* the course is brought to the table.

- Wine and beverages are poured *before* the course is brought to the table.

- Water levels are consistently being observed, and every person who walks past a table is noticing those levels. (I used to cringe when I saw a guest pour their own water at the table; that's OUR task.)

- Any used item that a guest has finished should be cleared from the table as soon as it's noticed. This is a skill. Bussers, runners, servers, should be scanning the table anytime they are near.

- Clear tables in pairs, so no one is ever stacking plates at a table or making unnecessary noise.

- A napkin is folded or a new napkin is provided should a guest leave the table

- Chair is re-aligned if a guest leaves the table

Arms

Similar to watching how people move and stay small in the kitchen, employees on the floor should be aware of the space around guests. This can prove tricky in small restaurants. I like to establish a common approach point at the table — an agreed upon spot (i.e. between seats 2 and 3). This way, for the most part, guests know which way we are coming from and it's consistent.

Arms are important when employees are constantly reaching around and across a table to put items down or take them away. Sometimes servers are so quiet I've been startled as they slip in and out from every direction. Someone on my right, someone on my left. It will be necessary at times, but the team should be aware of the experience for the guest. While it's important to put down that steak knife or grab an empty martini glass, a guest doesn't need to be shocked and startled because of great table maintenance. Stay aware.

Employees should be aware of reaching across a guest with the back of their hand coming close to the guest's face. If a server uses their *open arm* to reach across a guest for an item, they will have automatically created extra space between themselves and the guest. This was taught to me many years ago as the "open heart" rule. If I am using my left arm and the guest is on my right, my heart will be open to them. If I use my right arm with the guest on my right, my heart would be closed off, they would be looking at the back of my right arm and my right hand as I reached across.

In restaurants we will often hear, "Leave from the left, remove from the right." This basically provides a similar framework of creating space and keeping your heart open to the guest. This also helps avoid showing the back a hand to a guest that is being served. If reaching across a table, employees should be deliberate, quick, graceful, and conscious of the space they are taking.

Water Service

While I covered the basics of water service in Part 2: Upscale, on page 86, in elevated restaurants a little more information and details are required by employees:

Anyone touching the bottle of water at the table should know the type of water they are serving and where it's from. If the water is filtered or aerated in-house from a machine, know what type of machine. Often guests are attracted to the sustainability consciousness of the restaurant and may ask for more information.

Communication is key when it comes to types of water a guest is having. Some restaurants use different glassware, napkins, or other ways to communicate to the team which water is being enjoyed. A few points about water service are:

- Only open the new bottle in front of the guest, at the table.

- Serve the water while keeping your heart open to the guests.

- Be careful not to splash water onto the table when pouring. Pay attention to the sound of the water. The pouring should sound smooth not "glug, glug, glug" like someone is quickly dumping the whole thing out into a bucket. It should be graceful. Use a nicely folded serviette to catch any spillage from the bottle or carafe.

- Just as one would do if they were pouring wine, face the water bottle label toward the guest when pouring the water.

- Ideally a coaster should be used if the bottle is placed on the table. This looks nice but also creates a catch for condensation.

- If placing the bottle on the table, do not plop it. Very little sound should be heard when it's *placed* on the table. Ensure the label is facing the guests.

- Do not place the lid back on bottle. (An argument can be made for bubbles escaping, but honestly, you will not lose much through a small opening over the course of the meal. A server can keep the cap handy, in case a request for the cap is made.) Ultimately, the restaurant standard decision should be followed.

- When the glass is one third from the bottom, offer more water. All employees should be paying attention.

- Pay attention to any guest that has asked for ice in their water. If their cubes have melted, a nice anticipatory gesture may be to come to the table and offer more ice. I've spooned a few cubes from a glass of ice in my hand directly into a guest's glass.

- If a second bottle is needed, always ask the person who ordered if they would like another for the table.

- Some elevated restaurants do not want any bottles, water or wine, placed on the table. The option may be to have it on a designated table nearby or in a bucket (water, white wine) close to the table. In view of the guest is preferred. When you commit to this style, you really have to stay on top of your water and wine maintenance, because a guest cannot pour themselves at a table. Nor should they. Everyone needs to be ultra focused on beverage levels. It's painful to watch a guest get up from their table, walk over to where their wine is, and bring it back to pour their own wine. This should never happen.

- I recently ran into a gentleman I had met years ago at Ray's & Stark Bar, a wonderful Patina group restaurant, helmed at the time by my friends Kris Morningstar and Viet Pham. Not only was the food exceptional, but this gentlemen, Martin Riese was their Water Sommelier. A water sommelier?! It was news to me. I'd never heard of a water sommelier before. You want to talk elevated offerings? This was without a doubt an elevated water experience. I can easily say that Martin Riese is the most passionate person I've ever spoken with about water. Just as we speak with guests about what the best wine to pair with their meals are, Martin had the same knowledge, but with water — 20 waters to choose from.

Bread Service

Elevated restaurants will either outsource their bread or make their own in-house. Baking a few exceptional bread options is a great way to showcase the talents of the chef and the kitchen team.

When it comes to bread service, it's important to introduce the types of bread at the table. I've worked places where the bread was brought tableside and the guests were asked what type they would like as they were shown three different types. For instance: baguette, olive, brioche. Whomever is handling service should be able to communicate clearly to the guest what each type is. If it is made in-house, this should be stated. The bread server will place the requested types on each guest's bread dish. It should also be clearly stated to the guests what *type* of butter, olive oil, or accoutrement is placed on the table to accompany the bread.

If the bread is placed on the table in a basket or other type of vessel, the person doing so should announce the different types to the table. Some restaurants will outsource their bread to a local company. This should be described at the table as well. Guests like to know if their bread is coming from a local bakery.

Taking bread away can be a bit tricky, but in restaurants with smaller table spaces, servers may be encouraged to take the bread away after the first course, freeing up space. Some guests really want to keep that last bite or may want to have bread throughout their whole meal. The person clearing the bread course should always ask the guest before they clear the bread.

Managing the Pace of Your Table

I highly recommend reading this section in Part 2: Upscale on page 87. All of that advice still applies and now we're going to add a little more foresight, attention to detail, and communication with teams. In an elevated atmosphere, pace is vital, not only to keep the table moving, but more important, the restaurant team should be intentionally controlling the experience. Everything in this style is intentional and deliberate, so communication with each member on the team is massive.

It's important to note that pace or moving the table along should always be in the interest of the guest experience. Karim Guedouar, now the Director of Operations for the Dinex Group, told me this about lunch service when he was the GM of Restaurant Daniel in NYC: "The timing and style of the guest is much quicker, and you have to adapt to that. You can have the same person that will spend 2 ½ hours for dinner and wants to be out of here in 45 minutes for lunch. **Timing becomes a form of service for lunch. The service therefore needs to be much more efficient.** The efficiency of lunch is the speed. The guest actually wants that. So, you are not rushing people within that."

Working in what was always referred to as "fine dining," I learned that an intentional dining pace has to be created by the team. We were very dependent upon others and how we set up each service moment. It required paying close attention to timing and consistency.

Prep Times

You need a top-notch expeditor at an elevated restaurant. Coursing and time management requires great communication between the server, runners, and expeditor. The most successful service teams I've been a part of had stellar communication between these three roles. Often, the runners are intermediaries because they are moving between the two areas: front and back of house. Servers also need to manage prep times for cocktails, wine bottle service, wine pairings, and food. The server needs to know how long each of these tasks take so they can create the flow of the experience. It requires a lot of brain space and finesse. Some common issues to arise are:

- If the server puts a cocktail order in late and follows it with the starters, the risk of the food arriving before the cocktail exists. Knowing prep times for both are important so they can mitigate this issue.

- If the correct wine glasses aren't down by the time the sommelier arrives to pour the proper wine pairings, this puts a hiccup in the timing. The sommelier needs to pour that tasting before the course is placed in front of the guest. It's all connected.

Courses

You do not want a guest waiting too long between courses. There are a lot of tasks that need to happen in that short time frame: clearing, resetting with proper utensils, pouring wine or managing wine pairings. Communication is vital and service can't look rushed. There has to appear to be a flow to it all. Service needs to match the food here, so that table needs to be set correctly and serviced by the time that food course comes up in the pass. There is no, "Give us a minute, chef." That just isn't going to land well in a restaurant of this caliber.

Wine Pairings with Tasting Menus

Oftentimes with tasting menus, the guests will have the option of wine pairings. These are selected smaller amounts of wine, chosen specifically to go with the flavor profiles of that dish. A guest may have 7 courses and 7 wine pairings with their meal. Wine will tend to be 2oz-3oz pours.

Wine pairings with tasting menus require a lot of coordination between sommeliers, servers, and support staff. Timing is critical as the wine glass needs to be place and the specific wine poured just before the next course is set in front of the guests. Appropriate glasses for the style of wine should be placed, with time allowed for a brief explanation of the wine. This rhythm of service in coordination with the timing of the kitchen is what makes this type of experience so unique and special for guests.

Hand Signals

When my guests at The Dining Room ordered a bottle of sparkling, flat, or regular tap water, as soon as I left their table the back server was behind me with the water they ordered, ready to pour. There would at times be a small gasp. "How did they know that? How did the other server know what water we ordered? I don't see a headset or an earpiece." It created a little giddiness in the guest, and execution of this "magic trick" was very simple: we used hand signals. When I asked for their water preference, I had my hands behind my back. A one finger meant still; two fingers meant sparkling; closed hand, regular tap. The back server or busser was tasked with watching my hand from across the room and grabbing the corresponding water. It was that simple and guest amazement was pretty consistent. Most important, we were saving time and being efficient. Hand signals, eye contact, and other ways to communicate are absolutely necessary at this level of restaurant.

Your hand signals and cues should be discreet. If everyone on the team knows to look for discreet signals at certain moments, it can really improve the non-verbal communication and save crucial time. Signs are usually dependent on the task that is being executed. If I touch my right lapel after I take a wine order that would be different than if I touched by right lapel after I took the dessert order. These all have to be set up with the team prior, so everyone knows what play is being called. I've seen and heard of a few non-verbal cues used, such as:

- Leaving the table, if I touch the right side of my lapel, it means two Burgundy glasses, if I touch the left side, two Bordeaux glasses.

- Leaving the table and placing your left hand with four fingers extended at your side meant to bring bread to the table

- Leaving the table with a closed left fist at your side meant the back server was to start prepping the table for the first course of a tasting menu.

- Hands behind the back, with one hand extending 4 fingers, thumb across the palm means, "I need help getting out of here, please interrupt me."

- Hands behind back, closed fist: fire this table's next course

You don't want to overuse hand signals, and it shouldn't look like anyone is working as a third base coach at a baseball game. It needs to be subtle to work, so it's vital that everyone is looking for the cues at key moments. When pulled off well, it lends to a more refined dining room, helps the pace of the table, and creates a little magic in the dining experience.

Marking / Plausing

If the reader hasn't read the previous section on Marking/ Plausing in Part 2: Upscale, they can do so on page 89. Every course is marked or plaused with clean utensils that are appropriate to the type of cuisine that is being served. Additional utensils at this style of restaurant may include:

- Chopsticks
- Demitasse spoon
- Cocktail fork
- Oyster fork
- Fish knife

The clean utensils should always be on a CLEAN surface of a tray. A lot of restaurants will use a clean, small utensil tray or small designated plate for marking. When it comes to elevated dining and utensils, there are often very high-end, expensive specialty utensils being used. Anyone handling these should know the maker and be able to communicate that if a guest asks. I've mostly been asked about knives. This too, is part of that elevated experience.

Use a Tray

Always use a tray. Any employee taking items to or from tables should have a clean tray to place the item on. I love the small trays because they make it easy to access different areas of the table without accidentally brushing into anyone. Because of the size of most plates, a tray is not necessary when clearing plates from a table. Here are a few tips:

- The tray needs to be clean. If a used item is placed on it, the tray should be cleaned and sanitized before any more items are placed on it.

- Place items on the tray so there is no sound when doing so. A clean under-liner can help with sound and sliding issues.

- Be aware of items that are touching each other when on the tray together.

- There should be no sound or reverberation of glassware or silver on the tray.

Do A Lap

I haven't worked in an elevated dining room that wasn't dependent on everyone assisting each other. It's essential in this atmosphere. Seeing the whole room and assisting others, where and when you can, is vital to this style of service. Everyone needs to buy into creating an extraordinary experience for guests. To do that, employees need to see the whole room, avoid tunnel vision, and ensure that when their own section is going well, they step out and see where they can assist other team members. Great leaders are always coaching on this and encouraging this type of unity and teamwork.

Clearing a Table

Clearing a Table is covered in detail in Part 1: Casual on page 24 and Part 2: Upscale on page 90.

Dessert and Beyond

After-Dinner Drink Offerings

There is a lot of opportunity to enhance the dining experience at the end of the meal. Being able to offer excellent beverage pairings with desserts is an experience most diners won't find at a more casual restaurant. Offering dessert wines, ports, amaros, brandies, aged bourbon, or crafted non-alcoholic options can really enhance the last course of the evening. I recently dined at a restaurant in Los Angeles with an amaro cart they would bring to the tables during dessert. It was an exceptional offering in a beautiful Italian restaurant. These are great ways to enhance the meal, improve sales, and go next-level.

Servers and managers need to know how to manage this latter part of the meal, which could be just dessert or...cheese course and dessert, and/or after dinner drinks and coffee. This can quickly and unpredictably add a lot of time to the last segment of the meal, effecting table turn times and other incoming reservations.

I can understand why some restaurants may not want to extend the meal from 2 to 2.5 or 3 hours. Every restaurant will have their steps of service and game plan around this part of the evening. Certainly, on the last turn of the night, if table turn times aren't a factor, this becomes a great time and space to upsell and create a memorable after-dinner experience. I loved showing guests how many great after-dinner options we had at Capo. Not only was our Wine Spectator Grand Award-winning wine list amazing, but Capo did not disappoint with after-dinner, ultra-premium drink options.

If timing is an issue, here are a few ways to shave a bit of time off the last segment of the dining experience:

- If the server has memorized the after-dinner drink list, is confident and well versed in this area, it will allow them to offer the options without the table needing to look at the after-dinner drink menu. The menu should *always* be offered, but veteran severs are also able to verbally offer those items first. For instance, "If you were interested in a dessert pairing or after-dinner drink, we have some amazing options." The server could list a few favorites and then say, "I would also be happy to bring our after-dinner drink list."

- Getting the drink order in with the desserts will save time as opposed to making it the course *after* dessert. At times, a guest will have dessert and then order a cognac to sip on. If that is what they want, then it is what it is. But if time is short, I suggest the effort to condense the two together.

Coffee Service

Every restaurant will have its specific style of coffee service. It may be traditional or tableside service. Anyone delivering or making the coffee tableside should know your coffee brand and where it is from. They should also be familiar with the items used to make the coffee at the table. Guests will ask. This is part of that elevated experience.

If you are serving decaf to a table that requested it, be specific about it being decaf when it is placed in front of the guest. Here are some examples of what some steps of service encompassing coffee service may look like:

- The coffee should be placed on a saucer with the handle at the three o'clock position in front of the guest.

- A spoon should accompany the coffee and be placed at the top of the saucer with the handle running parallel to the cup handle.

- A caddy containing sugar and various sweetener offerings should be full, clean, and presented with the coffee.

- If milk is requested, steamed milk in a small pouring vessel should be placed near the caddy.

Tea Service

As with the coffee, tea services can range from simple to complex. In elevated dining, a knowledgeable server ensures that a specific tea is steeped for the correct time. I knew nothing about steeping teas before working at The Dining Room. Just learning that each type of tea had a proper steeping time (the time you leave the ball or bag in the hot water before it is removed) was a game-changer. I thought I hated green tea because it was so bitter. Wrong. I was just leaving it in the water too long and it was pulling more tannins out of the bag than necessary. Tannins create a bitter taste. The fix is to pull the bag before too much tannin is extracted. This is why recommended steeping times exist.

Learning and becoming knowledgeable about the basics of tea service is essential in an elevated dining atmosphere. We would deliver the tea to the table and let the guest know we would be returning shortly to pull the tea ball or bag. "I will be back in 6 minutes to pour your chamomile tea. I would like it to steep for the proper time." Not many restaurants were paying attention to the smallest detail of tea service. Everyone else would just drop off your tea and it was up to the drinker to pull their own ball or bag out of their pot.

This tiny step, returning to the table, removing the ball or bag, and pouring the tea for the guest, truly elevated the tea experience.

We also trained a bit on the history of tea and the types of tea we served in the restaurant. We knew our teas like we knew our wines, liquors, and coffees. We needed to be prepared for that conversation with the guest. It wasn't often, but when an inquiring guest wanted to know a bit more, it felt great to be able to engage on that subject and provide an elevated tea experience for them.

Recommended steep times:

- Black Tea: 3-5 minutes
- Green Tea: 2-3 minutes
- White/Yellow Tea: 2-3 minutes
- Fruit & Herbal Tea: 3-5 minutes

Tea accoutrements may include lemon, honey, milk, sugar, fresh herbs.

Cheese Service

Before I started working at The Dining Room, I was invited by the chef and director of service to dine and experience the room. One of the most impressive moments was when a cheese cart arrived after dinner with 25 cheeses on it! I was shocked, and scared. I was going to have to do this?! Our server, briefly, explained every single cheese. The name, the type, where it was from, and 2-3 descriptors. FOR 25 CHEEESES! I was in awe. I love cheese, but how was I going to remember all of this? Flash cards. Books. Videos. I became an expert.

Some restaurants offer a cheese course and it's an option that guests may choose to start or finish their meal. I've seen pre-selected cheeses served on a cheese plate. I've also seen a full cart rolled up to a table, as it was at The Dining Room. Overflowing with cheeses and accoutrements. Whether we're placing a plate on the table or building each personalized dish tableside, it's an elevated offering to enhance the dining experience.

The team should know which cheese is which. This was the hardest part. We would test each other before service and the more we did this the easier it became. It was built into our pre-shift. Robert would apologetically add cheeses last minute to a collective groan from the front servers, who would then start rapidly memorizing tasting notes and pronunciations. I bought books on it. It was fun to dive into the world of cheese.

I've seen it many times where a server or runner in a restaurant is asked what type of cheese is on the plate and they give the guest a blank look, a pause, and then, "I believe...." Or "I think it's...." This isn't what you want a guest to hear from a service professional trying to provide an elevated experience. It's up to the leaders to ensure the team have the correct information and are able to retain it.

Post-Dessert Course

Many elevated dining restaurants offer a post-dessert course. This is taking the old-school after-dinner concept of chocolate mints on the check tray and finishing the meal with a slam dunk. This can be as simple as an unexpected, shared cookie plate for the table, custom made mini-dessert for each person, or arriving at the table with a post-dessert cart consisting of a variety of house-made miniature sweets for guests to choose from. The server can then create a dish for each person at the table consisting of mignardises (bite-size desserts) and petit fours (small cookies or cakes). Joel Robuchon, famous for his complex tasting menus, is also known for his after-dessert cart consisting of dozens of bite-size desserts, chocolates, cookies, canneles, pralines, and more.

Dropping the Check

When the guest is ready for the check, this should be handled quickly. A server or manager should *already have accounted for everything* on the check by the time this moment in the evening comes. Often, last minute, time-consuming clean-ups of a check include deleting possible mistakes, comping items, and adding items such as forgotten bottles of water that were served. The team can avoid these last-minute additional check tasks by applying a few rules in their process through the evening:

- All items provided to the table during service should be put into the computer PRIOR to that item arriving at the table. Occasionally, items are needed "on the fly" or it may be easier and faster to get the item to the guest and then go to the computer. It needs to be remembered by the team that this item should be put in as soon as possible. It's easy to forget about items and this is where mistakes happen. All items and costs need to be accounted for.

- If items are comped for a table, it's ideal for that to be put into the computer for tracking purposes. Even though that item may be a gift to the table, there should be a record of it and it's also important for the guest to be reminded when they look at the check that it was a gift from the restaurant.

- Any items that needed to be replaced or were mistakes should be removed or coded properly prior to the guest asking for their check. These tend to be the main reasons a check is delayed. The restaurant doesn't want to have this final moment be frustrating for the guest. Every item on the check should be correct and if a service fee is applied, it should be clear that is the case when presented to the guest.

- Employees should always thank the guest when the check is placed at the table. To be clear, "Thank You" and "Goodbye" are two different moments. I'm not a fan of, "Here is your check. Thank you. Have a good night." Not squished together, and not at this level of restaurant. The goodbye should be a moment that is reserved for *after* the guest has paid and is now getting up from the table or is on their way to the door. I understand that servers can get busy, but these two moments need to be split. This point should be coached by managers.

- Everyone should say goodbye. This is a moment that needs to be met. Not only should the team be appreciative, but wishing the guests a good day or evening and letting them know you hope to see them when they come back are essential ways to engage with guests as they are leaving the restaurant.

Resetting the Room

In elevated restaurants, all tables should be reset within three minutes of guests leaving the table. Whether or not other guests are waiting for the table, the goal is that the restaurant should look as delightful and organized as it did before the doors were open for the first guests of the shift. If the reader skipped past Resetting the Room in previous sections, they can find those in Part 1: Casual on page 27 and Part 2: Upscale on page 94. A few additional tips on the resetting the room for elevated dining are:

Often the table set will require the use of a couple of tablecloths: one for the underlining and one for the over. Ensure the length of the tablecloths match and the inside seams are facing down.

- The space under the table and chairs should be checked for any crumbs.

- Chairs should be wiped down and when re-set, should just slightly be touching the tablecloth that is falling over the table.

- If using live candles, the height of the candle should be observed and changed if it looks like it may expire within the next two hours.

- If vases with flowers are used on tables, ensure flowers look fresh throughout the shift and the water is fresh.

- Although any glassware should already be free of marks, double checking these before a guest is seated at the table is essential.

Side work

Earlier lists of side work can be found in Part 1: Casual on page 29 and Part 2: Upscale, on page 95. Please reference these sections if you need guidance in this area. Some additional side work in elevated restaurants may include:

- Polishing all flatware/ silverware

- Polishing glassware and/or decanters before and after service

- Cleaning windows, mirrors, or any glass tables before service begins
- Ironing/ steaming tablecloths and napkins, if applicable
- Pre-setting any items that will be used for tableside service
- Ensuring coat storage area, if applicable, is clean and ready for use

41

VISION

THE 8 RINGS

The first time I heard "vision" referenced in hospitality, I was bartending. We would be so weeded on a busy night, three people deep at the bar, and I'd lock-in and get super-focused on the drinks and only the person right in front of me at the bar. A fellow bartender, Gary Twinn, told me, "Hey Josh, you need to look up; you are getting tunnel vision. The drink is important, but you need to make eye contact with the people that are waiting, even a few behind those in front. It will let them know you see them and put them at ease even though it may be a while before you get to them. They need to know you've seen them." He was talking about vision, and that was a lesson I needed to learn over and over.

Next, I heard it in restaurants. I would be so focused on my tables in own my section that I'd get tunnel vision and not be able to help others out. A great front man told me, "You are doing well in your section, but you need to get out of there, Josh. Help others. Look up, read the room, see what it needs. It's not only about your section. Your team needs you. Have some vison."

When I got into hotels, it was really easy to focus on just my part, my department. But hotel departments are so integrated and connected that if I wanted to succeed, it required me to understand other departments. This way I could see how I fit into the whole operation. Understanding how the other parts worked allowed me to excel in my position because I could see exactly what my position's purpose was inside of the whole experience.

220 SERVING UP EXCELLENCE

But back to restaurants. Improving my vision—seeing and reading the table, the room, the kitchen, the whole operation—refined my game immensely. By the time I got to the Langham, I had a vision for my vision: I'm a visual learner, so I drew eight rings. This is the visual framework I built for myself as a server and have continued to use in many roles in hospitality.

Think of a restaurant as having eight aspects or rings. They go from small to large.

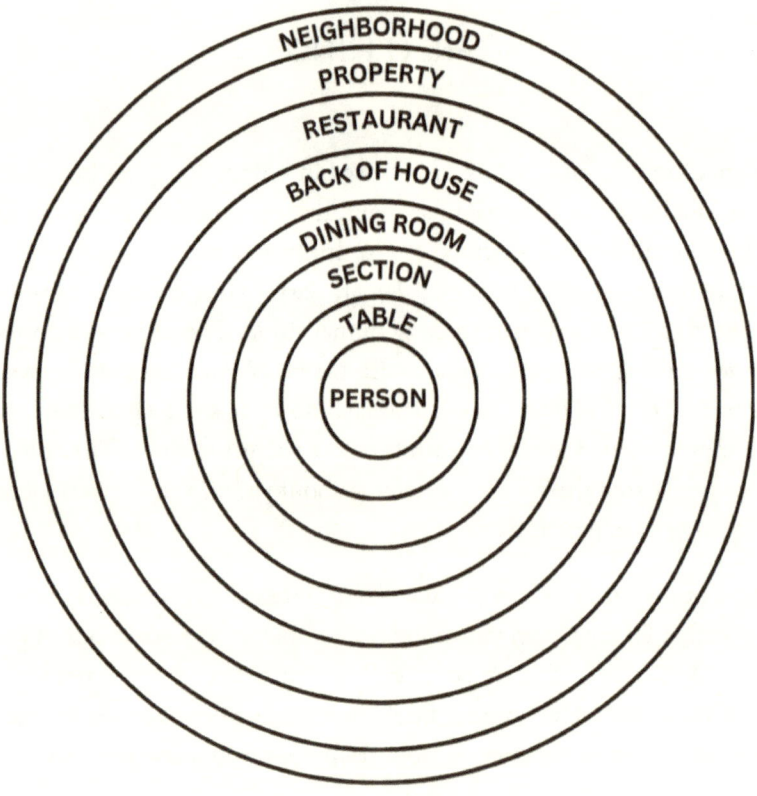

THE 8 RINGS

- The first ring surrounds the person at the table.
- The second ring surrounds the table.
- The third ring surrounds the section.

- The fourth ring surrounds the dining/bar areas.
- The fifth ring surrounds the back of house.
- The sixth ring surrounds the restaurant.
- The seventh ring surrounds the property.
- The eighth ring surrounds the neighborhood.

This helped me visualize the style of service I wanted to give to my guests and the type of team player I wanted to be with my co-workers. This has also served me well as I've trained people on what vision is and how to slowly work on these areas. Here's how I broke these rings down:

The First Ring: The guest. Read the person. What do they want? What kind of experience? How are they feeling? How am I going to make sure they leave feeling better than when they came in?

The Second Ring: The group at the table. Who is this couple or group at the table? What kind of experience are they looking for? Do they just want to eat and get out quickly? Is it a special occasion? How much interaction do they want or need? Is the table maintained?

The Third Ring: My section of tables. How busy am I? Am I giving enough attention to each of my tables? Am I firing courses on time? Is every table on time and ready to turn?

The Fourth Ring: The dining and bar areas. Am I paying attention to getting out of my own section and helping others? Am I assisting with table maintenance, taking an order, checking beverage levels, seeing if the bar needs anything cleared? Can I run drinks for the bartenders? Am I checking on the restrooms to make sure they are cleaned and stocked during service?

The Fifth Ring: The kitchen. Am I communicating well with the BOH team? Putting orders in correctly, firing courses on time, listening to updates on counts, helping the runners bring food out, assisting with marking tables or making room to drop food?

The Sixth Ring: The restaurant. Am I knowledgeable about our chef, our restaurant, and other restaurants we may operate, so I can share that with my guests? Am I aware of upcoming special dinners, unique menu offerings, and holiday menus and informing our guests about those?

The Seventh Ring: The property. If I'm in a hotel or our restaurant is in a complex, am I educated on what other offerings exist? Can I answer commonly asked questions that might pertain to other hotel outlets or amenities that are offered? Can I use this information to have a more in-depth engagement with my tables?

The Eighth Ring: The neighborhood. Do I know the surrounding area? Can I confidently recommend other places or things to do on our street or within a couple of blocks? If I drive to this job from far away, is there a way I can educate myself on a few things in the half mile that surrounds our restaurant? This is an amazing way to engage with the guests and offer great recommendations.

This quick checklist always provided me a good visual and guide to ensure I'm hitting points of service that are important to me and not getting stuck with tunnel vision. It always helped me connect with fellow employees and improve the guest experience. This list supported me well as I coached others. When you use this same approach as a supervisor or manager, the framework allows you to isolate any area of the ring and coach on it. Ensuring each employee is seeing the whole room, not just their section and tables, is key to executing great service at this level.

JOANN CLEVENGER

Restaurateur- Upperline

Being Kind

Our business to our guests and customers is to make them feel good and we bring a special feeling to those people. It is a gift to be nice. It's a gift for both sides. Being pleasant and making someone else's day is such a gift. You get such a good feeling out of it, and you may make a difference in someone else's life. We forget to be kind to others. Some things in life, if you give them away, they are not renewable. Like oil is not renewable. But kindness and giving pleasure to others is a renewable resource. A server smiling at you doesn't mean they can't smile and engage in the next ten seconds; it's a renewable resource and each of us has that potential. The ideal goal is that when someone leaves the restaurant, they are excited about the idea of coming back. We win; they win.

Reading the Table

The thing about interacting with guests is you learn from each encounter, and every encounter makes you more of an expert at listening carefully, watching the customer, and trying to ascertain what *they* are looking for. Do they want to be left alone, want some interaction, maybe a story? Are they looking for the exotic experience of dining in New Orleans? Listening to the guest and carefully observing what they seem to be hoping for gives us clues as to how to make them happy. It's all about making them feel special.

Restorative

The original meaning of the word *restaurant* is "restorative." It gives me incentive almost every day. The world is full of obstacles sometimes. You are in the wrong line at the bank; your ID is out of date—you have these hassles during your daily goings-on about your life. But you come to a restaurant, and you can be restored [from] the hassles of the day. And when we give, we make a difference in other people's lives. And it doesn't have to be a fancy restaurant. It can be a diner or a little café where you just go to get coffee and toast. You can leave feeling restored. That is a remarkable thing to be able to do for people!

The Mental Hug

One thing that is important is to not be anonymous. You go to these big grocery stores or banks and the people that are interacting with you do not look at you. They don't look you in the eye. Sometimes they smile, but they are not really looking at you. It's almost mechanical. But in a restaurant that does it well, the guest is not anonymous—you have a personal relationship. You are looking someone in the eye so they don't feel anonymous, and they are not just one more person in line to say hello to. It is very special. It's like a mental hug. The idea of the mental hug is that it makes the guest know that we care about them, and we are going to look after them. It's a place of safety. The eye contact, the smile, all those things give a mental hug to the guest, from people that really care. And we can do it with people that are not the guest. We can do it with the mailman or the person that delivers the fish and the way we speak to them. We spread this joy and delight among the people we encounter.

That Extra Touch

I have a piece of paper that I type up. I call it "Upperline Favorites." It's art, antiques, books, wine, and food shops. It has my favorite radio station, the whole back of it is about independent bookstores, there is a little sandwich store I admire very much, etc. And I will give some people this piece of paper and say, "Here are some of my favorite bookstores and this is my favorite radio station," and I tell them why.

Sometimes I tell them that almost everybody that comes for JazzFest takes this radio station home with them. They can stream it on their PC—and you see this spark in their eye—they can have New Orleans with them every day. So, I'm giving them a gift.

Learning Kindness

Before I was a waitress, I was not a kind person. I was sort of an intellectual bookworm who didn't really have much interaction with other people. My nose was always buried in a book and as a result of being in the fantasies of books, I had too high of expectations of everybody. And so going to work as a waitress was fantastic for me. I had to put myself out to please someone else. And it came to me pretty easy because I had been around nice people in my life: my mother, people at church.

But I wasn't that kind of nice until I started working as a waitress. Going to work as a waitress, you had to interact with people. You had to go up to a table and say, "Good evening, how are y'all tonight?" And that brings out the best in me. And I think it has the potential to bring out the best in any of us.

43

CAPO

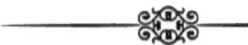

Learning a Fast Room and Selling an Experience

Capo is a great room: a neighborhood restaurant with little pretention. I had heard about it for years because somebody I had worked with knew somebody who knew somebody who worked there and told me the servers made good money. I asked how much. She said, "The few I know own homes." Well, I guess I could drive to Santa Monica for that gig.

A year later I was at a friend's bachelor party playing a flag football game in a park near Sherman Oaks, and I'm talking with the guy I'm guarding. He tells me he is a set designer, and he also had a job as a server at Capo. I asked him if it was as hard to get a job there as everyone says it is. He told me the most recently hired person had been there for two years and after that it started at five years. After the game, I said, "Hey, do you mind if I text you my number, and you can let me know if anything ever comes up? "Sure," he said. That's how I met Davis Campbell. A couple of years later my phone rang.

I had a pretty good amount of confidence coming from The Dining Room. The Dining Room had won a lot of awards, and I felt I could easily coast into any other job. That dream was shattered the first time I witnessed service at Capo. It was like nothing I had really seen. It was fast. Super-fast. Not anything like a three-hour tasting menu in a "fancy" restaurant. Not fast for the guests. But for the servers. The reason the servers made a good amount of money was there were no back servers, no bussers. There was one bartender, one runner, four or five servers. This meant the tip pool was small, and it was an even split. I liked this because it immediately took away any money disparities within the front of house team. With a smaller team, you still had to give great service. I had to learn how to multitask like I'd never experienced in a restaurant before, while maintaining grace and composure.

Environment

Capo is one of the most unique rooms I've ever been in, and it's one of my favorites. It's one room with a patio. There's a live fire in the dining room where you can see food being cooked, and a small bar, and it was always packed with famous people. I've never seen anything like it, and I had worked in a pretty popular bar in the middle of Hollywood for years.

What I love is that the room doesn't feel precious in any way. It has hardwood floors, white tablecloths, and the lighting is soft and perfect. The music has varied over the years, through different tenures, but has always been one of the better playlists I've heard in dining rooms of this caliber. The room is comfortable, inviting, low-key, and really expensive.

And this is all because of the boss, Bruce Marder. He is a great chef who created one of the best rooms in Los Angeles. It's filled with his amazing art collection, and every tiny detail in the room is intentional.

Bruce is one of the toughest bosses I've had. And smartest. He saw the whole room, every detail, and didn't mince words about his standards and expectations. He couldn't care less that I came from The Dining Room. He was glad I was trained, but what was important—and made very clear to me—was that I could adjust to his style of service and not mess it up. So, it was like starting new. I got notes on everything in my first few months there. I had to check my ego a lot, forget some service styles I had lived by, and start over. It was hard. But it was a great lesson in having to adjust at any point in your career to fit your new job and a new restaurant's established culture. If I didn't, I was out. Over my time there, I saw a quite a few people with great resumes, from world-renowned restaurants, last only weeks. They couldn't adjust to Capo's culture; they couldn't keep up; **they didn't meet the pace with grace.**

Some of the hardest things for me to do out of the gate were:

- Get the order in quickly

- Tighten up my course-firing times

- Get out of my section. This was the hardest.

- Talk less with my tables: it wasn't a 2 ½-3-hour turn; for a two-top we aimed for 1 ½ hours and a four-top, 2 hours.

- Turn my tables

- Ramp up my wine knowledge very fast. This led to me eventually earning my level two sommelier certification.

- Learn to offer more expensive wines than I ever had sold before.

- Hit all the points of proper wine service, but don't look stiff. Who cares if it's a $1,600 bottle of wine?

I told my family that it was amazing food in a beautiful, eclectic room with fine-dining prices. But it was the farthest thing from traditional fine dining that I had experienced at that point in life. And I loved it. It was cool, hip, accessible and ridiculously expensive. We were expected to just be ourselves, talk to tables, be comfortable, but still hit all the right steps of service. It was a very specific balance of professionalism with relaxed, authentic interactions.

Selling an Experience

Money wasn't an issue for most of our guests at Capo. I asked Davis in the first couple of weeks how he had the nerve to simply point at an $800 bottle of wine for a table. He casually pointed at a two-top that had just bought a bottle in that price range and said, "Look at those guys in their expensive suits at table 12. The one on the left is wearing a Brioni. The one who booked the reservation is staying at Shutters, a luxury hotel a block away. He is spending $800 on a room tonight. For himself. His company is probably paying for it. I don't know that $800 would be considered expensive to him. Think about their perspective. Let's say one of those guys is trying to close a million-dollar deal with the other guy. Do you think a $2,000 bottle of wine is a crazy option if you are trying to get someone to lock into a million-dollar deal?" He had a point.

The second thing that Davis told me is something that I carry with me to this day. He said, it's not about the money. Don't get hung up on it. **At this level, the money really isn't the issue. It's about the experience. We have something they can't get anywhere else. At least not tonight. And that is what we are selling: an experience.** They can go buy a veal chop from Bristol Farms and put it in their oven. They can try to make a Bolognese and have some expensive wine with it. They could find white truffles at a fancy store. They could even try to play the same music we have here. But they can't have this—this room, with this art, this fireplace, with these people, this food, these vintages of wine, and our service. We have something they can't find anywhere else, and these people are willing to pay for it.

After I understood that, I was able to relax a bit. He framed it for me. I was just a specific part of this whole experience Bruce had put together. They liked my personality. They wanted me to engage with the tables. Pay attention to their details of service, be a little quicker with my turns, and try to sell some more expensive items. We had one of the Top 90 wine lists in the world, Wine Spectator Grand award, with over 2,500 wines on it. A block from the beach, packed with famous and wealthy people who felt they could let their guard down and relax. That was Capo. And it helped me buy a home.

44

STEVE SCOTT SPRINGER

Former General Manager- Spago

Prepared

We have a highly detailed plan for every single service. You have a plan for who is doing a tasting menu, who tends to stay a long time, and who is usually a quick diner. You are making either educated guesses or going off the knowledge of prior visits. We take really good notes on all of our guests and try to plan those sections, so [a server] is not getting multiple sat at the same time in their section. We find that the stronger structure and plan we have in place for the whole night, the better we can adapt to the changes. We can see what's moveable, not moveable, and recognize the if/and scenarios.

Line-up

It's about motivation. There are times at a pre-shift meeting when it's not about 'Don't do this' and 'Don't do that.' I like to apply the same mentality that you would have in equity theatre: there is a rule that you can't give notes a half hour to curtain. It's the same thing in a pre-shift meeting. You can't stand up there and berate them and expect them to go out a deliver great service. **You need to motivate staff and make sure you are recognizing positives at work.** I think it's not just about saying, "Put the fork down at the right time." There is a whole other way to connect to your employees.

The Story

It's not about listing ingredients so somebody doesn't experience an allergy. It's about telling stories, so I need people to understand the story behind the dish. One of things we often say is, "What's special about the special?" Wanting to really dig deeper, beyond the ingredients to really understand what the story is behind this that will engage the guest. What can we do to tell something to the guest about this dish that they didn't know? Maybe it's, "This is Chef's pâté platter today. Wolfgang and Chef have been sparring about who can make the best pâté, so Chef got excited and went crazy on pâté, here is your course." Or "Here is our tuna; we serve it at the Oscars every year. I know you are visiting from out of town, so we thought we'd send it over to you."

45

SHORT MEMORY

THE BENEFITS OF FORGETTING

In this type of work, it's important to develop the ability to forget quickly and move on. I've spoken on stage with scripted material quite a bit and when you miss something in a speech or in a play, you can either keep kicking yourself about messing up or move on. The more you kick yourself around about the past moment, the more you rob yourself of being 100% in the present moment. This happens in restaurants quite a bit. Especially when you have a team that is trying to play to a high standard and execute great service. Sometimes they will miss. It's guaranteed. The question is how well are they able to get past that mistake quickly and refocus their energy on what's ahead?

Roger Federer, the great Tennis player said this during a commencement speech at Dartmouth college: *"In tennis, perfection is impossible... In the 1,526 singles matches I played in my career, I won almost 80% of those matches... Now, I have a question for all of you... what percentage of the POINTS do you think I won in those matches? Only 54%. In other words, even top-ranked tennis players win barely more than half of the points they play. When you lose every second point, on average, you learn not to dwell on every shot. You teach yourself to think: OK, I double-faulted. It's only a point. OK, I came to the net, and I got passed again. It's only a point. Even a great shot, an overhead backhand smash that ends up on ESPN's Top Ten Plays: that, too, is just a point. Here's why I am telling you this. When you're playing a point, it is the most important thing in the world. But when it's behind you, it's behind you... This mindset is really crucial, because it frees you to fully commit to the next point... and the next one after that... with intensity, clarity and focus. The truth is, whatever game you play in life... sometimes you're going to lose. A point, a match, a season, a job... it's a roller coaster, with many ups and downs. And it's natural, when you're down, to doubt yourself. To feel sorry for yourself. And by the way, your opponents have self-doubt, too. Don't ever forget that. But negative energy is wasted energy. You want to become a master at overcoming hard moments. That to me is the sign of a champion. The best in the world are not the best because they win every point... It's because they know they'll lose... again and again... and have learned how to deal with it. You accept it. Cry it out if you need to... then force a smile. You move on. Be relentless. Adapt and grow. Work harder. Work smarter. Remember: work smarter."* (Kottke, Jason. 2024/6/20. Kottke.org. https:// kotte.org/24/06/a- few- lessons- from- Roger- federers- dartmouth- commencement- speech)

I've struggled with this myself. Getting past an awful moment of service in the restaurant: spilling red wine on a white table cloth in front of the company's president, being yelled at by a guest in front of everyone in the restaurant, having a guest tell me I've ruined their anniversary. I've been in the game a long time. Failure is going to happen. From a management standpoint, how can you best assist your team with the tools to move past these challenging moments that may distract them moving forward? How can you better set them up for success? I think this is a good topic to discuss with your team because we aren't all perfect and, in this world of restaurants and bars, we need to be able to bounce back quickly. The more this issue is openly discussed with the team, the better. Here are a few things to help you and your staff in a moment that seems like it may linger and disrupt the immediate needs of service and the team:

- Remember, there will be time to review what went wrong after the shift. It's important to let it go. Remind yourself that mistakes can make you better.

- If you need it, take a quick minute and step off the floor. Breathe. Use this time to re-center. Slowly count breaths, etc.

- Get yourself back on a clear objective. Shift your intention to the next most important thing in the restaurant.

- After your shift, think about what you can learn from the mistake. Often there is a positive that can be pulled out of every experience.

Write this down. Sometimes taking a pen to paper rewrites the experience and allows you to let go of the mistake a little quicker.

- I used visualization when I worked at The Dining Room. Especially if I had been kicking myself overnight for a mistake during service. The next day when I pulled into the parking lot, I'd sit in my car for a few minutes and visualize a great night where I hit all the points of service.

This is not a green light to just say, "Well, I'm not going to dwell on that, stuff happens." It's important to know what you can control in the moment, what you can't, and save the investigation into why it happened for after service. It's necessary to go back and review it, though. You don't want the same issue arising shift after shift. At a certain point, if a pattern exists, it needs to be addressed. Keep a short memory, when necessary, but don't let mistakes become bad habits.

46

JOSIAH CITRIN

Chef/Owner- two-starred Michelin restaurant Melisse

The Casual Guest

At Charcoal we try to give the detailed service and the excellence in the guest experience without obviously doing everything we do at Melisse. We really want to focus on the guest feeling great. I don't want to shoo away great service because I have a more casual restaurant.

Know Service

If you are a chef in the back of the house and you want to have a successful restaurant you need to understand front of the house—whether you are managing it or not. I started off with very little front-of-the-house experience. In 18 years at Melisse, I've worked as the maître d', manager, done everything I've had to do at different times. And I think it is super-important to know that and understand that. And to know service!

I think I can see the dining room better than most anyone that works for me. I can see what's going on and how the service is going. Are we taking care of these tables? When I'm in the restaurant I'm always focused on what's going on with service. I realized after a time that I really needed to focus on that and understand that and be a part of it. I think it's helped because it's tough and you are going to have people come and go. If you don't have that input into how everything works than it is always going to change based on who is coming in and running your restaurant. This restaurant runs how I want it to run all the time, as Capo runs how Bruce wants it to run, no matter who is running it. And that is important. That's the identity of the restaurant. And [whether] it's good or bad will be to the detriment of the restaurant or the greatness of the restaurant.

"Walk in My Shoes"

At Melisse, we used to pair a cook and a server together. One night the cook would work with the server on the floor and another night the server would work in the kitchen with the cook. And then they would come in and experience a meal at Melisse together. We used to call it "Walk in My Shoes." It was a great.

LARRY NADEAU

Dining Room manager- Two-starred Michelin restaurant, Enclos. Former Maitre'd- The French Laundry.

First Impressions

We've all heard the hostess is the first person you see when you walk in the front door. We, at The French Laundry, probably spent more time training that position, as to what we are looking for, than really any other position. I think so many restaurants fall short. It's one of my pet peeves. It's the biggest one. And regardless if it's a Michelin restaurant or Joe Blow's diner down the block, that welcoming you get when you walk in that door is so important. And it has got to be sincere.

That's the thing in the restaurant; you've got 45 minutes or 5 hours depending on the restaurant. But if I walk in the door and the hostess doesn't even look up at me and just grabs three or four menus, escorts me to the table, and doesn't even give me a smile or at least an "Enjoy your dinner," you are already starting in the negative, and you have to make that up someplace. You end up losing an important moment. And you have to get that back.

And it's not hard — doesn't take any more time, any more energy — to do it a better way. I always blame that on management. The management just doesn't do a good job of training that particular position. That person has to understand what it is they are doing. All restaurants need to pay more attention to that job.

Be Present

You can't read a table when you are in your own head. So, if I'm walking through the dining room and my mind is filled with 100 things—the twelve things I need to do next or other things; my mortgage, my girlfriend, my kids, all that other stuff—there is no way to be open to reading a table when my mind is filled with my own stuff. That's one thing I love about the restaurant business: you have to drop all that stuff to really be present for the guest. And when you're present—and you can't do it 100 percent of the time—then you can really start to pick up stuff really quickly. You can start to notice things that the guest might need, so they don't have to ask. You notice when a woman is cold, so she doesn't have to ask for a pashmina. You notice right away that she is rubbing her shoulders, for example. Nonverbal signs. But you can't pick up on that stuff if you are not paying attention or you are too wrapped up in your own stuff. That is the fun part, picking up on all that stuff. (those signs)

Sense of Urgency

At The French Laundry, we talked about focus as opposed to speed. A sense of urgency is a big saying of Thomas Keller's. You hire somebody new and you talk about a sense of urgency, and they thought it meant running the food out of the kitchen as quickly as possible and then getting back to the kitchen as quickly as possible. Sure, that's part of it. But it doesn't involve running or looking like you are in a hurry. So, what we talk more about is focus, pace, control, and confidence.

Failure

One of things that was amazing was how many people we hired that thought The French Laundry ran perfectly, service to service. That would usually be one of the first things I would tell somebody when we hired them. "Hey man, we are just 16 individuals trying to do a really good job every night. We screw up, we make mistakes." Thomas always talked about perfection being something you are always trying to achieve, but that it is not a static thing;

it's a fleeting moment where you might get it, but it's gone as soon as you get it.

The VIP/Regulars Trap

Your first priority should be that [a regular guest] has a better time than the last time he was here. Or better service than the last time he was here. You can be comfortable in your conversation with him, but don't forget that he is not coming here to see you. He's happy to see you, but he's not coming here to see you. And you might be taking care of people on table 3, but table 2, who is your table, is paying attention to you, as well as table 4. Guests don't really like when one table is sucking all the energy from their captain. I'm always reminding [servers] that they have to take care of the other tables as well.

Water Service

Pay attention. You know how it is: you walk by the table and no one needs water, and you walk away and two of the guests down their water glass completely. What are you going to do? Pay attention. If you have an 80-year-old lady in the restaurant and she has to pick up her water glass and it is FULL, you are not doing a really good service to her...there is a really good chance she might have little bit of a shake in her hand. The water glass is going to be heavy and you trying to keep filling up that water glass is a disservice. So, fill it up three-fourths full, keep an eye on it, and when it gets down to a third—pay attention to it. It's an individual thing. It shouldn't be a table thing or a dining room thing — "I'm going to go around and pour the dining room." And yet that happens, busser grabs a pitcher and walks around the dining room. I get it, there are places where that is appropriate, but it's not good service for sure.

48

WHY SO SERIOUS?

The Importance of Keeping a Playful Attitude

One of my favorite teachers in graduate school and now a friend, Larry Hecht, once told me about the difference between important and serious, and why it was essential to draw a line between the two. If something is important, it can still be playful and essential. If something is serious, you run the risk of leaving playful out of it.

For me, I don't want "serious" in service. Serious brings to mind furrowed brows, trickles of anxiety sweat, shaky hands, servers rushing around the room without looking at people, taking people in. Seriousness can suck the air out of the room. When people used to mention a "stuffy room," it's this type of seriousness and preciousness they were talking about. There may still be a space for this protected experience, but we don't have to be serious about it. It can be important without seriousness.

Important vs. Serious

People can still be held accountable for not meeting standards and expectations, but it may not be necessary to bring the dread vibe with it. Remember this server or employee still has to go speak with guests. They have to bring some positive energy to the room, so if a manager "Debbie Downers" the whole group and only speaks about mistakes with serious tones, that manager may be making the situation worse. This is not a green light to avoid constructive feedback discussions, coaching during service, or the pursuit of always improving; those should always be a part of line-up and discussions, but leaders should pay attention to tone and intention. Stay positive. One can still stay positive while addressing important issues of service. Look at your approach. Is it effective? How do we keep a balance? Here are a few ways:

- Bring some levity to your line-up. Think of leaving your team inspired instead of warned.

- Give praise in front of the group for good things that you notice.

- Smile with your team, don't just save it for the guests walking in the door.

- If you are a server, use the words *thank you* a lot with your support team; it can lighten the mood while keeping the direction of service moving forward.

- If you are going to complain, try to phrase it in a positive light and offer possible solutions.

- Be nice to yourself. You are going to make mistakes. It's important to note them and tomorrow is another day to get back up and try it again. That's important, but it sure isn't serious.

- Take a break. If you are overwhelmed and you feel service is getting too intense, take a quick breather.

- Stay aware of your mood. Your energy is going to affect the room, so it's important for you to have an awareness of that energy, be in touch with that, and find a counterbalance when you need it.

When you can stay positive, it can really affect the whole team and may blossom in ways you can't see. Chef Stuart Brioza mentioned to me, "I need my day to be very positive and that trickle-down effect works and everybody adds something and everybody matters. And when everybody matters, everybody feels important. And when people feel important, they feel empowered. When you have a whole flock of people that are empowered, great things happen and you can have leadership that can take a big step back and merely guide."

DAWN AGNEW

Former Maitre d'- One-starred Michelin restaurant, Gary Danko

New Culture

We have people come in and say, "I've worked all over the country. The best places." Well, that's not Gary Danko. "Why don't we do it this way or that way? When I was at such and such, we did it this way." That's not Gary Danko. It's so essential to be open to change and learning the differences of wherever you are. We want new people to be excited to come into our culture and learn, and that means they are going to be flexible and excited to learn from the guest as well, which in turn is going to make the guest trust them.

Training

Training is huge. At Gary Danko, everyone is part of the training process. It's a tight team, and everyone has to be as successful as the person next to them. We aren't afraid to tell you what you are doing wrong and what you are doing right. And it's a pooled house, so everyone is accountable. There are many solutions to certain issues or mistakes.

Attitude Adjustment

If someone throws me attitude, they are going home. You think they are going to do it again? I'm not working with the attitude. You can't be afraid to send someone home—you're going to have to work harder, but it's the beauty of lateral service—we will be fine without you. We have runners that can be bussers, vice versa. We have floaters that know how to be servers, and we have the maître d' that can do all roles and cover responsibilities. It's really important to have that ability and support in the room.

Customer for Life

It's all of these little steps we have in place to make sure people feel they are wrapped up in a little blanket and feel great when they leave. And if they are not happy, we are going to jump through a massive number of hoops to make sure they are when they leave. If you can do that before a guest walks out the door, you've probably created a loyal customer for life. Instead of calling them two days later and going back and forth about what went wrong.

50

REFRESHING ENTHUSIASM

Inspiring Employees Back to Standards

I've had a lot of conversations with restaurant managers about the following questions: How can I re-inspire employees that just seem like they've lost that pep in their step? How do I restore that bright energy that they had early on and get them to re-engage with our guests? At a certain point in a restaurant career, some employees fall into simply hitting the steps of service. They think walking through the steps is enough and forget that a sense of warmth and gentle enthusiasm has to enhance those steps. The phrases "Phoning it in" and "Accomplishing the bare minimum" come to mind. If not addressed, this issue can be detrimental to the whole team.

This energy drop is common with teams that have been working together for a long time. It makes sense that some employees will occasionally lose their shine, lose that passion to truly engage with guests. Our job as managers and leaders is to pay attention, see where this is happening in the team, and find ways to get those employees back on track.

I wish one conversation with this person could solve this issue, but in reality, it may be a bit of a process to bring these employees back to top form. When I was bartending in Hollywood in my mid-20's, I needed a manager to have this talk with me. I had lost my pep, was taking gratuities for granted, and in retrospect, was a little tired of my bar gig. I felt I could do my job in my sleep and I was slipping into judging customers a lot. My manager, Hiko, had to take me aside and call me out on it. He was very nice; I was very defensive. It was a tough conversation. I soon came back around to providing great service again. It took a bit. He kept checking in on me, asking how I was doing. I am grateful for his transparency and direct communication with me about the issue. I saw it as getting "called out," but he probably saw it as "good leadership communication." He wanted me to stay, but he had to remind me of the standards I needed to follow. He held me accountable. Here are some ideas for how to help employees refresh that service enthusiasm:

- Find a private space to talk with them about the issue.

- Recognize them for what they are doing well. Be specific. Recognize them in front of others.

- Be straightforward about what the issues are. You have to be able to name specifics so the two of you are on the same page.

- Let them know they need to be more engaged at work. Continue to have more one-on-ones with them and listen to their feedback.

- In terms of service, engage them by asking what they are going to focus on during a shift:

    - Finding out two bits of information about the table (see *bits of information game below) is a good engaging game.

    - Practice smiling authentically during their intro to the menu.

    - Suggest three open-ended questions they may ask during the course of the meal.

    - Pick a basic: pulling chairs, keeping beverage levels proper.

    - Focus on thanking each table and being there to say goodbye as they leave.

- Have the employee teach a class to the team on a subject this employee is passionate about.

- Have them lead a line-up once a week with the team.

- If it's someone you have invested in, think about taking them to a restaurant that has service a little more impressive than your own. Make it an R&D trip: Research and Development. The mission is to notice some points of service the two of you can learn and bring back to your restaurant.

- Provide opportunity for growth. If they are stuck, maybe a new objective or the idea of an expanded role will provide a needed spark to their engagement.

*Bit of Information: At the Langham we once played a game where the objective for each of us was to find out a bit of specific information about the table, come back to the server station, and share it with each other. This was beyond the information on a chit. You would engage with the guests, return and say, "45 is from New Zealand, 31's kid just graduated from USC, 22 is a dentist in Pasadena, or 51's son is in the Rose Bowl game tomorrow, he's the quarterback for Oregon!" At one point, we even wrote the info on our huge whiteboard in the server station. While we were always conscious of guest privacy, we were showing each other that we weren't just offering a smile, we were engaging a little deeper. We were finding details about our guests that allowed us to assess their needs. This made it fun and reminded us of how each table really is unique. This game gave us a clear objective that immediately put us into action: engagement.

SARAH CLARKE

WINE DIRECTOR, REPUBLIQUE

Know Your Wines

If you work in an Italian restaurant, you should know the Italian wine basics: what main varietals grow in the major regions. I don't need you to know the obscure wines of Sicily, but you should understand what comes from Tuscany and Piedmont. [You should have] at least heard of barbera, Barolo, brunello, and have some familiarity with them. Do your research. I give people a pretty good pass when it comes to Italian wines because they are tricky. But you have to show a willingness to participate. Have a clear understanding of our wines by the glass and over time have five or ten bottles that you know and can go to on our list. So if a guest says, "I like pinot noir," you know where you can lead them.

Clarifying the Wine

A good way to make sure they ordered the right style of wine is to present the bottle and say, "Is everyone at the table familiar with this wine?" Because you don't want to insult the person who ordered the wine—because you are assuming they know—but you are giving them an out by someone else at the table not knowing if it's what they want. It doesn't put them on the spot, but it gives them an out. It doesn't make the server look like a jerk, but it can clarify the order before you open that $175 bottle.

Prioritization

Multitasking is essential because you need to be able to switch speeds at any given time, and the flow of the restaurant can change so fast. **The servers that are the most successful are the ones who are mentally organized and can prioritize quickly what they need to do.** If they are going to delegate, they immediately know who to delegate to. The flip side to that is the server who lets things stack up. The server that has three tables that haven't ordered and then four tables. You can just see they are cruisin' for a bruisin' because they haven't asked for help, are not going to get to it all, and when they do, they are going to pummel the kitchen with tickets, and it's just a disaster.

Basic Principles

Proper basics matter. Whether you are serving a cup of coffee or an incredible glass of Burgundy at a Michelin-starred restaurant, there [are] still basic hospitality principles. You speak politely, you say please and thank you, you address someone correctly, and you make eye contact. The employees at the Starbucks near me are so nice. They know so many people's names. It's just Starbucks, but they are so nice, know people, talk to people, and that is very valuable. This is what we do. This is hospitality. Unfortunately, these days, it is entirely too cool to seem like you can't be bothered. The employees that can't be bothered with basic hospitality, I don't understand what they are doing—there are other ways to make money.

52

DIRECTOR OF SERVICE

Coaching, Auditing, Leading

I've always enjoyed the role of the director of service. Although he was the General Manager of The Dining Room, Robert had the title, Director of Service. Very similar to a maître d'. This used to be a very common role and title in elevated restaurants: a leader whose main focus was on the service performance of staff and the quality of the experience for guests. Robert observed everything. He was the same way when he was owner of Blue Velvet, the first restaurant he hired me in. He was a very involved owner who knew how he wanted service executed. He had high expectations of managers that were skilled in the area of coaching and directing. Both Sam and Rick were master technicians in the dining room. One came from Balthazar in New York and the other from Spago in Los Angeles. And since I was new to serving in upscale restaurants, I assumed this was the way all restaurant managers were.

It's really important for managers and leaders to make time to observe the details of service. Watch the sequence of service: are the steps clean? Is the timing on? Is the team communicating well about table maintenance? Time has to be specifically made during the shift to observe the service. Targeting a small pocket of time, or a specific part of the sequence, allows a manager to still tend to the needs of the night but to also step out of the action and be objective. Watch the game. Take some notes and offer coaching later. Create a list of sequences, time blocks, you can pick from to observe/coach, for instance:

- The host welcoming guests and sitting them at the table

- The server greeting the table, introduction of the menu, and initial drink order

- The server, busser, runner, clearing a course and resetting the table for the next course

- The runners dropping a course at the table and properly announcing it, asking if they may bring anything else out to the table, etc.

- A server or sommelier presenting a bottle of wine and pouring it at the table and placing the bottle down

The point is managers need to carve out time to do this. Coaching for standards and improving efficiency will allow leaders to back away from having to assist in those areas and refocus on table touches and engaging with guests.

Coaching the First 25 minutes

Eighty percent of mistakes will happen in the first 25 minutes of the guest's experience. If you think of a great track relay team running and handing off the baton, the first 25 minutes of the dining experience is that. But instead of having four relay team members, you have seven: the valet, host, server, busser, runner, bartender, and cook will be tightly involved in the first 25 minutes of every table's experience. This many hand-offs leaves plenty of opportunities for mistakes. If a team can guarantee a tight first 25 minutes, hitting all the standards correctly and getting the order into the kitchen, then they will be setting themselves up for success. Communication is key. I always felt I could take a deep breath after the order was in the computer and the first drinks and starter course were placed on the table. The first 25 minutes is a critical, finite block of time that a manager should be able to audit and coach.

DONATO POTO

Co-owner/GM- Three-starred Michelin restaurant, Providence

Being Present

McDonald's or Providence — it doesn't matter the level of the restaurant. If somebody is not present and doesn't know how to approach a guest and make them feel comfortable, then it doesn't matter if they have been working in the business for 30 years, because a guest will be unhappy.

Learning

No matter how much I think I know, no matter how well I think I run my restaurant, I always learn every day from other people and other places. I've learned a lot from working with servers that have worked all over the world.

Be Friendly, Not Familiar

Interactions depend on the restaurant and expectations. It's all about reading the guest. Even if you are very comfortable with the guest, you have to be aware of the fine line not to cross. Be friendly, but not familiar.

Bring in the Suit

When there is a major problem, a server needs to know when you bring in the suit. If things are going wrong and the server has tried their best and it didn't work, and the guest thinks the server is only making it worse, the server should realize this. The manager is the next obvious person to step into the situation when the guest is not happy. The manager then needs to smooth things out and the next dish should be brought out by a manager instead of the server...it's about a whole team winning the table.

New Kid on the Block

Very often, when a restaurant is busy, they may not care about the guest because there are so many. They may think, we have 100 reservations, 100 walk-ins, and a two-hour wait list; everything is going well, and people are waiting every day, so if a guest is not happy and they leave, who cares, there is another one.... That is the biggest mistake. Everyone goes to busy restaurants at the beginning, but if you are a host or manager who receives the guest and you do not appreciate that guest at busy times as much as you appreciate a guest when you are half empty, then you are in for failure. A year from that opening day, the door is not going to open as often, because you are not the new kid on the block. So, those guests that you lost at the beginning are not going to come back. And that happens often in this industry, when you open up and it's an instant success, you forget that it's not going to be a success forever.

54

GREAT WHEN I NEED TO BE

The Consistency of Performance and Behavior

I worked with this guy, Tim, who was a great server and had seniority. He was excellent at what he did. Really, really good — when he chose to be! Tim was smart and had a lot of experience in the industry. He had worked at high-end, well-known restaurants in different cities and had obviously been well-trained. At that point in my career, he was one of the best servers I had ever worked with. He had phenomenal table presence, food knowledge, kitchen etiquette, and he could sell big wines.

The problem was: Tim would decide when he wanted to do his job and when he wanted to be lazy and not do it. He decided to do his job when there were important people in the room: owners, celebrities, TV chefs, his friends—people he deemed important enough for him to bring his "A game." Whenever these people came into the restaurant, he went into Super Server mode. You could sit back and watch with amazement. Charming, working hard, fun to be with on the floor, great team player, generally happy about his job. It was like he had a cape on under his shirt that said, "Super Waiter." And it was actually enjoyable to work with him.

Since we had all seen Tim's capabilities on the floor and witnessed his Super Waiter greatness, it was obvious to us all when he decided not to be. When he decided not to be a part of the team. When he decided not to give 100 percent. Which was a lot of the time. When the guest wasn't important enough to him, he went back to ordering co-workers around, not paying attention to guests' needs, and belittling other employees.

This behavior, if unchecked, will seep into other team members. Soon, a server is leaving the floor 15 minutes early to go check Instagram on their phone and doesn't think anyone notices. The server who sells a $300 bottle of wine at one of their tables and thinks they can coast the rest of the night. Great service can't work like that. A player doesn't make a great catch for a touchdown in the third quarter and take the fourth quarter off, congratulating themselves. They play hard through the final whistle. Consistency is everything in a restaurant: food, service, behavior.

Consistency

I've seen managers and leaders behave this way as well. They may treat people differently depending on who is in the room. They might be very nice with certain guests or specific employees and turn around and be very rude to other employees. The more employees see the manager putting on different masks for different people, the warier they become of that manager. Even if that employee is on the "good" side, the behavior they are witnessing will always have them asking, "Am I next?" "Will they turn on me?" It amazes me when a leader thinks variations in their behavior witnessed by the team won't lessen their status. There is no strength in having your team wonder, "Who is going to show up?" when you've given them multiple personas to choose from. It's important to be consistent in your behavior. You are establishing the tone for the rest of the team. Excellent service and behavior is a standard you must set for yourself.

DOMINIQUE CRENN

Chef and co-owner- Three-starred Michelin restaurant, Atelier Crenn

Knowledgeable Guests

What I love about most of my customers is they have [food] knowledge, and it's beautiful when they have knowledge because you get to know them, and they come back and it's kind of an exchange you have with your customer. You allow them to discover something they have never had before, and you allow yourself to learn from them and maybe an idea comes from that. It's this exchange of ideas and this dialogue that happens. And I think it makes the restaurant better.

Evolution

Our motto at Atelier, in the company, is that we don't believe in perfection, we believe in evolution. So, every day is another day where you can learn and improve. I am learning all the time. If you go out there and you say, "I know everything and what I'm doing is the best," you are kidding yourself, that is crazy. Humility needs to be there in our profession, especially with chefs. Because there is so much we need to learn every day. Things are moving. The world is moving. I'm always in movement and I love that. My brain is always in movement. My eyes and my ears and always absorbing new things. And I think that's beautiful.

Improvement and Growth

Criticism needs to be constructive. I always tell them it's not because you think you are weak in some area; it could be a strength too. So, when you learn about your weakness — and things you need to improve on — they might become a strength to you. We all need to get pushed by people. I need to get pushed every day. I want people to tell me things that I may be doing wrong. It's important.

At the end of night, we always have a meeting with the team. And we ask questions and we are curious. And we also listen and that is very important. That is what makes a team become most successful. The server, cook, chef, GM — at the end of the night, this discussion about how people feel. You have to keep the communication open and be willing to hear what people think and also listen to yourself and look at yourself and really rate yourself. Sometimes you know you didn't do well. Just acknowledge that, take the responsibility on yourself. This is how you develop and grow.

Chain of Command

When you have a team, you have to make sure there is a chain of command. They need to talk to each other. They can't go to me right away. I want my crew to go to my sous-chef or my chef de cuisine and talk to each other. Talk between yourselves. I want people to communicate when they need to communicate. If you have a problem and you don't want to talk to your direct superior, then you can come to me. My door is always open.

56

STAYING AHEAD

Creating a Culture of Innovation

When I went to The Dining Room, our goal was to achieve two Michelin stars. It was a very clear-cut goal. We would have regular meetings at the restaurant and come up with ways to innovate and improve the dining experience. To do this required an openness, a sense of adventure, and a room where you felt you could risk ideas without being judged or mocked. This healthy culture was set up and completely supported by Robert Hartstein and Chef Craig Strong. All of us were encouraged to come up with ideas to elevate the experience just a little more. We would bounce the ideas around, test them out in service: the good ones stayed; the not-so-good quickly disappeared.

I always appreciated this because they were smart enough to use the employees they had assembled and trusted us to help innovate. They were empowering us. We were bringing our own experiences, we were out eating at restaurants, as were they, bringing back great ideas from other dining rooms, and we were competitive. Massively. We wanted to win! We wanted a second star, a higher Zagat rating, the best OpenTable service, and a James Beard nod. You could feel it; it was an exciting team to be a part of.

By including us and our ideas, they built an immediate buy-in from the team. If you only treat your team as just a way to execute your own "brilliant" ideas, that may work for a bit, but there is a weak heartbeat in that. The excitement is thin and will dissipate quickly. But when you include your team's ideas, guide the group, filter and balance those ideas with your vision, you create a force to be reckoned with. Robert knew we could only crush it if we were all personally invested in our style of service and believed in each other.

Cheese Cart

We were always trying to personalize our restaurant experience in any way we could, and we would have meetings to bounce some ideas around. One of those times I came up with an idea about the cheese cart. My own frustration with cheese was that I could never remember what cheese I was eating or had enjoyed at a restaurant or party. I had a hard time with the names and types. I pitched the idea that we had a piece of paper, 5 inches by 8 inches or so, cardstock, on which we could pre-print the names of the cheeses. A box next to each one that the server could check. This way, after we had plated each custom plate of cheese for each person at the table, we could quickly check the box of the cheese they had and place the card to the right of their dish as they started to enjoy their course. Robert loved the idea. He suggested to put on the back of the card the closest cheese shop to the hotel. We picked Nicoles in South Pasadena because that is where Robert had picked the cheeses for the cart. Another server pitched in that we should add two more shops: Silverlake Cheese shop and the one at the Farmers Market in Mid-city, Monsieur Marcel. This way, we were offering our guests a guide to continue their cheese experience when they left our restaurant and the hotel. We had a lot of people do staycations at The Langham, all having their own homes within a one-hour drive. So, these shops covered a wide area. The cards were a huge hit! Low cost. Innovative. Memorable.

One night, many months after we introduced the cards, a woman came in with her husband and waved me down from her table. She said, "Hi, I just wanted to say thank you for that card with the cheeses from a few months ago. We had a dinner party last weekend, and I found it in the kitchen drawer and those were the cheeses we used for our party. They were a hit! And we showed everyone the card too. They were impressed with how many cheeses you have here." Not only was the card functional, but it also brought back her memory of dining with us. That experience. And here they were again, a week after finding that card in the kitchen drawer. And they shared their story — they told their friends about us. Win.

INTO ACTION: PROMPTS

Building Engagement, Connection, and Culture

I hope you are inspired by what you read in this book and maybe you are already putting inspiration into action. I decided to include some prompts for any restaurant professional that is looking for more ways to connect with their teams. As mentioned previously: practice, repetition, and consistency can rapidly build skillsets, level up teams and — with focused leadership — shift the culture of service in a restaurant.

While there are plenty of skills exercises peppered throughout the book, here are some additional ways you may be able to help yourself, your colleagues, or your teams stay consistent in the pursuit of always doing better. As my friend Tim says, "Celebrate the redundancy" and have fun with these. The five categories these focus on are: Coaching, Team Engagement, Guest Connections, Improvements, Knowledge.

GM to Managers

1. List 10 restaurant needs you'd like managers to focus on. (Improvements)

2. Have each manager tell you three key points they would like to improve on, personally, over the next six months. Discuss strategy. Follow up. (Improvements)

3. Have managers select five items you feel the restaurant needs improvement/coaching on. (Improvements)

4. Select, in order, ten essays from the book for your manager(s) to read, and meet once a week for ten weeks to discuss each essay. (Coaching)

5. Ask each manager to pick a favorite paragraph to share at the monthly manager meeting. (Team Engagement)

6. Have your manager(s) create a list of their 30 favorite quotes from the book and use those at daily line-ups for a month with your staff. (Team Engagement)

7. Have your managers (s) pick a specific section from The Rundown and report back to you three ways your restaurant can improve that specific area of service. (Improvements)

8. Have your manager(s) do a brainstorming idea based on the vision chart and list local recommendations that they can share with the team and with inquiring guests. (Guest Connections)

9. Find a local online source and have manager(s) put together a quick hit list of three interesting things going on during the weekend. Share these briefly at line-ups and/or post on a line-up board for BOH and FOH to enjoy. (Guest Connections)

10. Work with the chef and target a few trips to the kitchen for the front of house staff to visit specific stations and get a detailed explanation from the line cook that works that station. (Team Engagement)

11. Have a manager pick a specific skills exercise from the book and fine tune it to fit the needs of your restaurant, style of service, and food. (Team Engagement)

12. Depending on the size of the team, schedule a brief meeting every 180 days with each team member and ask them to self-review and share with you where they think they can challenge themselves and make improvements on their service. (Team Engagement)

Managers to Servers

If you are a manager, hopefully you've been able to use the information provided in this book to lead your teams. I've also included a few prompts here as ways to engage with your employees.

1. Hand the book to someone at shift line-up and have them randomly pick a page in the book without looking at the content. Have them read that section. Discuss it with the team. (Team Engagement)

2. Look through the Rundown section in any of the three parts of the book and pick a section to speak about at line-up. Stay focused on the subject of that section with the team throughout the shift. (Improvements)

3. Find a few favorite quotes from interviewees that speak to you and your restaurant style and share them with your team. (Team Engagement)

4. Using sections in the Rundown, ask your team to tell you the top five areas they think the team could improve on. (Improvements)

5. Using the Description Food essay on page 103 as a jumping off point, ask the team to have a description battle. Two people face off, describing the same dish, and the group decides who wins. This should remain fun, the point is discovering good descriptions, not making anyone feel bad. (Team Engagement/ Improvements)

6. Explore some of the wine-heavy interviews in the book; pick a section from an interview, read it out loud, and discuss it with the team. (Team Engagement)

7. Find a brief passage about the importance of the initial greeting of guests in the restaurant. Share it with the team. Have them tell you what they like about it or where they think improvements can happen in making a great initial greeting. (Guest Connections)

8. Pick a team member and have them explain a bottle of wine they like to sell and three sentences about the wine. Where is it from, who

is the producer, and what is special story element about the wine, winemaker, wine process, or wine family. (Improvement/Guest Connections)

9. Using the vision chart, have team members share recommendations in the neighborhood with other team members. (Guest Connections)

10. Pick a drink on the menu and ask a team member to tell you one ingredient in it. Go around the group and have each person add one ingredient. When the drink is complete, have the next person describe the drink to the group. (Improvement)

11. Ask the team if anyone has eaten anywhere recently. Ask them to describe the food, atmosphere, music of the place and if they would recommend it. (Guest Connections)

12. Ask team members to choose one of the aspects in the Rundown and express to you which one they are going to focus on during the shift. (i.e. pulling chairs, getting the order in within a certain time, clearing tables with minimal sound, marking tables before courses, keeping water levels maintained, upselling desserts, etc. There are a lot to choose from. Having some intention and stating it out loud to the team is a nice focus to start the shift with. (Improvement)

13. Pick a step of service and observe the whole team doing that one isolated step. (Coaching)

14. Read through the linking tasks section on page 107 and find a few steps of service you can link together and observe. Every manager should have a list of linked steps they can observe and coach on. (Coaching)

15. Find an employee that may need a little coaching on getting back into form. Make time for this person. Set up a meeting. Discuss goals, timelines, and specifics that you would like them to focus on. Use the book. It's about support and positive feedback on raising the level of service. (Coaching)

Servers to Servers

You may be a server who is using this book to improve you own service or working with a friend or co-worker to improve your service. Reading this book alone for self-improvement will definitely help you tighten up your service standards, but teaming with another server and working through the book together may help with retention and goal setting. Have fun with these. Over time, these all become so natural they give you more time and ways to connect with your guests. Here are some ways two servers could use this book together.

1. Read the book together. Agree on some dates to meet up to discuss. (Knowledge)

2. Quiz each other on the wines and cocktails, improving descriptions for guests. Role play with each other, each playing a guest who is looking for recommendations. (Knowledge)

3. Quiz each other on menu items, describing them, not just listing the ingredients. Role play these by one of you being a guest and asking about items and certain dietary restrictions or allergies. (Knowledge)

4. Build the item —- you can go back and forth with each other, adding items to a dish or drink until you have built it. Then each of you offer a description for the guest. (Knowledge)

5. Quiz each other on what wine, beer, or cocktail would pair with what dish the best. Provide an answer and tell each other why it would pair well, same as you would do with a guest. (Guest Connections)

6. If you tend to set up the dining room with someone, you can play the "50 or 100." I usually pick the number based on the total number of items. You can do this with multiple servers as well. The goal is to make it through all the items — food, wine, and cocktails — describing them to each other as you set up for the shift. If you mess up or leave an item out, the next server has to describe the same

dish but correctly. (Knowledge)

7. Pick an essay or interview to read once a week. Get together before work for 15 minutes and talk about what the ideas in the essay or the interview mean to each of you and how it can help connect with guests or improve your own performance. (Improvements/Guest Connections)

8. Tell each other before service about one element of service from the Rundown that you are going to focus on: greeting, steps of service, upselling wine or cocktails, getting your order in quickly, offering desserts with better descriptions, making sure water levels are always full, etc. Watch each other during service and check in with each other. Make it fun. (Improvements)

9. Timing. Time each other. If there is an area you think you could speed up — for instance, the time between a guest sitting down and getting the order into the system, making latte foam, etc. — time yourself or have a partner do it. (Improvements)

10. "Wasn't Asked." My friend Akili Steward liked to challenge himself to make it through service without a table asking him for anything. It was a measurement of anticipating the needs of the guest at the table. As I like to say, "Beat the guest to the request." Make it a game with another server and see who wins. Keep it fun. (Guest Connections)

11. Ask each other to pick out various cooking methods/techniques your kitchen uses and describe them. This can be helpful in understanding the kitchen, details of preparation, and improving descriptions. These can be used at line-ups as well. Methods may include: Brining, aging, grilling, baking, poaching, steaming, en papillote, searing, roasting, fire roasting, torching, fileting, sous vide, confit, aeration, emulsification, reductions, demi-glace, pickling, or molecular gastronomy techniques. (Knowledge)

12. Connect with the chef or sous-chef and ask for a tour of the kitchen and stations. Find out which person cooks which items, gain a little more understanding about back of house operations. (Team

Engagement)

13. Play a game where you report back to each other something cool or interesting you found out about your guests: where are they from, what neighbourhood do they live in, what are they doing for the weekend, etc. This shouldn't be invasive to the guest experience, but come from your natural engagement with them. (Guest Connection).

14. Keep a count on how many guests you welcome into the restaurant and how many you say goodbye to as they are leaving. Keep a tally of it for the evening. This is a great opportunity to use varying ways to welcome and say goodbye to guests. (Guest Connection)

15. Practice presenting wine to each other. Pick a bottle of wine. One of you presents it to the other as if they are the guest. Show the label and introduce the wine saying the vintage, producer, varietal, and region. Practice how you play. The more you practice the more comfortable the process will become. Repeat the process with other wines.

16. Practice opening wine. Davis Campbell mentions on page 147 about offering to help the bartender open wines before the shit to improve this skillset. For a proper example, the Court of Master Sommeliers, Americas has amazing free videos available on YouTube about opening wine, sparkling wine, and decanting a bottle of wine.

RECOMMENDED RESOURCES

Books and Podcasts

I've learn a lot from following my favorite restaurant and bar people on social media. I'm always inspired by their creations and it keeps me involved with what is going on in our business around the globe. My bookshelf is also peppered with many books I've used to learn about service, food, and beverages. Here is a list of a few of those as well as a couple of podcasts I enjoy.

SERVICE

Setting the Table by Danny Meyer

Lessons in Excellence from Charlie Trotter by Paul Clarke

Unreasonable Hospitality by Will Guidara

Counter Culture by Joshua Farrell

FOOD

The New Food Lover's Companion by Sharon Tyler Herbst

On Food and Cooking by Harold McGee

The Flavor Bible by Andrew Dornenburg and Karen Page

The Vegetarian Flavor Bible by Karen Page

The Flavor Matrix by James Briscione and Brook Parkhurst

The Art and Science of Food Pairing by Petery Coucquyt, Bernard Lahousse, Johan Langenbick

Cheese Primer by Steven Jenkins

French Cheese (DK Publishing) by Kazuko Masui and Tomoko Yamada

WINE

Great Wine Made Simple by Andrea Immer Robinson

The Sommelier's Atlas of Taste by Jordan Mackay and Rajat Parr

The 24-Hour Wine Expert by Jancis Robinson

Windows on the World Complete Wine Course by Kevin Zraly

Jancis Robinson's Wine Course by Jancis Robinson

One Thousand Vines: A New Way to Understand Wine by Pascaline Lepeltier

The World Atlas of Wine by Hugh Johnson and Jancis Robinson

Vino Italiano: The Regional Wines of Italy by David Lynch and Joseph Bastianich

The Wines of Burgundy by Clive Coates

COCKTAILS

Imbibe! by David Wondrich

Death & Co: Modern Classic Cocktails by Alex Day, David Kaplan and Nick Fauchald

Roundbuilding by Daniel Waddy and Kevin Armstrong

Jigger, Beaker, and Glass by Charles H. Baker Jr.

Whiskey by Michael Jackson

BEER

Tasting Beer by Randy Mosher

The Brewmaster's Table by Garrett Oliver

Great Beer Guide by Michael Jackson

Ultimate Beer by Michael Jackson

NON ALCOHOLIC (MOCKTAILS)

Good Drinks by Julia Bainbridge

The Mocktail Club by Derick Santiago

Mocktails by Caroline Hwang

COFFEE AND TEA

The World Atlas of Coffee by James Hoffmann

The Coffee Dictionary by Maxwell Colonna-Dashwood

The Story of Tea: A Cultural History and Drinking Guide by Mary Lou Heiss and Robert J. Heiss

Serendipitea: A Guide to the Varieties, Origins and Rituals of Tea by Tomislav Podreka

FOOD AND BEVERAGE PAIRINGS

What to Drink with What you Eat by Andrew Dornenburg and Karen Page

Wine Simple: Perfect Pairings by Aldo Sohm with Christine Muhlke

Wine Pairing for the People by Cha McCoy and Layla Schlack

PODCASTS

Gastropod with Cynthia Graber and Nicola Twilley

The Sporkful with Dan Pashman

Copper and Heat with Katy Osuna

I'll Drink to That! Wine Talk with Levi Dalton

The Vinepair Podcast with Adam Teeter, Joanna Sciarrino, Zach Geballe

Somm TV Podcast with Jason Wise

The Craft Beer and Brewing Podcast with Jaime Bogner

All About Beer with Em Sauter and Don Tse

Drink Beer, Think Beer with John Holl

INDEX

1-10 Game, xxii
A.O.C., 115
accountability, xxi, 64, 168, 115, 262, 264, 267
adapting, 13, 188, 229, 252, 256
after-dinner drinks, 92, 182, 211-214
Agnew, Dawn, 242-243, 286
ai, 138-140
allergies, 5, 15–16, 19, 77, 83, 140, 187, 200, 263
Alinea, 157
Altman, Sam, 139
anticipation, xix, 23, 49, 171
arms, 24, 91, 123
Atelier Crenn, 255-256

atmosphere, xv-xvi, 100, 122-123, 202, 206, 211, 213, 262
attendance, 113-114, 151
attitude, xii, 14, 16-17, 98, 123, 161, 164, 242
awards, 158, 194, 226, 282–283
awareness, 112, 142, 164, 241
balance, 43, 89, 123, 133-134, 164, 190, 228, 241
Balthazar, 249
bartender, xiii, 37, 39, 51, 59, 65, 68, 83, 89, 114, 121, 123, 137, 147, 126, 250
Bauer, Michael, 154
Beard, James, 257, 282-285
beer, 7, 31, 43-44, 59,

67, 131, 159, 183, 263,
    267-268
behavior, 125, 150, 163-
    164, 254
being present, xi, xiv, 10,
    108, 138, 188, 194, 232,
    238, 251
Bit of Information game,
    246
Blau, Elizabeth, 80
BOH (back of house), 4,
    59-60, 178-179
Borowski, Brian, 112, 277
Bouchon, 230
bread service, 77, 87, 206,
    209
breath, 46, 125, 153, 233, 241,
    250
briefing, see also line-ups
Brioza, Stuart, 95, 241
Burgundy, 248, 266
burnout, 137, 173
bussing (bussers), 4, 37, 46,
    58-59, 61, 78-79, 89, 94,
    98, 164, 186, 208, 226,
    243, 250
Caine, Michael, 153
Campbell, Davis, 147-149,
    226-229, 285
Cannon, Jackson, 136-137,
    285
Capo, 54, 107-108, 133, 160-
    161, 182, 226-229, 236, 279
captain, 59, 118, 177-178, 193
chain of command, 256
Chambers NYC, 166
champagne, 196
Charcoal, 235
chargers, 191

checks,
    dropping, 26-27, 93-94,
        117, 215-216
    averages, xiii, 8, 117, 133-
        134, 148
checklists, 29, 40-42, 95-96,
    217-218, 222
cheese, 212, 214-215, 258,
    266
chef, xvii–xviii, xx, xxii, 38,
    57, 59–60, 62–64, 73, 75,
    77, 80, 85, 87, 92, 95, 105,
    127, 129, 144, 171, 177, 179,
    181, 187, 195, 197, 200, 206, 208,
    214, 227, 235, 253, 255–257,
    260, 264, 281–283
Chez Panisse, 171
Cicerone certification, 67
Citrin, Josiah, 235-236, 286
Clarke, Sarah, 247-248, 287
cleanliness, 7, 28, 44, 63, 94,
    108, 192
clearing, xv, 22, 24-25, 58, 61, 70,
    90-91, 95, 201, 206, 208, 210-
    211, 250, 262
Clevenger, JoAnn, 223-225, 286
cocktails, 65, 120, 136-137, 181,
    207, 263-264, 268
Connie and Ted's, 251
coffee, 101, 212-213, 269
Cole, Adam, 105-106, 283
collaboration, 172, 182
communication, xii, xvii, 22–23,
    47, 59, 68–69, 81–82, 87–89,
    99, 113, 119, 123, 127, 138,
    142, 146, 185, 194–195, 201,
    206–207, 209, 245, 256

company culture, xiii, xvi, xviii, 9, 29, 42, 64, 85, 164, 182, 185, 201, 227, 242, 257, 259, 265, 285
complaining, 37, 138
components of a dish, 105
concierge, xix, 52
confidence, 33, 101, 103, 199, 226, 238
building, 9, 18, 28, 82, 120, 131, 134, 148, 157, 168, 170, 194
connected, xii-xvi
guests, xix-xxi, 36–37, 39, 52, 61, 64-65, 72, 79, 83-84, 107, 123, 127, 129,130, 139, 148, 150-154, 161, 172, 183-184, 194, 199, 207, 259-264
teams, xvii, 14, 36-38, 64, 76, 124, 131, 164, 186, 230, 259-264
consistency, 14, 17, 114, 123-124, 207, 253-254, 259
control, 7, 19, 63, 71, 96, 122–123, 150–151, 158, 163, 198, 234
cooking methods, 105-106, 286
courses, 22, 61, 77–78, 80, 88–90, 92, 107, 156, 177–178, 187–188, 195, 208, 262
Court of Masters Sommeliers, 161
Crenn, Dominique, 255-256, 287

criticism, 116, 163, 166, 256
culture, xiii, xvi, xviii, 9, 29, 42, 64, 85, 164, 182, 185, 201, 227, 242, 257, 259, 265, 285
curiosity, 151, 160–161, 166
customer, xii, xix–xx, 8, 14, 17, 19, 22, 29, 43, 67, 123, 148, 151, 172, 223, 243–244, 255
Danko, Gary, 242
delegating, 118-119, 146, 195
delivering food, 8, 20, 84, 108, 128, 200, 212, 250
runners, 60-61
synchronized service, 201-202
describing, 32, 103–104, 106, 111, 259-265
dessert drinks, 92, 148,
desserts, 25, 45, 68, 80, 92, 134, 211–212, 215, 262, 264
dietary restrictions, 19, 81-84, 96, 140, 186–187, 194, 197, 200, 263
Director Of Service, 249-250
discovery, xv, 8, 255, 261
dishwashing station, 26, 93
do a lap, 24, 90, 211
Eastern Standard, 129, 136
education, xiii, 116, 130–131, 137, 166–167, 178, 182, 281
efficiency, 24, 28, 61, 81, 107-109, 119, 134-135, 141-142, 145-146,169, 187
ego check, 153-154, 162-163, 227
El Encanto, 157
empathy, 131, 150, 153, 171

empowering, 146, 241, 257
Enclos, 237
encouragement, 46, 68, 68,140, 161, 257
energy, xii, 17, 76, 85, 108, 138, 160, 188, 232–233,' 240–241, 244
engaging employees, 9, 35-36, 58, 130, 165
guests, 96, 245-246, 250
Equal Measure, 129, 136
evaluate, 108, 139, 145-146
Even, Josh, 186
Evvia, 124
expectation, xvi, 9-10, 31–32, 161, 184–185, 190, 193, 227, 240, 249, 251
failure, xx, 115, 128, 169, 233, 238, 252
fairs, 45
fairness, 49, 163
family style, 126-127
Federer, Roger, 232
feedback, xx, 14, 48-49, 75, 107, 116, 172, 240, 245, 262
fileting, 170, 264
finances, 115
firing food, 61, 89, 107, 221, 228
first impressions, 97, 237
flavor profile, 7, 65, 116, 127, 139, 183, 208
focus, xi, xvi, 10, 12–13, 47, 59, 75, 82, 108, 138, 151, 180, 182, 186, 208, 232, 235, 245, 249, 259, 262, 264
FOH (Front of House), 4, 58-59, 73, 177-178, 186, 260

food knowledge, 59, 143, 172, 180, 253
food runner, *see also* runner
forgetting, 232-234
friendly, 16–17, 51, 81–82, 96, 98, 138, 147, 251
front server, 59, 118, 177– 178, 186, 193, 200, 215
Gladwell, Malcolm, 169
goals, 13, 35, 71, 75, 152, 262
Golden Road Brewing, 43
Goldman, Josh, 120-121, 282
grace, 131, 142, 203-204, 227
gratitude, 224
gratuities, 114
grooming standards, 10-11, 71–72, 189
Guedouar, Karim, 207
guest cues, 23
guest details, 124, 200
hand signals, 208-209
hand written notes, xii
handheld device, 141–142
Harker, Garrett, 129-132, 284
Hartstein, Robert, 38, 154-155, 193, 215, 249, 257-258, 281
headset, 142, 208
Hecht, Larry, 240
Herrschaft, Joe, 96
hiring, 7, 46, 62, 110, 113, 124, 130, 172
Hollywood, 123, 227, 244
hosts, 33, 58, 65, 77, 96, 98-99, 195, 197
Hotel Bel Air, 162
Houston's, 110
improvement, 107, 112, 146, 164, 256, 259-264

Ink, 105
innovation, 126, 138, 142, 145–146, 257-258
intention, 21, 33, 69-70, 72, 98, 101, 112, 122, 128, 141, 146, 185, 189-190, 198, 206-207, 227, 233, 241, 262
James Beard Awards, 282-283
judgement, 150, 257
Keller, Thomas, 238
kindness, 125, 223, 225
Kirby, Robin, 124-125, 284
Kokkari, 124
labor costs, 113, 139, 179
Langham Huntington Hotel, 46, 155, 187, 190, 220, 246, 258
lateral service, 243
leadership, 112, 119, 124, 134, 146, 241, 245, 259, 287
Lepeltier, Pascaline, 166-167, 285
lighting, 32, 52, 122, 227
line-up meetings, xvii, 13-14, 39, 53, 75, 76, 164, 182, 190, 192, 230, 241, 245, 259-262
listening, 21, 69, 98, 182, 221, 223
local options, xii, 52-54, 65, 87, 167, 172, 206, 222, 260, 262
Lucques, 115
Maitre D', 96-97, 195, 237-239, 244, 249

Marder, Bruce, 226, 229, 236
Marder, Max, 107, 133, 160
marking, 61, 89, 108, 210, 221, 262
McCracken, Tim, 76, 281
McPherson, Iain, 65-66
meal break, 113-114
Melisse, 235
menu maintenance, 17, 30, 40-41, 75, 141
Messi, Lionel, 169
Michelin, xiii, 133, 190, 237, 248, 257, 282–285
micro-managing, 115, 146
mindset, 10, 38, 71, 74, 76, 107, 146, 166, 188, 232
mistakes, 6, 39-40, 115, 153-156, 168, 202, 215–216, 232–234, 242, 252
molecular gastronomy, 38, 264
money, xi, xiii–xv, 31-32, 35, 37, 45, 57, 82, 87, 107, 112–114, 120, 133, 140, 147, 149, 167, 226–229, 248
Monferrato, Marino, 98
Morningstar, Kris, xxii, 63, 188, 205
motivation, xiii, 230
multi-tasking, 34
music, xv, 12, 28, 32, 100, 122–123, 136, 158, 227, 229, 262
Muto, Hiko, 244
Nadeau, Larry, 237-239, 284
neighborhood, xii, 52-54, 65, 87, 167, 172, 206, 222, 260, 262

research, 66, 143, 161, 245, 247
reservations, 16, 39, 212, 228, 252
reservation system, 7, 14, 41, 96-99, 113, 139-140, 195-196, 200
resolution, 122-124
rest break, 113
Restaurant Daniel, 207
restorative, 224
retention, 63–64, 137, 259-265
return guest, xix, 52, 103, 155
Ribalta, 123
Riese, Martin, 205
The Ritz-Carlton, 144
Robuchon, Joel, 215
Rouge Tomate, 166
Rose Bowl, 246
Rossman, Lewis, 33-34, 283
Sam's Chowder House, 33
scheduling, 99, 113, 179
seat numbers, 6, 9, 61, 69, 77, 186–187
Sebastiani, Sam, 160
self-education, 131, 167, 267-270
selling, 13, 65, 75, 111, 120, 148–149, 161, 182, 199, 228–229
serious, 240-241
Seward, Akili, 23, 264
shadowing, 5, 70
shared plates, 78, 91, 126-128, 185
short memory, 232-234

side work, 28-29, 42, 95, 107, 217
Sizzler, xiii
skills exercises, 39, 98, 199, 259-265
smell, 11, 72, 104, 158, 191
smiling, 223, 245
social media, xi, xx, 143, 183, 267
sommelier, 23, 64, 77, 80, 100, 159-161, 178, 181, 183, 199, 201, 205, 207-208, 228, 250, 268, 282
Sonoma, xvi, 96, 182
sound, 103–104, 136, 164, 204, 210–211, 262
Spago, 230-231, 249
speed, 5-6, 18, 121, 145–146, 186, 207, 238, 248, 264
Springer, Steve Scott, 230-231, 286
stand-up, *see also*, line-ups
Standard Italian, 129, 136
standards, xvi, xxi, 7, 10–11, 57–59, 62, 71–73, 85, 180, 189, 193, 227, 240, 245, 250, 263
State Bird Provisions, 95, 241
steps of service, xiv-xvi, xxi, 14, 77-78, 80, 107-108, 116, 127, 178, 192-194, 202, 212-213, 228, 244, 262, 264
story, x–xii, xiv, xxii, 37, 43, 51, 64, 147, 160–161, 163, 172, 182, 231, 258, 261, 277
Strong, Craig, 187, 257
Stuckey, Bobby, 21-22
Styne, Caroline, 115-116, 282

non-alcoholic options, 67, 183, 211, 269
non-verbal communication, 23, 99, 123, 208-209
Obligacion, Gary, 157-158, 285
observation, 43, 50
Oscars, 159
over-describing, 106
pace, 19, 23, 87, 134, 145, 206–207, 209, 227
paging system, 141
pairing, 68, 178, 181–183, 187–188, 200, 207–208, 211–212, 230, 267-269
Parr, Raj, 161
patience, 85, 125, 140
perfume, 11, 72
Perry's, 51, 54
personalization, xix-xx, 8, 16, 19, 77, 81-82, 92, 129, 157-158, 186, 193, 214, 258
Petit Crenn, 255-265
Peyton, Nic, xix
Pham, Viet, 205
podcasts, 269-270
point of sale, 5, 11, 15, 62, 73, 138, 180, 186, 189
policies, 7, 63, 113–114
positive, xi–xii, 13, 17, 37, 47, 113, 130, 139, 158, 172, 230, 234, 262
Post Ranch Inn, 157
Poto, Donato, 251-252, 287
Providence, 251
practice, xvii, xxi, 6, 17–18, 50, 63, 89, 104, 121, 147, 164, 168–170, 182–183, 194, 199, 202, 245, 259-265
Prairie, Justin, 161
praise, 183, see also feedback; criticism
pre-shift meeting, 8, 19, 88, 207, see also line-ups
prep times, 8, 19, 88, 207
prepared, 9–10, 46, 53–54, 70–71, 73, 76, 86, 127, 188, 190, 214, 230, 241
mentally, 10, 71, see also breathe
prioritizing, 241
prix fixe menu, see also tasting menu
proactive education, 167
professionalism, 48-49, 82, 150-151, 228
profit and loss statement, 113
Puck, Wolfgang, 231
qr code, 141
Ray's and Stark Bar, 205
reading the guest, 9, 33, 251, see also non-verbal communication
reading the table, 220, 223
real estate, 87, 133-135
recovery, 153-154
regulars, 16, 43, 82, 96, 124-125, 232
Reilly, Paige, 43, 281
repetition, 5-6, 14, 168-169, 202, 259-265
Republique, 247
requests, 26, 97, 195

synchronized service, 201-202
Tabish, Alex, 201
table maintenance, 22, 24, 61, 84–85, 90, 134, 202–203, 211, 249
table turning, 6, 8, 19, 61, 79, 88, 92, 99, 107, 133-135, 140-141, 212, 228-229
taking orders, 18-19, 83, 199
tasting menus, 126, 129, 177–178, 181, 187–188, 200, 208, 215, 226, 230
tea service, 109, 213-214, 269
teaching, 167
team building, 259-265
technology, 69, 138-139, 141
texting, 10, 140
The 8 Rings, 219-222
The Dining Room, 40, 64, 73, 75, 94, 139, 173, 234, 249, 257, 277, 279, 281, 282
The French Laundry, 237
The Greenbrier, 105
The Langham, 46, 155, 187, 190, 220, 246, 258
The Line Hotel, 235
The Magic Mistake, 153-154
The Roister, 157
The Rundown, 3-30, 57-95, 177- 218
The Swarm, 95
The Swiss Hotel, 160
time blocks, 107-109
tips, 148
tone, 85, 98, 123, 164, 240, 254

Tony's Darts Away, 43
training, xxi, 4–6, 62, 64, 68–70, 97, 105, 114, 121, 123, 169, 180, 242, 287
trays, 23, 25, 27, 68, 89-91, 94, 100, 108, 210-211
Trotter, Charlie, 267
trust, 9, 146, 172, 199, 242, 257
Twinn, Gary, 219
uniform, 10-11, 71-72, 100, 162, 189, 198
Upperline Restaurant, 223
upsell, 19, 65, 68, 82, 181–182, 199, 212, 262, 264
utensils, 13, 16, 23–26, 60, 78, 86, 89–91, 93, 109, 122, 128, 185, 190, 202, 208, 210
V.I.P, 239
valet, 135, 250
value, 31–32, 35–36, 60, 97, 122, 139, 150–151, 171, 180–181, 183– 184, 193, 199, 202
vision, xvii, 24, 211, 219, 257, 260, 262
visual learner, 5
visualization, 234
Voltaggio Brothers Steakhouse, 143
Voltaggio, Michael, 143-144, 285
Walk In My Shoes, 236
warmth, 244
Washington, Doug, 100-101, 283
water service, 58, 74, 78, 85-87, 95, 108, 128, 178,

188, 198, 202, 204-205,
208-209, 239, 262, 264
Waters, Alice, 171, 286
Wells, Marvin, 110, 284
Wine, xiii, xv, 57–59
   clarify type, 247
   clarify price, 49
   dessert, 80, 92, 182, 211
   education, 64, 66, 100,
101, 116, 131, 147, 159-160,
161, 166-167, 182, 228,
247, 268-270
   management duties,
62-63
   pairings, 181, 183, 187-188
   preparation, 73, 8, 95,
147, 178, 189, 191, 233
   practice, 147, 169-170,
261-264
   selling, 109, 129, 148-149,
160,182, 199, 228-229
   service, 86, 100, 128, 187,
196, 204-205, 208-209,
224, 248, 250, 253
   steps of service, 77-78
   tasting notes, 177–178,
181, 187–188, 194, 200,
208, 215
Wine Spectator Grand
Award, xiii, 212, 229

ACKNOWLEDGEMENTS

This industry is built on our ability to share our skills, teach each other, and learn from each other. It's one of the aspects of our industry that I'm most proud of. I've worked with some amazing teams in many restaurants, bars, and hotels.

Thank you to Dean Kuipers for editing this book and Christo Downs for the great cover design.

Thank you to the many people who have been encouraging and helpful in the process of writing this book including Tim McCracken, Terry Scannell, Robert Hartstein, Brian Borowski, Andrew Pettingell, Ken Concepcion and Michelle Mugcal at Now Serving, and Paolo Lucchesi for making an introduction that kicked this whole thing off. And to my co-workers, colleagues, managers, and bosses at Capo, The Dining Room, Lava Lounge, Blue Velvet, and the many places we've spent time connecting with guests, making a buck, and depending on each other.

Thank you to the passionate individuals that shared their thoughts on service and the pursuit of excellence in this book. Hearing your perspectives inspires me and makes me want to continue to raise my game in our hospitality industry.

And of course, Kirsten. Thank you for the many years and post-shift late-nights of talking about service, crazy restaurant stories, and endless moments of, "I have an idea, what do you think?" And most importantly all of the laughs. Your support means the world to me. I love you.

ABOUT THE CONTRIBUTERS

All interviews by Joshua Farrell. (In order of appearance.)

Lewis Rossman

COO/Partner of Shenkman Hospitality, overseeing Sam's Chowder House. Former founder/operator of Osteria Coppa and Campo, as well as Chef de Cuisine at the acclaimed Acquerello, in San Francisco.

Paige Reilly

Owner, Upside Pub, Co-founder Artisanal Brewers Collective, Former GM Golden Road Brewing and Tony's Darts Away.

Doug Washington

Former partner at Jardinière, as well as Stock & Bones Company: Town Hall, Salt House, Anchor & Hope. Current Principle/Creative director at Doug Washington Design focused on designing restaurants and hotels.

Adam Cole

Chef. Consultant. Former Sous Chef; Ink, The Dining Room, The Greenbrier.

Marvin Wells

Currently serves as Director of Hospitality for Far Out Hospitality, after a distinguished 22-year tenure with the Hillstone Restaurant Group. He's known for his operational excellence, team development, and commitment to exceeding guest satisfaction.

Caroline Styne

President and Wine Director of the Lucques Group: Lucques, A.O.C., Larder, and various partnerships with hotels and event venues. James Beard award winner for Outstanding Restaurateur. Sommelier.

Josh Goldman

Hospitality & Beverage Consultant, Advanced Sommelier. He is a veteran of the Los Angeles bar and restaurant scene. Formerly of The h.Wood Group, Soigne Group, Ink, The Dining Room.

Robin Kirby

Robin's love language is *acts of service*. She has been instrumental in running several fine dining establishments in the San Franciso Bay Area. For the last 20 years she has worked alongside her husband, Paul, overseeing the operations at two Bay Area fine dining institutions; Kokkari in San Francisco and Evvia in Palo Alto.

Garrett Harker

Restaurateur: Eastern Standard, Standard Italian, Equal Measure. Known for his hands-on approach to service, he has achieved national recognition for his unique and highly effective style of hospitality. The James Beard Foundation has recognized him as a semifinalist for the esteemed Outstanding Restaurateur Award four times.

ABOUT THE CONTRIBUTERS 285

Jackson Cannon

Beverage Director for ES Hospitality: including Eastern Standard, Equal Measure, and Standard Italian. He has been recognized by *Tales of the Cocktail* as a finalist for *Best Bar Mentor* and *Best Restaurant Bar*. As creator of The Hawthorne, it was a James Beard semi-finalist celebrated for its elevated yet welcoming cocktail experience.

Michael Voltaggio

Chef, Author, and Restaurateur: Voltaggio Brothers Steakhouse, Vulcania, Wye Oak Tavern. Formerly Ink and Ink Sack. Top Chef Winner.

Davis Campbell

Sommelier in Nashville, TN. He is the founder of Wines Together, an in-home tasting experience and wine education company. He has almost 20 years of experience in top restaurants in New York City and the Los Angeles Area.

Gary Obligacion

General Manager of El Encanto hotel in Santa Barbara. Gary was previously Vice President of Food & Beverage for Aparium Hotel Group; spent 8-1/2 years as Director of Operations and then Director of Development for The Alinea Group in Chicago; and served as the General Manager of Post Ranch Inn in Big Sur.

Pascaline Lepeltier

Beverage Director; Chambers. Former managing partner at Racines, NY, and beverage director at Rouge Tomate. Author of *One Thousand Vines: A New Way to Understand Wine*. Master Sommelier. Best French Sommelier winner.

Alice Waters

Chef, Author, Restaurateur; Chez Panisse. She is the recipient of seven James Beard Awards, a food activist who was a leading proponent of the "slow food" movement, and founder of the Edible Schoolyard Project. She is a recipient of the National Humanities medal.

JoAnn Clevenger

Restaurateur; Upperline Restaurant. New Orleans. Frequent James Beard Outstanding Restauranter nominee. Recipient of the Craig Claiborne lifetime achievement award.

Steve Scott Springer

Former General Manager, Spago. Los Angeles. Former General Manager, Bouchon.

Josiah Citrin

A culinary expert and veteran of Los Angeles's gourmet dining scene, he is the Chef/Owner of Citrin (a one-star Michelin awarded restaurant), Melisse (a two-star Michelin awarded restaurant,) and Charcoal. Citrin is a partner in Dear Jane and Dear John, and also oversees the hotel food and beverage program and the restaurant Openair at the LINE LA.

Larry Nadeau

Dining Room manager, Enclos: two-star Michelin restaurant. Former Maître d' The French Laundry: a three-starred Michelin restaurant.

Dawn Agnew

Managing Director of Hotel Drisco in San Francisco. Hospitality consultant at TruNew Consulting. Dawn led the opening of the renowned restaurant

Gary Danko, where she was instrumental in laying the foundation for a world-class Michelin-starred restaurant.

Sarah Clarke

Sommelier. Wine Director; Republique, Former GM and Beverage Director, Osteria Mozza.

Donato Poto

Co-Owner/GM of Providence restaurant, a three-star Michelin awarded, and James Beard awarded restaurant. Co-Owner/GM of Connie and Ted's. Previous accolades for Providence include "Top 50 Restaurants in the United States" by *Gourmet* magazine and the #1 ranking in "Jonathan Gold's 101 Best Restaurants" in the *Los Angeles Times*.

Dominique Crenn

Chef, author, and co-owner of the three-star Michelin awarded Atelier Crenn and former celebrated restaurant Petit Crenn and Michelin-star awarded, Bar Crenn. She's received numerous accolades, including James Beard Awards, a place on *The World's 50 Best Restaurants* list, and the 2021 Icon Award from that same organization. In 2024, she was named one of TIME Magazine's 100 Most Influential People.

ABOUT THE AUTHOR

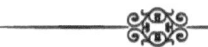

Joshua Farrell has worked in the hospitality industry for over 30 years. He started out as a teenager washing dishes in a pizzeria, worked in many food and beverage jobs, and many years later was a national semi-finalist for a James Beard Award for Outstanding Service with his team in a Michelin-starred restaurant. He has worked as a consultant in leadership, development, and training with a variety of hospitality-focused companies, from small franchises to multimillion dollar corporations. He is the author of the book *Counter Culture: An Essential Guide for Service*. He is currently Director of Learning and Development for two world-class luxury hotel brands in Los Angeles, where he lives with his wife, Kirsten, and their two cats, Easy and Mouse.

www.ingramcontent.com/pod-product-compliance
Lightning Source LLC
Chambersburg PA
CBHW030305080526
44584CB00012B/450